PEOPLE
AND
PLACE

PEOPLE AND PLACE

*Studies of Small Town Life
in the Maritimes*

EDITED BY
LARRY McCANN

Advisory Research and
Editorial Committee

Berkeley Fleming
Carrie MacMillan
Larry McCann, *Chairman* (1982-86)
John Reid
Tom Storm, *Chairman* (1981-82)

Thaddeus Holownia
Chapter Frontispieces

ACADIENSIS PRESS
Fredericton, New Brunswick
and
COMMITTEE FOR STUDYING
SMALL TOWN LIFE IN THE MARITIMES
Mount Allison University
Sackville, New Brunswick

People and Place:
Studies of Small Town Life in the Maritimes

Canadian Cataloguing in Publication Data

   Main entry under title:

   People and Place

   (Sources in the history of Atlantic Canada; no. 6)
   Proceedings of a conference entitled Small Town Life in the Maritimes,
   held at Mount Allison University, Sackville, New Brunswick, February
   1985.
   Includes bibliographical references.
   ISBN 0-919107-09-5

   1. City and town life - Maritime Provinces - Congresses. 2. Maritime
   Provinces - Social conditions - Congresses. I. McCann, L. D. (Lawrence
   Douglas), 1945-   . II. Series.

   HT127.P46 1987   307.7′62′09715   C87-093973-4

This book has been published with the help of grants
from Mount Allison University and the Social Science and
Humanities Research Council of Canada.

Designed and printed in Canada by
MORRISS PRINTING COMPANY LTD.
Victoria, British Columbia

For Berkeley, Carrie, John,
Tom and Thaddeus

CONTENTS

PART THREE: *Contemporary Small Town Life*

PEOPLE
AND
PLACE

Preface

THE MARITIMES IS A REGION OF SMALL TOWNS. THE significance of this fact was recognized by a group of Mount Allison University faculty in the late 1970s when the opportunity arose to apply to the Social Sciences and Humanities Research Council of Canada for a grant in aid of research at small universities. Here was a theme that had meaning not only for the region, but also for the university community. The faculty of Mount Allison were people who lived in a small place, and in a sense, the opportunity to research the small towns of the Maritimes was an opportunity to learn about ourselves. Almost one-fifth of Mount Allison's faculty, and many student research assistants, participated in this research endeavour which lasted from 1981 to 1985, culminating in a conference on "Small Town Life in the Maritimes." Those involved in the research process were a truly multi-disciplinary lot: historians, geographers, economists, sociologists, anthropologists, and psychologists, as well as colleagues from the departments of Music, Education and Fine Arts. The conference in February of 1985 drew over 75 people from throughout the region, including Professors Gerald Hodge, of Queen's University's School of Urban and Regional Planning, and David Frank, of the History Department at the University of New Brunswick, who commented on the papers. This book is a collection of most of those conference papers, as well as several others by Mount Allison faculty or former students who participated in the research project. Several essays have been published previously in scholarly journals.

The essays group themselves quite naturally into three major themes: casting the pattern; the passing of traditional society; and contemporary small town life. The Maritimes is sometimes characterized geographically as a fragmented region, in which localism is a major shaping force in the personality of a place (Figure 1). This is clearly illustrated in the essays by historians Bill Godfrey and

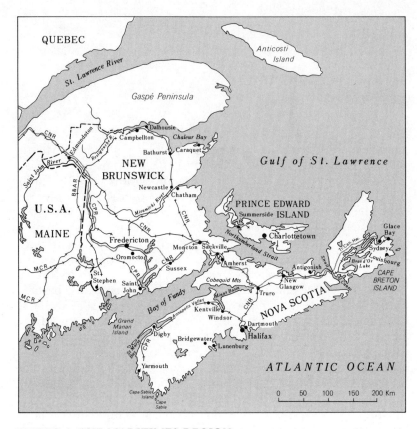

FIGURE 1. THE MARITIMES REGION.

PREFACE   13

Dean Jobb. Both emphasize how the political process, as exemplified by the likes of the eighteenth century opportunist James
Glenie or Josiah Wood, his late nineteenth century entrepreneurial
counterpart, is critical in shaping a community's fortunes, be they
political or economic. Another Maritime community that stands
out for its distinctiveness is New Glasgow, Nova Scotia, the birth-
place of the iron and steel industry in Canada. Larry McCann and
Jill Burnett examine the process of social mobility and the recruitment of the ironmasters, discovering that New Glasgow, despite its
rapidly changing population, was not an open society: to become a
member of the industrial elite, it was necessary, if not essential, to
be related through marriage to the pre-industrial, mercantile
leadership. Whether or not this casted pattern prevails elsewhere
awaits further research. Something of this cultural pattern is
suggested in the novels portraying the Maritimes, but as Carrie
MacMillan points out, there is a reluctance on the part of Maritime writers to fully convey the meaning of community as it applies
to the Maritimes. The heros and heroines of these novels are
frequently found in the "market" communities of Britain or the
United States, where the main readership of these books resided.
Such a pattern persisted well into the mid-twentieth century, and
has only recently diminished.

Some scholars would argue that traditionalism — the persistence
of cultural and other patterns over several generations — is also a
distinguishing feature of the Maritimes. Certainly the persistence
of the small town as a predominant regional settlement form
supports this assertion. But such an argument ignores the very real
changes that mark small town society in the Maritimes. Philanthropic foundations such as the Carnegie Corporation and the
Rockefeller Foundation played a crucial role in developing higher
educational and health care services in the Maritimes after the
First World War, but their prominence has waned with the rise of
the federal welfare state. Nevertheless, as John Reid argues, the
philanthropic agencies alerted Maritime political leaders to the
long-argued need for external intervention in the plight of the
regional economy. C. Mark Davis uses the temperance issue in
Amherst, Nova Scotia, as an example of another social issue that
has been taken over by the public sector, that is, by government
agencies. While private citizens and churches alike may still hold
concerns for intemperance, now it is the public purse that pays for
solutions to the problem. In fact, as Eric Ross argues in his study of
Pictou Island, government assistance in the form of unemployment

insurance greatly altered traditional labouring practices, putting
an end to the once essential seasonal round of work activities.
There is a relict landscape today on Pictou Island, just as many
crossroads and intersections reveal abandoned gas stations, senti-
nels of a more traditional way of buying gas. Thaddeus Holownia's
photographs vividly portray the changing relationship between
function and form in the retail gas industry, and his short essay
seems to lament the passing of more interesting — traditional —
forms. Group literary experiences are of course often short-lived,
their existence closely tied to the individuals who create these
movements. Gwendolyn Davies reminds us that a Maritime group
— the Song Fishermen — although short-lived, deserve recognition beyond the region. Her essay is the recording, in its fullest expression, of the relationship in meaning between people and place.

A major concern of contemporary small town life in the Maritimes is for the well-being of its people. Much of the recent
scholarship on the region, as shown by articles in journals such as
Acadiensis, has focussed on the process of regional underdevelopment. This theme is taken up by George De Benedetti and Richard
Price, economists, who analyze the underpinnings of small town
population growth between 1971 and 1981. Places dependent
upon traditional staple industries and aging manufacturing plants
did not fare well, but towns supporting new service industries had
at least an opportunity for population growth. There is need for
more research on this theme, a need which is currently being met
by Mount Allison's Rural and Small Town Research and Studies
Programme. This research group, funded by a generous grant from
Canada Mortgage and Housing Corporation, is a tangible benefit
of the research initiated by the Committee for Studying Small
Town Life in the Maritimes.

The essays by Patrick Baker, Richard Paul Knowles, and Christine and Tom Storm and Janet Strike-Schurman also deal with the
well-being of contemporary small town life. Baker's research demonstrates that the social structure of a small town can be all-
pervasive, shaping even the quality and content of newspaper
reporting to a very significant degree. Such social pressure can be a
creative force, however, as is the case surrounding the formation of
the Mulgrave Road Co-op Theatre Company. The Co-op has
done much to highlight the difficulty of achieving well-being in the
Maritimes, while at the same time showing just how resilient
individuals and communities in the region can be. In a sense, the
Maritimes is a caring region, with a strong attachment to people

and place. This statement applies to a concern for the elderly, as Christine and Tom Storm and Janet Strike-Schurman so clearly point out. Nevertheless, as seems true of Canadian society in general, the responsibility of government for ensuring well-being is evident even in this situation.

The essays in this book tell us a great deal about the character of the small town — or more broadly, about communities — in the Maritimes, but they do not tell the complete, nor even a comprehensive story. Many of the authors continue their research into small town phenomena, and their future research papers will contribute much to the very real need to understand more about such a vital force in the character of the Maritimes region.

Many people have supported this project, including Willie Eliot, Vice-President Academic of Mount Allison, who readily discussed the idea for the project in its initial stages. Later, Deans Charlie Scobie, Jean Bour, and Bill Godfrey provided necessary encouragement. The various drafts of the essays were typed speedily and accurately to meet tight deadlines by Miss Mary Ann Lorette and Mrs. Cathy Colwell. Andrew Ferguson, Sharon Myers, and Anne-Marie Smith provided careful proofreading of the manuscript. The maps were drafted by Mrs. Stephanie Kucharyshyn of the Department of Geography, University of Alberta. They were her last project before retirement, and it is a pleasure to acknowledge again her excellent work and friendship over the past twenty years. The same co-operative spirit marks the work of Phil Buckner of Acadiensis Press, who has shared his enthusiasm for research on the Maritimes to assist in publishing this volume. We are also grateful to the editors of *Acadiensis* for permission to republish the essays by Dean Jobb and John Reid. The essays by Carrie MacMillan, Richard Paul Knowles, and Christine and Tom Storm and Janet Strike-Schurman are republished by permission of the editors of *Studies in Canadian Literature*, *Canadian Drama / L'Art dramatique canadien*, and *Canadian Journal on Aging*, respectively.

The book is dedicated to several colleagues who gave willingly of their time to shape the ideas surrounding the theme of small town life, commented on research proposals and papers, and helped with the organization of the Conference. Tom, especially, deserves our thanks for initially suggesting the small town theme and for organizing the committee that carried forward the need to research and write about this important topic.

L.D.Mc.

PART ONE

Casting
the
Pattern

W. G. GODFREY

James Glenie and the Politics of Sunbury County

I N EARLY LOYALIST NEW BRUNSWICK BOTH JAMES Glenie and Sunbury County were rather unique. Glenie was a colourful and opinionated Scot who dared to oppose Thomas Carleton and his loyalist advisors on any number of issues — a decidedly unloyalist figure. Sunbury County likewise was distinctly unloyalist in its orientation. Settled some time before the American Revolution, 1762-1763 to be precise, it was one area of New Brunswick that had a substantial pre-loyalist population. Moreover, it did not welcome with open arms the loyalist refugees who poured in after 1783. Not surprisingly, in 1789 Sunbury County elected the outspoken James Glenie as one of its representatives in the provincial assembly where, for roughly the next fifteen years, he would be a constant critic of New Brunswick's ruling elite.

Recent research and writing has revealed that the traditional picture of James Glenie as New Brunswick's first heroic reformer and leader of a reform party badly needs revision. His political motivations have been questioned, and the brevity, timewise, of his reform convictions has been established, along with the reality that any following or faction he might have commanded had largely disappeared by the early 1800s.[1] Even as his support at the province-wide level declined, Sunbury continued to return Glenie as one of its representatives, although admittedly by 1802 with a considerably reduced majority. A closer examination of Glenie's county-level support could further illuminate the basis of his

---

[1] See W. G. Godfrey, "James Glenie," in F. G. Halpenny, ed., *Dictionary of Canadian Biography* (Toronto, 1983), V, pp. 347-58. See also W. G. Godfrey, "Thomas Carleton," in *ibid.*, pp. 155-63. For many years G. F. G. Stanley, "James Glenie: A Study in Early Colonial Radicalism," Nova Scotia Historical Society *Collections*, 25 (1942), pp. 145-73, has been the accepted interpretation of Glenie.

appeal and test whether the erosion of sympathy for his cause(s) was at all matched in loyally unloyalist Sunbury County.

In 1784 the loyalist founding fathers of New Brunswick had good reason to view the old settlers of Sunbury County with considerable suspicion. Maugerville, at the heart of the county, which sits astride the St. John River near present-day Fredericton, had, after all, enthusiastically endorsed the American revolutionary cause and contributed, in 1776, twenty-seven of its native sons to Jonathan Eddy's rag-tag army of liberation when it moved through the Fundy region.[2] Once Eddy's siege of Fort Cumberland collapsed, however, and British authority was reasserted, the leading citizens of Sunbury, Israel Perley for example, pleaded a version of temporary insanity as grounds for such disloyalty. Isolation from English officialdom and protection, and alleged intimidation by New England privateers, brought on this unseemly display of support for the American cause. Now Perley hoped there would be "a general pardon and no attempt to distinguish the loyal from the disloyal."[3] The healing of wounds would be disrupted considerably when the new province of New Brunswick took shape as a refuge and reward for true loyalists. An established Anglican Church, emphasis on a landed gentry, a controlled assembly and powerful executive, a judiciary and bureaucracy packed with good loyalists only, and the threat of seeing their land possibly lost to loyalist claimants, these were the new realities with which the old settlers of Sunbury County now had to cope.[4] To religious dissenters, small farmers, unrepentant believers in a more egalitarian society and representative system of government, their interests had to be protected by vigilant representation in the assembly.

Enter James Glenie: a brilliant mathematician and military engineer whose first military career in the British army had ended in a court martial brought on by his insubordination. His career was rescued, and rank restored, by the intervention of powerful English patrons, but another attack on those in power dashed any

[2] For a recent overview of Nova Scotia's rejection of revolution, see W. G. Godfrey, "Revolution Rejected: The Debate in Nova Scotia over Whether to Become Part of the United States," *Horizon Canada*, 2, No. 24 (August, 1985), pp. 553-59.

[3] Stephen E. Patterson, "Israel Perley," in F. G. Halpenny, ed., *Dictionary of Canadian Biography* (Toronto, 1983), V, p. 666.

[4] For a discussion of the loyalist elite's blueprint for New Brunswick, see Ann Gorman Condon, *The Envy of the American States: The Loyalist Dream for New Brunswick* (Fredericton, 1984).

chance of promotion and brought his resignation from the service. Capitalizing upon his knowledge of New Brunswick's timber resources, acquired while briefly stationed there in 1785, he arrived in Saint John in October of 1787 as a well-connected participant in the masting trade.[5] In November of 1789 he was elated when "the People unsolicited & contrary to my Wishes chose me Member of Assembly for the County of Sunbury." This victory was achieved allegedly despite "Every Strategem every low Artifice & Lie [which] was practised and made use of by the Govr's pitiful Junto for months before to prevent it." According to Glenie, the rulers of New Brunswick "are cursedly alarmed. For they suppose that a Majority of the House will follow me & that their villainous Practices will not only be examined into but brought to Light & exposed."[6] But it would be well over a year before the assembly met and Glenie could launch his attack there. In the interval, examples of "villainous Practices" were enthusiastically unearthed and used to underline the shortcomings and abuse of power by Thomas Carleton and his advisors. When Glenie's accusations and name-calling are digested — "Imp of Stupidity," "illiterate Moon-Struck Judge," "ignorant uncouth Dutch Boor," "a Person who is implicitly led through every Species of Absurdity by... ignorant unprincipled blundering Individuals," "ignorant stuttering Chief Justice," "a man on whom nature has fixed the stamp of Stupidity" were some of the thumbnail sketches applied to New Brunswick's leading citizens — they seem designed not to change the system but merely to replace one ruling clique by another. Instead of the "unprincipled Harpies" presently being appointed, Glenie proposed Jonathan Bliss as an excellent candidate for a judicial appointment, or "My neighbour Daniel Bliss." "For filling the Vacancies in the Council there are Capt. Phineas Shaw, Wm Gordon Esq. and several other European Gentlemen very well qualified who will not be Tools like those recommended."[7]

James Glenie was far from a tribune of the common people at this moment and if his electoral success in Sunbury County must be explained, it probably was patterned more on the approach and

[5] *Saint John Gazette, and The Weekly Advertiser*, 12 October 1787.

[6] James Glenie to Andrew Finucane, 30 November 1789, c.o. 188, 4/353-354, Public Record Office.

[7] Glenie to Finucane, 1 January 1790, M.G. 11, N.B., "A" Series, 4/107-112, Public Archives of Canada.

appeal of a William Davidson than on later issues such as assembly power. Davidson had been elected to represent Sunbury County in the Nova Scotia assembly and then in 1785 represented North-umberland in the New Brunswick assembly. In both instances, the fact that he was at the time of election the most prominent employer of individuals in each of the counties was a major help.[8] This deferential attitude on the part of the electorate was likely still present when Glenie moved into Sunbury with his masting con-tracts and, coupled with his outspoken anti-loyalist proclamations in an area with a substantial pre-loyalist population, contributed substantially to his acceptance. Admittedly, once in the assembly he became an active participant and soon demonstrated an alert sensitivity to the needs of his Sunbury constituents. Glenie was declared duly elected when the Assembly opened on 5 February 1791,[9] and within a few days presented "a petition from a number of the inhabitants of *Maugerville* praying an act of the Legislature for establishing permanent marks or bounds to the several rights or shares in the said township." He followed this with a motion for leave to bring in "A Bill for fixing permanently the Boundary Lines between the different Grants throughout the Province."[10] In late 1791 his friend and patron John Wentworth appointed him deputy surveyor of woods for New Brunswick, which was a boon both to Glenie and his constituents.[11] For Glenie, it would facilitate his exploitation of the province's timber while he could look the other way when his own constituents were illegally taking the King's wood which he was supposed to preserve.[12]

Again in the 1792 session he remained quite active. Spurred on by a petition from his Sunbury constituents, he called for an amendment to the Marriage Act permitting ministers of regular dissenting congregations "to solemnize, and celebrate Marriage, between persons of their own Communion...."[13] Apparently the

[8] See W. A. Spray, "William Davidson," in F. G. Halpenny, ed., *Dictionary of Cana-dian Biography* (Toronto, 1979), IV, p. 196.

[9] *Journals of the Legislative Assembly of New Brunswick*, 5 February 1791, p. 171.

[10] *Ibid.*, 8 February 1791, p. 176.

[11] Glenie to John [Flieger] 16 December 1791, Vol. 940, pp. 419-21, Public Archives of Nova Scotia.

[12] This is suggested in William D. Moore, "Sunbury County 1760-1830," unpublished M.A. thesis, University of New Brunswick, 1977, pp. 85-86.

[13] "The Humble Petition of Sundry of the Inhabitants of the County of Sunbury," 18 February 1792, R.S. 24, S6-P14, Provincial Archives of New Brunswick (here-after P.A.N.B.).

session ended before this was done but the gesture had been made. However, as early as July of 1788 Glenie had indicated his support for the dissenting religious beliefs of his old settler neighbours. At that time the Maugerville Congregational Church members, many of whom eventually would be Baptists and Methodists, were seeking pledges for an annual contribution to pay a dissenting minister's salary. Out of eighty-six contributions, forty-six individuals contributed less than one pound, thirty-five individuals contributed between one and two pounds, four individuals contributed between two and three pounds, no one contributed between three and five pounds, but one individual generously gave five pounds ten shillings — James Glenie.[14] Such a donation can only be considered princely, particularly from a Presbyterian Scot, one of whose sons would become an Anglican minister! In summary, in his early political career, James Glenie was an effective and responsive constituency representative.

The assembly session in February and March of 1795 brought consistent disagreement between the lower house and the council, which was allied with the lieutenant-governor, and time and again James Glenie emerged at the centre of the skirmishes. Once Thomas Carleton decided to attempt to secure a more amenable assembly through an election fought in September and October of 1795, Glenie was quite willing to take to the Sunbury hustings to outline his active and vigilant defence of the assembly's, and thus the people's rights. A proposed act concerning Supreme Court sessions, Glenie explained, was pushed "in order to carry the administration of Justice by that Court into every County and to every Man's door as much as possible; The very purpose, I conceive, for which the Judges receive their salaries." He pointed out that this bill had been passed by the assembly five times only to be rejected by the council, and even when "I delivered a message myself putting them in mind of it as a Bill tending greatly to promote the happiness and convenience of His Majesty's subjects in this Province," no satisfactory explanation of "the reasons of the Council for setting it aside" was offered. The assembly's refusal to grant "Money for erecting Buildings of accommodation at Fredericton for the General Assembly and Courts of Justice" was explained as the result of the assembly's judgment that "the

14 "Documents of the Congregational Church of Maugerville," New Brunswick Historical Society *Collections*, 1 (1894-1897), pp. 139-41.

Province [was] not in a situation to bear without great inconvenience to the people, the raising of such sums as would have been necessary for these exertions." Moreover, Glenie expressed his opinion, growing out of his own considerable experience, that the buildings would be far more expensive than estimated: "I have erected, Gentlemen, more military works and public buildings than any other person in this Province, and I never saw an estimate for one yet, even when made by experienced, intelligent and skillful Engineers, who must be supposed much more capable of forming estimates, than the Gentleman who presented this, that did not fall greatly short of the actual expence of execution."

A concern about unwarranted or premature expenditures was also behind the assembly's unwillingness to approve "an allowance for a collegiate establishment." This "barely-existing Colony" could ill afford the proposed grant, which was in any case "not half sufficient." In addition, emphasis should be placed on a parish school system meeting local and broader needs first. The assembly, Glenie maintained, "very judiciously considered that Parish Schools, which disseminate generally a certain degree of information and learning, ought naturally to precede any endowment for a College, which without them is only calculated for the accommodation of a few Individuals, and has a tendency to monopolize education — And however much some persons may dislike the general dissemination of knowledge among the people and reckon it dangerous, it ought in my opinion to be the first object of attention in every well regulated state." Assembly refusal to accept Thomas Carleton's defence expenditures in Saint Andrews and Saint John was due to the responsibility resting elsewhere for such expenses: "I thought it my indispensable duty to point out the unprecedented nature of such an application, and the regular channel of payment for such expenditures which is through the estimates for army extraordinaries, annually presented to the House of Commons by the Secretary at war." Then turning to the most important issue of assembly power over the public purse, Glenie reminded his constituents that the council had claimed "that it is unparliamentary and unconstitutional in the House of Assembly to dispose of any public money for any other purposes or services than those recommended by His Excellency, or (which comes to the same thing) than those, which they choose to advise him to recommend, as they are a Council of advice as well as Legislation." To acquiesce in the fact of such an assertion "would have been tantamount to an absolute surrender of your purses, property, rights and liberties, into the hands of the Council at once... It is a proposition, to which I hope in God no House of Assembly will ever give its assent. For it is a parliamentary maxim as old as parliament itself, that those who have the sole right of granting have an unquestionable right to dispose of what they grant."[15]

Glenie had made a powerful case for a vigilant and active assembly sensitive to the needs of the overwhelming majority of New Brunswickers. Controlling needless and wasteful spending, bringing education and access to the courts first to the people, and enhancing the elected assembly's position and power within the governmental system were all issues which would have a definite appeal to many who were not among the privileged loyalist elite. In the election of 1795 the electorate appeared to approve of Glenie and the "assembly party's" conduct by returning a majority of members even more hostile to the "governor's party." Glenie himself won easily in Sunbury County, topping the poll with seventy-nine votes; his running mate, Samuel Denny Street, won his seat with sixty-three votes; the two defeated candidates, William Hubbard and Sylvanus Plummer, finished with twenty-two and twelve votes respectively. Fortunately, the polling book survives from that election listing all voters and how they voted, and providing a rare opportunity to examine more closely Glenie's support.[16] After deciphering the names of the voters, no easy task since comparison with other petitions was required to verify names, there were seventy-eight decipherable voters for Glenie and thirteen decipherable voters against his candidacy. These names were then checked against David Bell's recent listing of loyalists, Esther C. Wright's loyalist listing, James Hannay's Maugerville work that lists pre-loyalist settlers, and Congregational Church documents for Maugerville that provide pre-loyalist names.[17] The *Dictionary of*

[15] "Substance of Mr. Glenie's Address, To the Freeholders of the County of Sunbury, At the opening of the Poll on Tuesday the 1st of September [1795] instant: Explanatory of the Proceedings of the late House of Assembly, &c. &c.," Glenie Family, cb. 1, New Brunswick Museum (hereafter N.B.M.).

[16] "Poll Book on Election of Representatives for Sunbury. Poll opened 1st September 1795," York-Sunbury Historical Society Collection, MYO A 15, P.A.N.B.

[17] David G. Bell, *Early Loyalist Saint John: The Origin of New Brunswick Politics, 1783-1786* (Fredericton, 1983); E. C. Wright, *The Loyalists of New Brunswick* (Moncton, 1955); James Hannay, "Sunbury County Documents," New Brunswick Historical Society *Collections*, 1 (1894-1897), pp. 100-18; "Documents of the Congregational Church of Maugerville," *ibid.*, pp. 119-52.

Canadian Biography was also checked, but few of these individuals
have been examined in biographies, or are even mentioned in
others.

What needed to be ascertained was whether Glenie's support,
and the opposition to him, clearly demonstrated the pre-loyalist/
loyalist divisions. Of the seventy-eight legible voters for Glenie,
thirteen could not be identified as loyalist or pre-loyalist. The
remaining sixty-five legible and identifiable voters broke down
into forty-five pre-loyalists, or 69.2 percent, and twenty loyalists, or
30.8 percent. Of the thirteen legible voters against Glenie, one
could not be categorized as loyalist or pre-loyalist. Of the twelve
legible and identifiable voters, two were pre-loyalists, or 16.7
percent, and ten were loyalists, or 83.3 percent. What is note-
worthy is that 30.8 percent of Glenie's identifiable supporters were
loyalists, despite his anti-loyalist stance. Indeed, of the thirty
loyalist votes cast, twenty, or 66 percent, went to Glenie. The anti-
loyalist elite rhetoric of James Glenie apparently was quite accept-
able to a substantial number of the loyalist rank-and-file in Sunbury County. David Bell has established the non-monolithic nature
of loyalism in early Saint John, underlining the presence of opposition loyalists disagreeing with the elite in the 1783-1786 period, but
he describes that opposition as snuffed out quickly by the elite.
Moreover, he questions whether the divisions persisted and were
connected with the Glenie opposition group and the factiousness of
the mid-1790s.[18] The Sunbury returns confirm the continuing
existence of what could be labelled a moderate-reform-loyalist
group quite willing to support a challenge to the loyalist elite and
certainly not sharing the elite's dreams or aspirations.

During the ensuing constitutional crisis and period of turmoil
from 1795 to 1799, with assembly and executive deadlocked and in
constant conflict, Glenie's increasingly abrasive and abusive approach alienated many within this province-wide moderate-reform-loyalist faction. These members of the assembly wanted more
assembly power but proceeded to that goal in a more circumspect
and less confrontational fashion. Consequently Glenie was bypassed
or shunted aside in the assembly particularly after he attempted to
censure directly the lieutenant-governor in 1797, a motion rejected
by his colleagues in a 17 to 5 vote.[19] Through the guidance of Amos

[18] See Bell, *Early Loyalist Saint John*, pp. 133-35.
[19] *Journals of the Legislative Assembly of New Brunswick*, 27 January 1797, pp. 545-47.

Botsford, and other moderate loyalists within the "assembly party," compromise arrangements were worked out with the "governor's party" in 1799. Thus Botsford could report at that time that all disputes had been "amicably adjusted" in what he perceived as an assembly vindication and confirmation.[20]

What did James Glenie think of all this? Initially there was a strange silence, but before 1800 expired he had written and published a creed which revealed that he believed little had changed.[21] To quote some choicer extracts:

I believe in J--N. O--L.[22] S--Y of the Province of N.B. maker of Militia officers and Just Assess of the Peace, and plotter of all head quarter intrigues visible and invisible, the only beloved of Simple Tom, Beloved of all Britons, Men of men, head of heads, S--Y of S--Y's, beloved and not hated, being of one opinion with his Patron, by whom all Quonsillors are made ...

And I believe the Quonsil to be a faction of low bred Refugees who prefer the interests of the U--S to those of Great-Britain and the immediate creatures of the subtle Quack who can do no wrong.

And I believe T--Y C--N,[23] the disposer of all places, who together with his quack tutor are whorshipped and glorified by slaves, fools and knaves; who speak by Proclamation; I also firmly believe that they possess as much Malevolence and pride as Lucifer without one particle of his abilities ...

And I sincerely believe this City to be the most abominable of all Cities, over which the infamous whore of Babylon presides and always rides poor T---C--- as the phantom of Civil Government, and the Ghost of departed justice, and to be remarkable both for its attachment to Great Britain and attention to strangers, a few of the Citizens only excepted!!!!!!

But I now look for the coming of a new Governor to purge the Quonsil and to cause justice to be administered throughout the land, which God grant! Amen.

Obviously the compromise arrangements worked out by the assembly and council did not go far enough for Glenie. Nothing short of a purge of the upper house and a recall of the lieutenant-governor would satisfy him. The old Glenie, an abusive and bitter namecaller, re-emerged; the reasoned arguments for legal and

[20] Amos Botsford to Thomas Street, 10 October 1977, R.S. 24, S13-Z9, P.A.N.B.
[21] "Glenie's Creed," Glenie Family, cb. 1, N.B.M.
[22] Jonathon Odell.
[23] Thomas Carleton.

constitutional reforms were forgotten. His bitterness no doubt was heightened by the realization that even in the assembly, the cause of which he had briefly championed, he could no longer count on anywhere near majority support.

Could he count on the continuing support of Sunbury County, or would the changes in alignment within the assembly be matched at the county level? In the October of 1802 election, Glenie and Street barely squeaked back in, with one hundred and one and ninety-three votes, respectively, compared to their opponents' eighty-seven and eighty-two. Poll book results here would be revealing in that Glenie's support, slightly increased, and opposition, vastly increased, could be dissected. But the 1795 results are a rarity and the 1802 detailed returns are lacking. However, the elections of Glenie and Street were challenged and the resultant petitions for and against are revealing. The petition supporting Glenie and Street contained twenty names of whom thirteen were among the identifiable Glenie supporters in 1795.[24] Of the thirteen, ten were pre-loyalists (76.9 percent) and three were loyalists (23.1 percent). The opposition petition contained twenty-four names of whom thirteen had been among the 1795 voters.[25] Three were identified loyalists who voted against Glenie in 1795 and who obviously continued to oppose him. The remaining ten petitioners now opposing him had voted for him in 1795 and broke down into four pre-loyalists who had shifted, three loyalists who had shifted, and three voters, who cannot be identified as loyalist or pre-loyalist, who had also changed their allegiance from Glenie. Thus, if the petition evidence is representative, there was limited slippage among his pre-loyalist supporters and a more substantial loss among loyalist voters.

James Glenie's popularity in Sunbury County was based on more than anti-loyalist rhetoric in a pre-loyalist area. His supporters initially were drawn from both camps and his loyalist support was

[24] "Petition of Sundry Electors of the County of Sunbury complaining of the conduct of the Sheriff and of undue influence at the late General Election. Praying that Sammuel Dennis Street Esquire may be admitted to take his Seat in the House of Assembly," 16 FEbruary 1803, R.S. 24, S16-P17, P.A.N.B.

[25] "Petition of Sundry Inhabitants of the County of Sunbury complaining of False and inflamatory Speeches, and undue influence of James Glenie & S. Denny Street Esquires at the late General Election in the said County, praying that the said J.G. and S.D.S. may be declerr'd incapacitated to sit as members of the House of Assembly, pledging themselves to support the allegations by proof," 19 February 1803, R.S. 24, S16-P16, P.A.M.B.

much more substantial than realized, although admittedly the pre-loyalist commitment was stronger and deeper. At the same time, his economic activities would appeal to all constituents, as would his defence of expanded assembly rights and privileges, however brief. Moreover, there is no doubt about the rewards produced by his sensitivity to his constituents' needs and apprehensions, on the religious question for example. Above all, Glenie's shifting political fortunes, revealed in the changing alignments within the county, are a confirmation that the assembly and province-wide changes were being duplicated to a certain considerable extent in Glenie's home constituency. To be sure, there is strong evidence that Sunbury's pre-loyalist old settlers remained largely unrevised and unrepentant, but perhaps they merely wanted to provide a model that modern-day New Brunswick politicians still consider worthy of emulation.

DEAN JOBB

Sackville Promotes a Railway: The Politics of the New Brunswick and Prince Edward Railway, 1872-1886[1]

T HE RAILWAY EPITOMIZED PROGRESS IN NINETEENTH century Canada. Communities large and small vied with one another to secure the new technology of steam and steel. But while virtually everyone acknowledged the advantages of railways, few desired to risk the tremendous amounts of capital necessary to build and equip a line. Since railways would serve the wider public interest, government was called on to undertake their construction, or at least to subsidize the efforts of private companies to do so. Railways meant development and then, as now, development was good politics. A great deal has been written about the important role of railways in Canadian history, and recently historians have begun to take a closer look at the process whereby the goals of individual railway entrepreneurs became those of the general public.[2]

In New Brunswick a flurry of railway building followed the completion of the main line of the Intercolonial Railway (ICR) in 1876, accompanying a rapid expansion of secondary industry in centres such as Moncton, Saint John and St. Stephen. Railway mileage within the province increased by more than 50 percent between 1880 and 1890, reaching 1,132 miles of track by the end of

[1] I would like to thank Dr. Gerald Tulchinsky, Dr. Larry McCann, and Dr. William Godfrey for their comments on an earlier draft of this paper. The research was funded by grants from the Social Sciences and Humanities Research Council of Canada and the Bell Foundation, Mount Allison University.

[2] Brian J. Young, *Promoters and Politicians: The North-Shore Railways in the History of Quebec, 1854-85* (Toronto, 1978); Gerald J. J. Tulchinsky, *The River Barons: Montreal Businessmen and the Growth of Industry and Transportation 1837-1853* (Toronto, 1977); and Peter A. Baskerville, "The Boardroom and Beyond: Aspects of the Upper Canadian Railroad Community," unpublished Ph.D. thesis, Queen's University, 1973. For an overview of recent works on Canadian Railway history, see Baskerville, "On the Rails: Trends in Canadian Railway Historiography," *American Review of Canadian Studies*, 9 (1979), pp. 63-72.

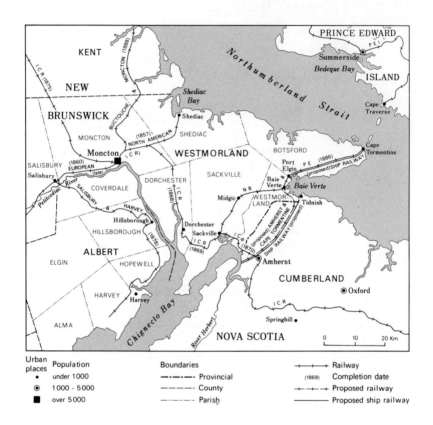

FIGURE 1. THE LOCATION OF SACKVILLE AND THE ROUTE OF
THE NEW BRUNSWICK AND PRINCE EDWARD RAILWAY.

the decade.[3] The history of one of the branch lines built during this decade, the New Brunswick and Prince Edward (NB & PE), offers an opportunity to explore the activities of railway promoters in the Maritime Provinces. The backers of the NB & PE Railway, a line stretching 36 miles from Sackville to Cape Tormentine in southeastern New Brunswick, sought to build this road in order to directly benefit their extensive business interests in the region. By virtue of their political influence on the federal and provincial levels, these businessmen succeeded in blocking rival schemes and securing massive government assistance for the project. The building of the NB & PE Railway illustrates the intimate relationship between politics and private business in nineteenth century railway promotion.

During the 1870s Sackville emerged as a small but active outport at the head of the Bay of Fundy. A total of 26 vessels — representing almost 9,000 registered tons — were launched at Sackville between 1870 and 1880.[4] Employment for these ships was readily available; the products of the fertile Tantramar marshes and nearby forests found a ready market in Britain, the West Indies, and, in particular, the United States.[5] Local merchants exported staples such as lumber, hay and other farm produce in exchange for manufactured goods from abroad. But an indigenous manufacturing base was beginning to take root. In 1871 the output of sawmills, forges, tanneries, and carriage shops in Sackville parish was valued at more than $190,000.[6] Another symbol of the industrial age had reached Sackville the year before when the town became a station stop on the Intercolonial Railway. As one observer noted at the

[3] Railway mileage is calculated from "Railway Statistics of Canada," House of Commons, Sessional Papers, 1880-81, vol. 4, 1891, vol. 11. The industrial expansion of the Maritime Provinces in the decade following the introduction of the National Policy of tariff protection has been documented in T. W. Acheson, "The National Policy and the Industrialization of the Maritimes, 1880-1910," Acadiensis, 1 (1972), pp. 3-28.

[4] Calculated from "Tables of Trade and Navigation of the Dominion of Canada," House of Commons, Sessional Papers, 1871-1880.

[5] In 1871, for instance, 24 of 28 vessels landing at Sackville came from American ports, while 16 of 22 clearances were to United States destinations: House of Commons, Sessional Papers, 1872, vol. 3, #3, statements 17 and 18. The development of the port of Sackville in this period is covered in greater detail in Dale C. Alward, "Down Sackville Ways: Shipbuilding in a Nineteenth Century New Brunswick Outport," unpublished B.A. thesis, Mount Allison University, 1978.

[6] Schedule 6, Industrial Establishments, 1871 census manuscripts, Public Archives of Canada (hereafter P.A.C.).

time, "the Sackville people can now begin to realize the fact of steam communication with the world."[7]

And realize they did. Some Sackville residents were alive to the possibility of forging a second transportation link eastward to capture the trade of Prince Edward Island. In the spring of 1872 W. C. Milner, editor of the local newspaper, the *Chignecto Post*, proposed the construction of a branch railway from the ICR at Sackville to Cape Tormentine on the Northumberland Strait, a distance of thirty-six miles. "Of the practical utility of such a road there can be no doubt," Milner claimed: "It would pass through a country already well settled and developed in an agricultural point. ... The construction of this road is however a necessity to Prince Edward Island. The distance from Cape Tormentine to Cape Traverse, P.E.I., is but eight miles. In the summer season, freight, passengers and mails, could be ferried across almost hourly, and in winter this is the only route by which P.E. Island maintains communication with the outside world."[8]

The prospects for such a line improved the following year when P.E.I. became Canada's seventh province. Under the terms of Confederation, the federal government agreed to provide year-round communication with the Island by steamer, a pledge which became increasingly important as the markets for P.E.I. produce shifted from Britain to the mainland in the 1870s.[9] The route from Cape Tormentine, the closest mainland point, to Cape Traverse appeared to be the likely choice for the institution of such a service. Small open dories called "ice boats" had been making the winter crossing for decades, ferrying passengers and mail over the hazardous ice floes of the Northumberland Strait.

Sackville soon made a bid to become the mainland centre for Island communication. In April of 1874 the New Brunswick Assembly incorporated the New Brunswick & Prince Edward Railway Company, with an authorized capital stock of up to $950,000, to build a line from Sackville to the Cape. The provincial government offered the company a subsidy of $5,000 per mile under this charter, on the conditions that surveys be undertaken within two years, construction begun within four, and the entire

[7] *The Borderer and Westmorland and Cumberland Advertiser* (Sackville), 2 September 1869.

[8] *Chignecto Post* (Sackville), 28 March 1872.

[9] Mary K. Cullen, "The Transportation Issue, 1873-1973," in Francis W. P. Bolger, ed., *Canada's Smallest Province: A History of P.E.I.* (Charlottetown, 1973), pp. 233-36.

line completed by 1880. The list of incorporators included Sack-
ville's most prominent citizens: Josiah Wood, J. L. Black, Amos
Ogden, John Fawcett, Edward Cogswell, Richard C. Boxall, and
Milner.[10]

For the most part these men controlled business interests that
stood to benefit from a branch line to Cape Tormentine. Wood,
just thirty-one years old in 1874, was undoubtedly the wealthiest
man in Sackville. Having inherited his father's wholesaling firm of
M. Wood & Sons, he carried on a thriving import and export trade
employing a small fleet of company ships. In addition Wood operated a private bank, sawmills, and a 500-acre farm; his total
assets were reputed to be in excess of $200,000.[11] Black, who carried
on a smaller wholesale and retail business valued at upwards of
$40,000, was one of the area's largest lumber producers. The firm
of J. L. Black & Sons controlled thousands of acres of timberland in
the eastern section of Westmorland County adjacent to the proposed route of the railway.[12] Ogden too was interested in lumber-
ing and, in partnership with Wood, owned at least two sawmills in
the same area.[13] Fawcett and Cogswell, proprietors of the town's
two stove foundries, shipped their products throughout the Maritimes and probably welcomed improved access to the Island
market.[14] Boxall, an English architect and engineer, and Milner,
the newspaper proprietor, apparently had no business interest

---

[10] *Acts of the New Brunswick Assembly*, 1874, pp. 185-92. The railway was originally
intended to be named the New Brunswick & Prince Edward Island, but the word
"Island" was dropped at the insistence of MLAs who thought it misleading. When
the line was incorporated by federal statute in 1889, the name was changed to NB &
PEI: *Proceedings of the New Brunswick House of Assembly*, 9 March 1874, p. 48; "An Act
Respecting the New Brunswick and Prince Edward Railway Company, 1889," File
24, Wood Family Papers, Provincial Archives of New Brunswick [P.A.N.B.]

[11] Dun, Wiman & Co., *The Mercantile Agency Reference Book for the Dominion of Canada*
(January, 1882), pp. 784-85. For a biography of Wood, see Dean Jobb, "Josiah
Wood (1843-1927): 'A Cultured and Honoured Gentleman of the Old School',"
unpublished B.A. thesis, Mount Allison University, 1980. To his business creden-
tials, Wood later added a public career spanning more than 30 years as a Member of
Parliament (1882-1895), Senator (1895-1912), and Lieutenant-Governor of New
Brunswick (1912-1917).

[12] I. Allen Jack, ed., *Biographical Review: Province of New Brunswick* (Boston, 1900), p.
239; W. B. Sawdon, "Joseph L. Black and Sons Limited Celebrate a Century in
Business," *Maritime Advocate and Busy East* (October, 1947), pp. 5-7; *Mercantile Agency
Reference Book* (January, 1882), pp. 784-85.

[13] *Chignecto Post*, 9 May, 12 December 1878.

[14] *Chignecto Post*, 26 December 1889; W. C. Milner, *History of Sackville, New Brunswick*
(Sackville, 1934), p. 81.

associated with the proposed route. As the company's chief engineer, however, Boxall soon became one of its most ardent supporters, while Milner actively supported the scheme in his editorial columns.

Local interest was high, and within a month the company reported stock subscriptions totalling $66,000. The bulk of these shares were taken up by Boxall and Amasa Killam, a lawyer who had promoted several branch lines in the Moncton area. Black subscribed for $2,500 and Wood, Milner, and Senator Amos E. Botsford for $1,000 each.[15] Because of his influence in political circles, Botsford was chosen to be the company's president. The patriarch of one of New Brunswick's most prominent Loyalist families, Botsford's "tall, unbowed, soldiery figure" belied his 70 years. Active in provincial politics as a member of the Legislative Council for nearly 35 years, he had been appointed to the Senate at Confederation.[16]

Backed by this show of local support and the promise of provincial assistance, the company pushed ahead with surveys and secured a contractor to build the line. At this point the promoters decided to approach the federal government to subsidize the project by supplying the rails. In 1876 a committee of the company, headed by Wood and Killam, met with the member of parliament for Westmorland, Albert J. Smith. As Minister of Marine and Fisheries, Smith was attempting to fulfil the terms of union with the Island by means of an ice-breaking steamer, the Northern Light, on the route between Pictou, Nova Scotia, and Georgetown, P.E.I. Should this experiment fail, however, Smith promised the delegation that the federal government would build the Cape Railway itself in order to improve winter communication with the Island.[17] Hopeful that the Dominion government would be obliged to build the line, the company cancelled its contracts and awaited the outcome of the steamer experiment.

The verdict was not long in coming. The Northern Light had been designed to operate in the St. Lawrence River and proved

---

[15] List of stockholders in the NB & PE Railway Company, 11 May 1874, File 24, Wood Family Papers, P.A.N.B.

[16] *Chignecto Post*, 29 March 1883. See also Lorna Milton, "Three Generations of Loyalist Gentlemen: The Botsford Men of Westmorland County," unpublished B.A. thesis, Mount Allison University, 1981.

[17] *Chignecto Post*, 21 December 1876, 5 September 1878. The federal government later aided at least three branch lines in New Brunswick by supplying second-hand rails: *Chignecto Post*, 18 March 1886.

incapable of breaking through the heavier ice of the Strait. Winter service was at best sporadic; the steamer was often unable to cross for weeks at a time, forcing the government to revert to sending mail and passengers over the Capes route in the ice boats.[18] The problems of the Northern Light did not go unnoticed in Sackville —the *Chignecto Post* closely monitored the steamer's infrequent trips and soon labelled the steamer connection a failure. In increasingly bitter editorials from late 1876 to early 1878, Milner assailed Smith for his refusal to aid the NB & PE Railway Company and called on the minister to uphold his "solemn assurance" by constructing the line to Cape Tormentine.[19] No action was forthcoming from Smith, however, and there was little the Sackville promoters could do to force his hand. Botsford spoke favourably of the project in the Senate on two occasions, but with his Conservative Party in Opposition he could do no more.[20] The company faced the same lack of political clout in the House of Commons. Only A. L. Palmer, Wood's uncle and a Conservative member from Saint John, came to the NB & PE's defence, advocating during the 1878 session that the Northern Light be abandoned and the Cape Railway subsidized in its place.[21] Despite these setbacks, the company took the precaution of reviving its charter in April 1878. The projected completion date was extended to 1884.[22]

In the general election of September 1878 the Liberal government went down to defeat at the hands of John A. Macdonald's Conservatives, but the results only added to the problems of the Sackville promoters. Smith, hardly a friend of the Cape Railway, was re-elected in Westmorland to sit on the Opposition benches. Even more disheartening was the outcome in the neighbouring constituency of Cumberland in Nova Scotia. There the victorious candidate for the Conservatives was Charles Tupper, the former provincial premier and a powerful figure within the party. Tupper was sworn in as Minister of Public Works in October 1878, and almost immediately ordered surveys of possible railway routes to the Cape with a view to improving communication with the Island.

[18] Cullen, "The Transportation Issue," pp. 234-35.
[19] *Chignecto Post*, 11 January 1877. For other editorials see issues of 21, 28 December 1876, 14 February 1878.
[20] Canada, *Debates of the Senate*, 20 February 1877, pp. 56-57, 18 February 1878, p. 48.
[21] Canada, *Debates of the House of Commons*, 20 April 1878, vol. 5, p. 2082.
[22] *New Brunswick Acts*, 1878, pp. 278-79.

This was not welcome news for the businessmen of Sackville. The largest town in Tupper's riding, Amherst, was only ten miles south along the Intercolonial and virtually the same distance as Sackville from the Cape. A growing industrial and commercial centre in its own right, by 1878 Amherst boasted a boot and shoe factory, a stove foundry, and a woodworking plant.[23] One resident claimed that a branch to Cape Tormentine would mean "numerous new factories and an increase of two or three thousand in the population" of the town.[24] Understandably, Tupper wanted these benefits for his own constituents. The report of the Cape surveys, submitted in April 1879, included estimates of two possible railways terminating at Amherst, but none to Sackville.[25] A dejected Milner expressed the mood of the Sackville promoters when he told his readers "We have played our card and lost."[26]

The Macdonald government moved slowly on the question of P.E.I. communication, however, and by 1881 no effort had been made to build an Amherst-Cape Tormentine Railway. Late that year, in an attempt to revive interest in the NB & PE Railway scheme, Botsford asked the company's engineer, Boxall, to prepare a report on the advantages of the Sackville route.[27] His report, completed just before Christmas, stressed the commercial potential of such a line to Westmorland County in general and the town of Sackville in particular. Lumber from sawmills along the proposed route, he estimated, would account for 650 carloads of freight annually, with another 1,200 tons of potatoes and 20,000 bushels of grain from local farms. Much of this traffic would pass through Sackville, which had a longer shipping season than the ports of the Northumberland Strait. Of lesser importance were the prospects for freight and passenger traffic to and from P.E.I.[28]

Boxall's optimistic report spurred what one observer described

[23] A. Robson Lamy, "The Development and Decline of Amherst as an Industrial Centre," unpublished B.A. thesis, Mount Allison University, 1930.

[24] *Chignecto Post*, 12 December 1878.

[25] Canada, *Journals of the House of Commons*, 1883, vol. 17, Appendix 3, pp. 80-84.

[26] *Chignecto Post*, 25 November 1880.

[27] In the nineteenth century it was common for railway companies to solicit such reports from engineers, who would provide an optimistic survey of the potential of the road in order to promote interest among the public and aid in the raising of capital. See the introduction to H. V. Nelles, ed., *Philosophy of Railroads and Other Essays by T. C. Keefer* (Toronto, 1972), p. 23.

[28] Boxall's report appears in vol. 139, pp. 57271-75, John A. Macdonald Papers, P.A.C., and was reprinted in *Sessional Papers*, 1882, vol. 10, #79, pp. 9-10.

THE POLITICS OF THE NEW BRUNSWICK AND PRINCE EDWARD RAILWAY

as an "eleventh hour movement of our business men."[29] Realizing the extent of the local trade at stake, Wood, Black, Ogden and other promoters of the NB & PE Railway met in February 1882 to discuss the situation. Those present feared "a reduction of business and depreciation of property would follow the diverting of the Railway from Sackville to Amherst," and called a mass meeting of local ratepayers for the following week to enlist municipal support.[30] At the ratepayers' meeting, Wood explained that the proposed line to Amherst threatened to divert the trade of eastern Westmorland County away "from its natural route to Saint John" via Sackville. He then moved that a provincial act be applied for to enable the parishes of Sackville, Westmorland, and Botsford, through which the NB & PE Railway would pass, to "raise money by assessment in aid of construction." When the assembled taxpayers displayed their support by passing the motion, Wood pledged he would devote his time and "any reasonable amount of money" towards making the railway from Sackville to the Cape a reality.[31]

More important than this promise of municipal aid was the willingness of Wood and Black, the town's most influential businessmen, to work together in the promotion of the NB & PE line. Four years earlier the two men had been rival candidates for the provincial assembly in a campaign marred by the emotional issue of sectarian schools. Black won,[32] but the bitterness of the fight lasted for several years afterward. By the spring of 1882, however, a common interest in the building of the Cape Railway ended the feud. "The two have had a regular funeral of hatchets — buried on the line of railway survey between here and Cape Tormentine," explained Wood's wife.[33] As an MLA, Black guided two important pieces of legislation through the New Brunswick legislature during March.[34] The first bill moved the completion date of the line ahead to 1887, but the original provincial subsidy of $5,000 per mile was

[29] *Chignecto Post*, 9 February 1882.
[30] *Chignecto Post*, 2 February 1882.
[31] *Chignecto Post*, 9 February 1882.
[32] *The Borderer*, 3 June 1878. Black polled 2,703 votes, enough to capture one of the four Westmorland County seats at Fredericton; Wood finished fifth with 1,915. See *The Canadian Parliamentary Companion and Annual Register*, 1881, p. 343.
[33] Laura S. Wood, "Journal of Everyday Affairs" [transcript of diary in the possession of Dr. J. L. Black, Ottawa] 12 May 1882, p. 33.
[34] *Journals of the New Brunswick House of Assembly*, 1882, pp. 68, 87.

pared down to $3,000. A further act enabled the parishes along the proposed route to purchase a total of $9,500 in NB & PE Railway stock, pending a vote by the ratepayers.[35] While Black handled these affairs at Fredericton, Wood travelled to Ottawa to deal with a new threat to the Sackville line.

Tupper, now minister for the new Department of Railways and Canals,[36] still wanted the Cape Railway for Cumberland County. But by 1882 he had also become interested in an ambitious scheme to construct a ship railway to convey vessels across the narrow Isthmus of Chignecto from Amherst to Baie Verte. The brainchild of H. G. C. Ketchum, an energetic New Brunswick engineer, the ship railway would provide a long-sought link between the waters of the Bay of Fundy and the Gulf of St. Lawrence at a fraction of the cost of a canal. Vessels and their cargoes would be lifted by hydraulic presses onto specially designed flatcars and then shunted overland by locomotives, thus saving hundreds of sailing miles around Nova Scotia. During 1881 Ketchum requested federal subsidies from Tupper, "who was inclined to look favorably upon a project which would bring large amounts of investment" into his own constituency.[37] Enthusiasm for the ship railway was high among the people of Amherst, who realized that "the expenditure of several millions in their vicinity would offer opportunities for profit," while enhancing the commercial importance of the town.[38] Tupper immediately submitted Ketchum's proposal to his department's engineers for study.

The businessmen of Sackville had long favoured the construction of a canal to Baie Verte, and saw the ship railway as a suitable replacement. Wrote Milner: "Sackville, as a vessel building and vessel owning community — the nearest to the Bay terminus of the

---

[35] *New Brunswick Acts*, 1882, pp. 70, 114-20. The reduction of the provincial subsidy to $3,000 per mile was reported in the *Chignecto Post*, 6 April 1882. Possibly as a result of an unfavourable vote by the ratepayers, the promised municipal support was never given. See *Sessional Papers*, 1886, vol. 10, #13, p. 49.

[36] Railways and Canals had been made a separate portfolio in May in order to deal with the building of the Canadian Pacific. Hector Langevin took over Tupper's old post of Public Works. Public Archives of Canada, *Guide to Canadian Ministries Since Confederation* (Ottawa, 1974), pp. 17-18.

[37] C. R. McKay, "The Chignecto Ship Railway," unpublished B.A. thesis, Mount Allison University, 1973, pp. 30-31. For more on Ketchum and the ship railway, see McKay, "Investors, Government, and the CMTR: A Study of Entrepreneurial Failure," *Acadiensis*, 9 (1979), pp. 71-94.

[38] J. W. Longley, *Sir Charles Tupper* (Toronto, 1916), p. 172.

Railway — would be greatly benefitted by the opening of this new channel of trade and new employment for vessels...."[39] But the promoters of the NB & PE Railway were taken aback by Ketchum's plan to make the ship railway part of a $4 million "transportation complex," including a conventional railway from Amherst to the Cape and a ferry service to P.E.I.[40] If this proposal were accepted, the NB & PE charter would be a dead letter. Tupper's chief engineer, Collingwood Schreiber, upheld the feasibility of the ship railway scheme in February 1882 and recommended that the government pay an annual subsidy of $150,000 for twenty-five years upon completion. He suggested a further subsidy of $500,000, payable at the rate of $20,000 per year over the same period, to build and equip the ordinary railway from Amherst to Cape Tormentine.[41] Not surprisingly, Tupper soon proposed that the government enter into a contract with Ketchum to construct "either or both of the lines suggested" on the terms outlined by Schreiber, reserving the ferry proposal for future consideration.[42]

Meanwhile, Wood and Botsford met at Ottawa in an effort to salvage the NB & PE Railway. Together they drafted a petition to Tupper in early March protesting that the Sackville company "could not exist as a rival line" if the government subsidized Ketchum's railway from Amherst to the Cape. They had "no objection to the Dominion Government constructing a line of railway from Cape Tormentine to the Intercolonial if they feel under obligation to do so," but insisted this connection be made at Sackville and not Amherst. The timberlands and farms along the Sackville route promised a better local traffic than Ketchum's line, a point which Wood and Botsford emphasized by enclosing Boxall's report of December 1881. Sackville also had the advantage of a good harbour (which Amherst did not) and was better situated to handle the trade of P.E.I. which traditionally flowed towards Saint John.[43]

[39] *Chignecto Post*, 23 February 1882.
[40] McKay, "The Chignecto Ship Railway," p. 30.
[41] Collingwood Schreiber to F. Braun, Secretary, Department of Railways and Canals, 4 February, 7, 10 March 1882, reprinted in *Sessional Papers*, 1882, vol. 10, #79, pp. 6-8.
[42] Memorandum by Charles Tupper, 11 March 1882, vol. 139, pp. 57248-50, Macdonald Papers, P.A.C.
[43] Wood and Botsford to Tupper, n.d. [submitted before 13 March 1882], *ibid.*, pp. 57267-69, reprinted in *Sessional Papers*, 1882, vol. 10, #79, pp. 8-10.

Both Wood and Botsford must have realized these arguments would carry little weight with Tupper, but at least their views were on the record. "Have devoted my time when not attending Parliament [to] working up a case for our Railway," Wood wrote home on 9 March 1882, trying hard to sound optimistic. "Make rather slow progress [since] every little thing requires so much labour. Members and especially ministers are so pressed with business it is hard to find an opportunity where they will give one the continued attention needed in business line mine."[44] Certainly the Minister of Railways and Canals had no interest in Sackville's protests. Tupper passed the petition on to Schreiber, who reported back in favour of retaining the Amherst-Cape Tormentine route. Ketchum's line was slightly shorter, he explained, and had the advantage of better grades since it would follow the practically level ship railway route partway to the Cape. In terms of trade, Schreiber rejected outright Boxall's estimates of the potential for local and P.E.I. traffic. Amherst was closer to the coal fields of Cumberland County, he pointed out, and the shipment of coal to the Quebec market via Cape Tormentine would "largely exceed any business which could reasonably be calculated upon in connection with the Prince Edward Island trade."[45]

The Sackville promoters refused to give up, and tried a different tack. On 21 March 1882 Boxall wrote from Sackville urging Botsford to continue the fight. At stake for the County of Westmorland was an estimated $500,000 worth of trade annually, he told the Senator, and predicted that "the Conservative party would suffer if this precious scheme of Ketchum's received their [sic] support...." Reviewing Ketchum's proposal, Boxall contended that construction of the ship and Cape railways combined would not exceed $1.5 million, but the government was being asked to subsidize the project to the tune of $4 million. Ketchum and his associates would thus pocket a "gift" of $2.5 million, something Boxall felt was "worth the consideration of thinking statesmen." To further discredit Ketchum, he included detailed projections of the earnings and expenses of the ship railway which Botsford was "at liberty" to use "on your discretion."[46]

[44] Josiah to Laura Wood, 9 March 1882, File 27, Wood Family Papers, P.A.N.B.
[45] Schreiber to Braun, 13 March 1882, reprinted in *Sessional Papers*, 1882, vol. 10, #79, p. 11.
[46] Boxall to Botsford, 21 March 1882, vol. 139, pp. 57245-46, 57254-60, Macdonald Papers, P.A.C.

Botsford knew at least one man in the cabinet who would be interested in these figures. His association with Samuel Leonard Tilley, the Minister of Finance, went back to the days before Confederation when both had been leading supporters of union.[47] As the ranking New Brunswicker in the cabinet, Tilley kept a sharp eye on affairs in his home province, particularly those which involved expenditures on public works.[48] Botsford sent him Boxall's statistics, noting in a covering letter that "if he is correct... Ketchum's scheme must prove a financial failure."[49] Boxall reiterated his charges in a second letter to Tilley, and reported that his business contacts in Saint John would not tolerate the diversion of the trade of Westmorland County southward to Nova Scotia. "Should the railway run from Amherst to Cape Tormentine," he warned, "St. John and New Brunswick must suffer."[50]

It was a warning Tilley could not afford to ignore. As the MP for Saint John he could hardly countenance a project which might prove harmful to the commercial interests of that city. In 1878 he had been elected by an extremely narrow margin — only nine votes — and 1882 was to be an election year.[51] Ignoring the fact that railways were Tupper's domain, Tilley immediately passed Boxall's figures on to Macdonald. "This," he told the Prime Minister on 24 March, "shows the necessity of our naming some definite estimates, before considering seriously the aid we might give" to Ketchum.[52] In a follow-up letter the next day, Tilley outlined a possible course of action. "State to the House that the Local Government are subsidizing the Road to Cape Tormentine," he suggested to Macdonald, "and that in order to give time to see if this work will be built by a company the Government will

[47] In April 1866 Botsford had introduced a motion that passed in the Legislative Council of New Brunswick favouring confederation. The acceptance of this motion by the Lieutenant Governor forced the anti-confederate government of Albert Smith to resign, paving the way for a new, pro-union administration. Tilley, one of the leaders of the pro-confederate forces, took office in the new government as Provincial Secretary. See *Chignecto Post*, 22 March 1894; W. S. MacNutt, *New Brunswick, A History: 1784-1867* (Toronto, 1963), pp. 446-47.

[48] Carl Murray Wallace, "Sir Leonard Tilley: A Political Biography," unpublished Ph.D. thesis, University of Alberta, 1972, pp. 369-70.

[49] Botsford to Tilley, 24 March 1882, vol. 139, pp. 57252-53, Macdonald Papers, P.A.C.

[50] Boxall to Tilley, 23 March 1882, *ibid.*, pp. 57263-66.

[51] Wallace, "Sir Leonard Tilley," p. 334.

[52] Tilley to Macdonald, 24 March 1882 (confidential), vol. 139, p. 57244, Macdonald Papers, P.A.C.

postpone a proposition for the building of that [railway]... until next Session." To indicate the government's desire to improve communication with the Island, however, Tilley felt $180,000 should be voted to build a branch line from the P.E.I. Railway to Cape Traverse. Probably thinking of his own seat in the House, he added that "this would tide us over the elections and would not compromise or embarrass any party in Nova Scotia, New Bk. or P.E.I." Two days later he met Macdonald in person to explain his case more fully.[53]

Macdonald followed Tilley's advice to the letter. Tupper had long been the Prime Minister's closest political ally and his probable successor, but by 1882 relations between the two had turned sour. Two years before they had a personal breach over the firing of Tupper's friend, Sandford Fleming, from the post of chief engineer of the Canadian Pacific Railway. As a result, noted one historian, Tupper "was never again the party's great electoral strategist or Macdonald's close advisor and confidant."[54] Tilley was now the government's leading supporter in the Maritimes, and the Minister of Railways and Canals was overruled. Tupper would have to be satisfied with the ship railway alone — still a massive undertaking — in the interest of placating New Brunswick, where the electoral fortunes of the Conservative Party had been relatively poor.[55]

On 10 April Tupper revised this memorandum on the ship railway scheme, deleting any mention of a companion line from Amherst to the Cape.[56] This was the basis of the final bill which he presented to the House on 9 May.[57] The following day, as Tilley had recommended, $189,200 was voted to build the Cape Traverse branch on the Island. It must have been galling for Tupper to have to rise and defend this motion. "We would have been prepared to bring down an estimate for the construction of the connection between the Intercolonial Railway and Cape Tormentine," he

[53] Tilley to Macdonald, 25 March 1882 (confidential), *ibid.*, pp. 57240-43.
[54] Alan Wilson, "Fleming and Tupper: The Fall of the Siamese Twins, 1880," in John S. Moir, ed., *Character and Circumstance: Essays in Honour of Donald Grant Creighton* (Toronto, 1970), p. 127.
[55] In the 1878 federal election the Conservative Party had carried only five of 16 seats in New Brunswick, the only province where they were denied a majority of the ridings. See J. Murray Beck, *Pendulum of Power: Canada's Federal Elections* (Scarborough, 1968), p. 37.
[56] Memorandum by Charles Tupper, 10 April 1882, reprinted in *Sessional Papers*, 1882, vol. 10, #79a, pp. 2-3.
[57] McKay, "The Chignecto Ship Railway," p. 32.

explained to the House, "but for the fact, that in the meantime that service has been provided for by the Government of New Brunswick, who have renewed the charter of a private company who propose to construct that work with the aid of a subsidy. Under these circumstances we felt that we could not ask Parliament to provide for a service which was apparently provided for by the Local Government."[58] By virtue of their charter and considerable political leverage at Ottawa,[59] the promoters of the NB & PE Railway had saved the line to the Cape for Sackville.

During April 1882 the company began to make the best of its new lease of life. A stock list circulated locally had brought in $80,000 worth of subscriptions by the end of the month. Wood, Black, and several other directors went to Fredericton to finalize subsidy arrangements with the provincial government.[60] And in May 1882, Wood took a step which was to have a profound impact on the future of the NB & PE Railway. At the request of some prominent New Brunswick Conservatives,[61] he sought and secured the party's nomination in Westmorland County for the upcoming federal election.[62] Well-educated, trained as a lawyer, and successful in business, Wood was a logical choice to contest the seat against Smith, the Liberal incumbent. But the deciding factor for Wood was his stake in the NB & PE Railway. On 6 June, just two weeks before the election, he succeeded Botsford as company president. With stock subscriptions totalling $50,000 he was by far the railway's largest backer.[63]

Campaigning on the Conservative platform of tariff protection, a transcontinental railway, and western development, Wood easily undermined his opponent. Smith, "the Lion of Westmorland," had represented the county since Confederation, but as a member

---

[58] *House of Commons Debates*, vol. 12, 10 May 1882, p. 1437.

[59] Gustavus Myers has suggested that one of the main reasons for securing a railway charter was to block rival schemes. See Myers, *History of Canadian Wealth* (Chicago, 1914), p. 165. If this was the intention of the NB & PE Railway's promoters, their strategy worked.

[60] *Chignecto Post*, 20, 27 April 1882.

[61] Both A. L. Palmer and Senator John Boyd later claimed credit for convincing Wood to run. See Palmer to Macdonald, 14 July 1882, vol. 386, pp. 182056-58; Boyd to J. H. Pope, 31 July 1885 (private), vol. 122, pp. 50038-40, Macdonald Papers, P.A.C.

[62] Wood was nominated by the local constituency association on the first ballot over Pierre A. Landry, a popular Acadian lawyer and MLA. *Chignecto Post*, 18 May 1882.

[63] *Chignecto Post*, 1, 8 June 1882.

of the Opposition after 1878 he wielded no power at Ottawa.[64] The most pressing local issue was the Cape Tormentine railway, and there was no doubt where Wood stood with regard to that project. On June 20 he defeated Smith by over 400 votes, and as the results were announced to the crowd assembled at the telegraph office in Sackville, "cheer after cheer rent the air for Wood and the Cape Railway."[65] "It was the greatest rejoicing Sackville ever saw," Wood's wife remarked proudly.[66] With the Conservatives returned to power, the NB & PE now had an effective voice in the councils of the government.

Wood immediately began to build a case for the granting of federal assistance to his line. During his first session at Ottawa in the spring of 1883 he secured an appointment to a select committee of the House set up to consider the perennial question of winter communication with P.E.I. At the committee's hearings, Wood elicited favourable comments on the need for a branch railway to the ICR, a wharf at Cape Tormentine, and the merits of the Capes route in general from witnesses familiar with the problems of Island communication.[67] The committee's report recommended that the government "adopt Capes Traverse and Tormentine as the points of communication for mails and passengers" to and from P.E.I., since travel "during the most severe part of the winter season can only be maintained between those points. . . ." The ice boat service operating on that route was to be taken over by the government and upgraded to provide daily crossings in winter. From Wood's point of view, the most important recommendation was that the government improve summer travel by building a pier at Cape Tormentine in connection with the NB & PE Railway.[68]

Actual construction of the line had begun at Sackville in the late summer of 1882, and the contractors took advantage of the winter months to clear the right of way through the woods and begin grading the roadbed. By spring more than 200 men were at work,

---

[64] Carl Wallace, "Albert Smith, Confederation, and Reaction in New Brunswick, 1852-1882," *Canadian Historical Review*, 44 (1963), p. 310.

[65] *Chignecto Post*, 22 June 1882. The results were Wood 2620 votes, Smith 2188, as reported in *The Canadian Parliamentary Companion*, 1883, p. 177.

[66] Laura Wood, "Journal," 21 June 1882, p. 44.

[67] See, for example, his questions to Samuel Prowse, p. 9, John Jenkins, p. 16, Captain Irving, pp. 45-46, and Senator J. S. Carvell, pp. 77-78, in the committee's minutes of evidence: *Journals of the House of Commons*, 1883, vol. 17, Appendix 3.

[68] *Ibid.*, p. 2.

and at the end of August about two-thirds of the line was graded and ready for rails. But railway iron was expensive, and the federal government turned down a request in April 1883 to supply used rails to the project. The company's stock subscriptions of $150,000 were insufficient; the provincial subsidy of $3,000 per mile was payable only upon completion.[69] The fact of the matter was that by the middle of 1883 the NB & PE Railway was in dire financial trouble. As was the case with so many other Canadian lines facing a shortage of local capital, the solution was seen to be investment from overseas sources. Armed with a provincial act empowering the company to borrow up to 72,000 sterling,[70] Wood went to England in July "with a view to get rails and open negotiations for the sale of the Debentures of the Company...." A London agent was retained to sell the company's bonds, and on his return, in September, Wood tried to restore confidence in the project. "I have every reason to believe the company is strong enough to complete the railway and put it in operation next year," he announced, "sale or no sale of bonds."[71]

Wood's timing could not have been worse. The world economy was sliding into a depression in 1883, and the failure of the giant Northern Pacific in the United States late in the year shook investor confidence in railway stocks and bonds.[72] Under these conditions it was unlikely that the NB & PE Railway would be able to float its bond issue in London. Wood seemed to realize this by the end of the year, and began to explore other avenues. In December 1883 he wrote to Tilley to get advance information on the railway companies the government planned to subsidize during the upcoming session, as well as the prospects for funding of the Cape Tormentine pier.[73] Wood secured an appropriation of $150,000 for the pier at the end of the 1884 session, but failed to obtain any assistance for the railway. The stumbling block was still Tupper. Although the federal government gave some $8.5 million in aid to private railway companies in 1884, Tupper fulfilled an

[69] *Chignecto Post*, 5 April 1883.

[70] *New Brunswick Acts*, 1883, p. 88.

[71] *Chignecto Post*, 13 September 1883.

[72] W. T. Easterbrook and Hugh G. J. Aitken, *Canadian Economic History* (Toronto, 1963), p. 433.

[73] Tilley to Wood, 21 December 1883 (private), File 23, Wood Family Papers, P.A.N.B.

earlier pledge to his Amherst supporters by turning down the NB &
PE Railway Company's request for a subsidy.[74]

By the summer of 1884 the Cape railway had a roadbed and
bridges, but no rails. Money was still the problem — the company
needed an estimated $160,000 to complete and equip the line. The
purchase of a small lot of rails, ten flat cars, and an old ICR
locomotive during July and August probably exhausted the company's funds, but at least allowed tracklaying to begin.[75] By the end
of the year, however, the situation had become acute, and at a
meeting on 9 November 1884 the shareholders agreed to raise the
necessary funds among themselves with a new stock issue.[76] Four
days later Wood bought $15,000 worth of used rails from the ICR
depot at Moncton.[77] This enabled crews to lay track as far as Baie
Verte, a village 17 miles east of Sackville, before winter closed in.

The company's financial position was brighter at the beginning
of 1885, and so were the prospects for federal assistance. Tupper
had resigned his portfolio and his seat in the Commons at the end of
the previous session in order to take up the post of High Commis-
sioner to London. A by-election in Cumberland during the summer
of 1884 returned C. J. Townsend for the Conservatives. An Amherst lawyer and businessman, Townsend immediately wrote to
Macdonald in an effort to block any bid by the NB & PE Railway
for a subsidy. "Very little, if any, private money has been expended
in the enterprise," he told the Prime Minister in July 1884, a
statement that was patently false.[78] If Amherst could not get the
Cape railway, its representative at Ottawa was prepared to do his
utmost to impede the progress of the Sackville line.

---

[74] Alan W. MacIntosh, "The Career of Sir Charles Tupper in Canada, 1864-1900,"
unpublished Ph.D. thesis, University of Toronto, 1959, pp. 271-72. In a speech in
June 1883 Tupper stated that the NB & PE Railway Company "had not asked for
aid, but would have to, and when they did he would remain firm to his pledges to
Amherst." *Chignecto Post*, 14 June 1883.

[75] *Chignecto Post*, 15 May, 24 July, 14 August 1884.

[76] *Chignecto Post*, 20 November 1884.

[77] David Pottinger, Chief Superintendent, ICR, to Wood, 14 November 1884, File 23,
Wood Family Papers, P.A.N.B. According to G. R. Stevens, Pottinger was selling
these used rails for the low price of $12 per ton. At this rate, some 1,250 tons, or close
to half of the rails used in the NB & PE Railway, came from the ICR. See Stevens,
Canadian National Railways, vol. 2: Towards the Inevitable, 1896-1922 (Toronto, 1962)
p. 310; and Boxall, "Estimated Value of Works to Date, 2 January 1886," File 24,
Wood Family Papers, P.A.N.B.

[78] Townsend to Macdonald, 17 July 1884, vol. 122, pp. 50066-70, Macdonald Papers,
P.A.C.

Townsend, however, did not inherit Tupper's influence with the government, and the new Minister of Railways and Canals, J. H. Pope, had no animosity towards the Sackville company. On 9 February 1885 Wood informed the House that he intended to apply for a federal subsidy on behalf of the NB & PE Railway. "The work, so far, has been carried on by the private means of the company," he emphasized, "Slightly aided by the local Government of New Brunswick... If we succeed in getting this [federal] aid the company will be able, during the coming season, to complete and equip their road...."[79] There was little Townsend could do to stop him — Wood had a charter, a half-finished railway, and two more years experience as a government back-bencher. When Townsend tried in March to introduce an act incorporating an Amherst line to tap the NB & PE Railway at Baie Verte, Wood had the bill withdrawn on a technicality.[80]

Four months later, on 15 July 1885, the NB & PE Railway Company was awarded the standard federal subsidy of $3,200 per mile, up to a maximum of $118,400. In Sackville, the *Chignecto Post* was jubilant: "the people of Westmorland will give due honor and credit to the men — headed by Mr. Wood M.P. — who have successfully engineered this undertaking."[81] But across the marshes in Amherst, Townsend was vehement. The subsidy had been granted to Wood, he complained in an angry letter to Macdonald, "notwithstanding my urgent, and repeated remonstrances" to the contrary. "You certainly must have forgotten your promise to me in writing last Summer that nothing of this kind should be done," he told the Prime Minister bluntly. His constituents were outraged: "How the Gov't can expect me to hold my own when treated in this fashion it is difficult to understand."[82] Other Conservatives demanded similar consideration for their own lines. Senator John Boyd of Saint John asked Macdonald to grant a subsidy to the Joggins Railway in Nova Scotia, while the promoters of the Moncton and Buctouche Railway were equally disgruntled at being passed over in favour of Wood.[83] Given such conflicting

[79] *House of Commons Debates*, vol. 17, 9 February 1885, p. 63.

[80] *Ibid.*, 4 March 1885, p. 349.

[81] *Chignecto Post*, 23 July 1885.

[82] Townsend to Macdonald, 23 July 1885, vol. 122, pp. 50072-75, Macdonald Papers, P.A.C.

[83] Boyd to Pope, 31 July 1885 (private), vol. 122, p. 50039; Tilley to Macdonald, 3 October 1885 (confidential), vol. 277, p. 127177, Macdonald Papers, P.A.C.

political pressures, it was a measure of Wood's influence at Ottawa that his railway received any assistance at all.

With federal monies assured to the company, the NB & PE was rapidly pushed to completion. At the beginning of 1886 Boxall estimated that almost $280,000 had been spent on the 32.5 miles of railway completed to that date, including $65,000 for rails and two locomotives costing a total of $11,000.[84] Construction of the remaining four miles was delayed while the federal government chose the location of the Cape Tormentine pier, but the entire line was in operation by September 1886. The government subsidies were payable upon completion, and Ottawa's share, totalling $113,440, was forwarded in two installments: $87,000 in September 1886, and the balance at the end of 1887.[85] The provincial government had paid the bulk of its subsidy — $90,000 out of $99,709 — by 31 December 1886.[86] Further public largess was given to the NB & PE with the completion of a 2,500-foot wharf at the Cape Tormentine terminus in 1893. Total expenditure by the federal government for the construction and repair of that pier had reached $240,000 by 1889.[87]

The NB & PE Railway quickly fulfilled the expectations of its promoters. As this was a major transportation route to and from P.E.I., passenger traffic was heavy, averaging some 15,500 people annually from 1887 to 1900.[88] In the summer months large numbers of people in the Sackville area took advantage of special excursion trains to the Cape, which developed into something of a local resort complete with fine beaches and tourist hotels.[89] The line was also the major carrier for the Island mails.

Freight traffic had been the reason for building the railway, however, and the shipment of local lumber commenced as soon as the first rails were laid in 1884.[90] During the first 14 years of operation lumber accounted for more than 40 percent of all freight

---

[84] Boxall, "Estimated Value of Works to Date, 2 January 1886," File 24, Wood Family Papers, P.A.N.B.

[85] *Sessional Papers*, 1887, vol. 12, #13, p. 63; and 1888, vol. 9, #8b, p. 62.

[86] *Chignecto Post*, 14 April 1887.

[87] *Sessional Papers*, 1890, vol. 8, #9, p. 59.

[88] Calculated from "Railway Statistics of Canada," Table 4, *Sessional Papers*, 1888-1901.

[89] *Chignecto Post*, 23 June 1887.

[90] The first carload of deals was sent over the NB & PE Railway to Sackville once nine miles of track were laid to Midgic. *Chignecto Post*, 23 October 1884.

carried, an average of 7.7 million board feet annually. Virtually all of this traffic originated at sawmills along the line and was bound for markets in the United Kingdom.[91] Railway access to the timber stands along the route greatly facilitated the shipment of this lumber to tidewater. Prior to the construction of the NB & PE, deals had been floated down rivers to Baie Verte and then rafted out to vessels for loading, or else shipped overland by teams to Sackville.[92] The lumber trade continued to use these outlets after 1886, but large numbers of ships began loading at Cape Tormentine once the pier was complete. The result was a better quality product. "It appears that deals, when shipped dry and clean, command higher prices in the English market, than when wet and bruised in the course of rafting," explained one observer, adding, "The deals shipped at Cape Tormentine are taken from the train directly on board the vessel in clean and bright condition."[93]

The directors of the NB & PE Railway were themselves heavily involved in the local lumber trade. Black and Ogden, two of the original promoters of the line, were the largest producers in eastern Westmorland County. Together they accounted for half the logs cut in the area during the winter of 1884-5, and produced a similar proportion of that region's lumber in 1892.[94] The sawmills and timber holdings of both men profitted handsomely from the railway. Black, with two mills just north of the NB & PE, had made "extensive purchases" of timberland in 1883, expanding his holdings to 12,000 acres. By one estimate, this was "enough log lands to guarantee an inexhaustible supply of logs for his mills for an indefinite period."[95] Ogden was also quick to take advantage of the railway, shipping 130 carloads of deals over the line during 1885 before it ever reached the Cape. W. F. George, an early promoter and a director until 1885, shipped smaller quantities of lumber over the railway.[96]

Wood, the NB & PE's president, had a variety of business

[91] Calculated from "Railway Statistics of Canada," Table 5, *Sessional Papers*, 1888-1901. In 1908, the first year which gave a breakdown of freight traffic by origin, fully 98 per cent of the lumber carried came from points along the line. *Sessional Papers*, 1909, vol. 11, #20b, Table 11.

[92] *Morning Herald* (Halifax), 13 June 1885.

[93] *Sessional Papers*, 1894, vol. 8, #9, pp. 70-71.

[94] *Chignecto Post*, 23 April 1885, 5 May 1892.

[95] *Chignecto Post*, 1 March 1883.

[96] *Chignecto Post*, 14 January 1886, 19 March 1891.

interests that were well served by his railway. His wholesale firm of
M. Wood & Sons exported 1.4 million board feet of lumber during
1885 alone,[97] and probably benefitted from access to the P.E.I.
market for other goods. Wood was also a major landowner in the
area, including a 500-acre farm and other lands along the route to
the Cape.[98] By the 1880s, however, the emphasis of Wood's business activities had switched to the nearby town of Moncton, where
he was a major investor in a cotton mill, a sugar refinery, and other
manufacturing concerns. These factories, noted the *Chignecto Post*,
were well situated to ship their products to the Island market, only
60 miles distant by way of the Intercolonial and NB & PE
Railways.[99]

Two Sackville manufacturers sat on the NB & PE's board for the
same reason. Charles Fawcett, a director throughout the 1880s and
1890s, obtained rail access to the Island market by building a short
spur line from the Cape railway to his stove foundry. W.B. Dixon, a
director from 1883 to 1886, enjoyed the same advantage but
without the effort. He was a managing partner of E. Cogswell &
Company, the town's other stove works, which was located within
a few hundred yards of the junction of the ICR and the Cape
line.[100]

The NB & PE Railway, then, was promoted and built by a
group of Sackville's leading merchants and manufacturers to serve
their own business interests. True, the shareholders expended a
considerable amount of their own money to finance the actual
construction, but they were more than repaid for their efforts upon
completion. Government aid totalled just over $213,000; the vari-
ous estimates of the cost of building and equipping the line average
out at under $300,000.[101] This means upward of $70,000 was

[97] *Chignecto Post*, 17 December 1885.

[98] Wood had inherited at least an additional 300 acres of farmland at Midgic, a station
stop on the NB & PE Railway, from his father. See deeds in File 50, Wood Family
Papers, P.A.N.B., especially James Hay to Mariner Wood, 1839 and 1844, and
John Patterson to M. Wood, 1843.

[99] *Chignecto Post*, 22 November 1883. Wood's investments in Moncton industry after
1879 are noted in Acheson, "The National Policy and the Industrialization of the
Maritimes," p. 8, and in R. T. Naylor, *The History of Canadian Business*, vol. 1,
1867-1914 (Toronto, 1975), p. 162.

[100] *Chignecto Post*, 12, 26 December 1889. The membership of the railway's board of
directors is drawn from reports of the annual meetings published in the *Post* and
Poor's Manual of the Railroads of the United States, 1896-1900.

[101] In 1891 the "Railway Statistics of Canada" gave a total cost of just over $270,000.
See *Sessional Papers*, 1892, vol. 8, #9b, Table 1. The secretary of the NB & PE

invested locally — a small risk for the shareholders considering the benefits which accrued to their other business activities. Moreover, NB & PE Railway stock proved to be a good investment in itself. In its first 14 years of operation the company never failed to show a surplus of earnings over operating expenses.[102] Direct government assistance, including an additional $240,000 for the pier at Cape Tormentine, enabled the promoters of the Cape railway to construct a valuable and profitable transportation artery with a minimum of private funding.

The construction of the NB & PE Railway was a success story in nineteenth century railway entrepreneurship. Within a few years of its completion, however, questions were being raised about the role of the promoters in securing government assistance for the railway. In particular, had Wood abused his position of public trust as an MP for private gain? The Opposition Liberals certainly thought so, and raised the matter in the House on 29 April 1890. Halifax MP A. G. Jones charged that Wood, "with the influence he possessed with the Government," had secured an appropriation of $160,000 for the pier at Cape Tormentine, and "expenditure of money not in the public interest, but in the interest of the small branch [railway] in which the hon. gentleman is a large owner." Wood immediately rose to defend himself, challenging Jones to show "that the road has not been of advantage to the section of the country through which it passes...." The appropriation for the pier and the subsidy paid to the NB & PE Railway, he pointed out, were made on the recommendation of a Commons committee in 1883. He did not add, of course, that he had been one of the five members of that committee. When the Liberals' Richard Cartwright repeated the charge of political influence, Wood flatly denied exerting any "undue" pressure on the government; he had received the same federal subsidy as had other railways in New Brunswick and other provinces. Support for Wood's case came from the government benches. Conservative T. E. Kenny of Halifax commended him "for the interest he has taken in securing

---

Railway Company later contended the line cost $288,000 to build. See Milner, *History of Sackville*, p. 87. *Poor's 1896*, p. 1029, gave a similar figure of $286,159. Probably taking into account later expenditures for improvements and rolling stock, a provincial government report in 1908 set the total cost of the line at $307,744. See New Brunswick, *Branch Railway Commission Report 1908*, p. 11.

102 For annual financial statements of the company, see "Railway Statistics of Canada," Tables 6 and 7, *Sessional Papers*, 1888-1901.

so important a public work for the county which he so well
represents," while the Prime Minister professed he had never
heard "a more unwarrantable, a more unjustifiable and uncalled
for attack" in his long parliamentary experience. The only influence exerted on the government in subsidizing the NB & PE
Railway, Macdonald maintained, was "the influence of its being
the right route, the most convenient and the safest mode of
communication."[103]

The matter did not rest there. The debate was picked up by the
Liberal press, with the Toronto *Globe* leading the attack on Wood's
role as president of the Cape railway. "One of the main objects for
constructing this line was to reach some mills owned partly by Mr.
Wood," charged the *Globe*. A further $160,000 had been voted "for
a pier at Cape Tormentine not required in the public interest, in
fact quite useless to anyone but Mr. Wood and his railways and
mills."[104]

These were serious allegations, and Wood felt compelled to
make a personal explanation in the House on 2 May 1890. The
Globe's report, he began, "is so much at variance with the truth that
I feel it my duty to refer to it:" "I own no mill, nor have I any
interest in any mill anywhere along this line of railway. I may
further say that I have no private property along that line, and I
have no private or personal interest to be served in any way by the
construction of that line." And yet this statement was clearly false.
Wood controlled lands, a wholesaling firm, and factories which
were "served" directly by the building of the NB & PE Railway.
Concluding his remarks to the House, Wood contended: "I should
have neglected my duty as a citizen, and should have been very
remiss in my duty as a public man, if I had not done everything in
my power to secure its construction."[105]

This was a telling point. The NB & PE Railway had been of
undoubted value to the eastern section of Westmorland County,
and Wood's constituents were well aware of that fact. "If there is a
public matter that Mr. Wood can claim the support and confidence of the people of Westmorland, it is the connection he has had
with this important public undertaking," the *Chignecto Post* stated
in his defence, for "it has certainly been a source of strength to him

[103] *House of Commons Debates*, vol. 30, 29 April 1890, pp. 4143-49.
[104] Quoted in *ibid.*, 2 May 1890, p. 4320.
[105] *Ibid.*, pp. 4320-21.

at the polls.''[106] The electorate judged its representatives at Ottawa not on their private interests, but on their contribution to local prosperity.

Gustavus Myers would not have accepted this argument. Members of Parliament promoting their own railways "were compelled by the exigencies of politics to put on an appearance of great concern for the public welfare," he charged in 1914, "while engaged in the very act of seeking to enrich themselves. . . ."[107] Indeed, such politicians did reap private gain from their activities, but more recent writers have argued that charges of political corruption must be assessed within the context of times.[108] The voters who returned men like Wood at the polls certainly did not feel the public interest was being sacrificed to private profit. For their part, the railway promoters in Parliament do not appear to have considered their actions as corrupt. Macdonald defended federal subsidies to private railway companies in 1890 as a means of encouraging development.[109] Wood used the same argument when charged with accepting "boodle" during his successful re-election campaign in 1887.[110] Nevertheless, such assistance went only to railway companies with the requisite political connections.

Politics and railways. In nineteenth-century Canada the two were inextricably linked. The businessmen of Sackville promoted and built a railway to Cape Tormentine because it was beneficial to their private interests to do so. The line assisted the exploitation of the staple resources — particularly timber — of the region through

[106] *Chignecto Post*, 8 May 1890.

[107] Myers, *History of Canadian Wealth*, p. 154. Wood himself did not escape Myers' wrath, but for his alleged role in promoting the wrong railway. In the House on 3 May 1886 a Liberal member charged that Wood, as president of the Caraquet Railway in northern New Brunswick, had received some $76,800 in subsidies for that line in a single year. This was an error — he really meant the member for Gloucester County, Kennedy F. Burns, who was president and chief promoter of the Caraquet line. Myers, however, did not detect the error and reported the charge verbatim. For his activities as president of the NB & PE Railway, Wood escaped unscathed. See *House of Commons Debates*, vol. 12, 3 May 1886, p. 999; and Myers, *History of Canadian Wealth*, p. 290.

[108] Kenneth M. Gibbons, "The Study of Political Corruption," in Gibbons and Donald C. Rowat, eds., *Political Corruption in Canada* (Toronto, 1976), p. 5, makes this very point. Another writer has explained that, in the nineteenth century, "the public ignored, condoned or was ambivalent towards the moral and ethical problems raised by the conjunction of railroads and politics." See Baskerville, "The Boardroom and Beyond," pp. 205-06.

[109] *House of Commons Debates*, vol. 30, 8 May 1890, p. 4627.

[110] *Chignecto Post*, 27 January 1887.

which it passed, and at the same time provided convenient access
to the P.E.I. market for local manufactured goods. Despite their
personal stake in the railway, its promoters were reluctant to risk
their own capital to effect its construction. Considerable time and
effort, therefore, were devoted to shifting the responsibility for
financing onto the public purse. The NB & PE Railway Company
constantly lobbied the federal and provincial governments for aid,
particularly in the form of direct cash subsidies or used rails. When
these efforts met with only limited success, the promoters turned to
direct political action to further their cause. Political power was
necessary to secure subsidies and stave off rival lines; as a government backbencher at Ottawa, the company president could do
both. Playing by the rules as they then stood Sackville's businessmen secured their railway and its attendant benefits for a fraction
of the total cost.

LARRY McCANN and
JILL BURNETT

Social Mobility and the Ironmasters of Late Nineteenth Century New Glasgow

The NEW INDUSTRIALISM OF THE LATE NINETEENTH century has often been characterized as a time of technological change and entrepreneurial opportunity. Some scholars, in analyzing this transformation in economy and society, have examined the cultural environment of change in an attempt to understand how people responded to emerging economic opportunities. A prominent and controversial issue focusses on the social origins of the leaders of the new industrialism, particularly the stereotype of the heroic labourer who was able to rise from "rags-to-riches" through hard work and acquired skills. Countering this view of open social mobility is the contention that industrial entrepreneurs evolved from within the merchant elite, signifying continuity of the established social order. This essay examines the nature of social mobility and the recruitment of industrialists in New Glasgow in the 1870s and 1880s, as this one-time shipbuilding community shifted to an economy based almost exclusively on the iron and steel industry.[1]

The literature pertaining to the recruitment of industrial entrepreneurs offers conflicting interpretations. Most comprehensive in scope is Thomas Cochran's *Frontiers of Change*[2] which examines the many causal forces that stimulate and facilitate industrial development. Generally, Cochran shuns environmental determinism in favour of a geo-cultural approach. While many argue that urban-industrial development is determined primarily by the availability

[1] The study extends the partial consideration of this topic found in L. D. McCann, "The Mercantile-Industrial Transition in the Metal Towns of Pictou County, 1857-1931," *Acadiensis*, 10 (1981), pp. 29-64. It does so by drawing upon new evidence researched by both authors, some of which is reported in Jill Burnett, "Wooden Ships and Iron Men: Social Mobility in Industrializing New Glasgow," unpublished B.A. thesis, Mount Allison University, 1984.

[2] Thomas Cochran, *Frontiers of Change* (New York, 1981).

of resources and accessibility to markets, the geo-cultural interpretation emphasizes the relationship between culture, resources,
and geographical location.[3] According to Cochran, environmental
and geographic factors play an undeniable and essential role in a
town's economic progress, but the fundamental shaping of a
society's economic development is largely dependent on the culture of the place: "the possibilities open to a people of a culture are
either limited or augmented by geography and natural resources."
Because the cultures of regions differ, "the esthetic or creative
responses" to the opportunity for material change can also vary.[4]
Cochran, by focussing on the causal forces of change, directs his
analysis to "culture-bound phenomena" which, by their very
nature, are immeasurable. Nevertheless, by offering a comprehensive commentary on the cultural stimulants of development, he
provides a basis for understanding the frontiers of industrial
growth. The fundamental characteristic of this frontier in America
was the Puritan pursuit of a pragmatic and utilitarian approach to
life. Cochran argues that economic rationality, rather than land or
family ties, was the common measuring rod of society.[5] Further,
because of the constant flow of immigrants and the regular migration of people between cities, the American population was com-
prised of adventurous frontiersmen. It was, in short, a society of
risk-takers. Americans developed a culture of risk for change that
exemplified their adaptability to a continuously growing and
developing society. For Cochran, the class structure was relatively
open, facilitating both social and economic mobility.

   Although Cochran's geo-cultural thesis provides a sensible contribution to our understanding of those forces that shape industrial
development, questions must be raised about his treatment of the
industrial entrepreneur. In his assertion that innovations are a
manifestation of the accumulated knowledge and experience of a
culture — "a joint-product of what we want and what we know"[6]
— Cochran tends to downplay the role of leadership within society.
While it is likely that innovators and entrepreneurs are motivated
and conditioned by their social and cultural milieu, one cannot

---

[3] Cochran defines culture as "the structures, beliefs and patterns of a society [and] the
   result of peoples' experience with life, their accumulated knowledge, and their
   aspirations. . . ." *Ibid.*, p. 3.

[4] *Ibid.*

[5] *Ibid.*, p. 13.

[6] Jacob Schmookler, *Invention and Economic Growth*, p. 12, as quoted in *ibid.*, p. 4.

discount the role of individual ingenuity. Clearly, as Burton Folsom and Peter George have argued, the quality of leadership in a society directly shapes economic growth and development.[7] While not displacing the environmental determinism thesis with a doctrine of entrepreneurial determinism, Folsom, George, and others have simply recognized that many forces are important in explaining urban-industrial growth.

Peter George further argues that the nature of the late nineteenth century economy ensured that individuals played a major role in shaping patterns of industrial growth and development: "...a dramatic and perhaps overriding feature of the American economy during the late nineteenth century was its predominantly private nature;... although... governments guided and promoted economic development... a large range of economic functions was concentrated in the hands of individual decision-makers...." Because these individual decision-makers were acting in the context of a transitional period from a mercantile to an industrial economy, the social and economic environment was "peculiarly favourable" to the pursuit of new opportunities. New products were introduced, innovative methods of production were applied, and new markets and resources were exploited. "All of these changes," George suggests, "were introduced by individual merchants and industrialists."[8]

While the innovative role of the industrial entrepreneur is crucial to our understanding of urban growth and development in the nineteenth and twentieth centuries, the problems of analyzing the nature of entrepreneurial influence are formidable. For example, although one may refer to the work of psychologists and sociologists for interpretations of entrepreneurs and entrepreneurial behaviour — and turn to historical studies for evidence of the social origins of the industrial elite — there is difficulty for all in deciphering the precise influence of the entrepreneur amidst the complex data pertaining to markets, technology, and other economic factors.

However, a number of studies have collectively given much insight about the nature of these problems. Here we will focus attention on the nature of the pre-industrial social structure and the concept of social mobility in the recruitment of the industrial

---

[7] See Burton Folsom, *Urban Capitalists* (Baltimore, 1981) and Peter George, *The Emergence of Industrial America* (Albany, 1982).

[8] George, *Industrial America*, p. 55.

elite during the mercantile-industrial transition, about which socio-
logist E. Digby Blatzell provides an interesting commentary. For
Blatzell, "the status balance of the early industrial period, when
long established kinship and community ties bound together socially prominent families, was upset by the new wealth generated
during America's late nineteenth-century Gilded Age, when the
increasing complexity of society and the larger number of urban
families commanding wealth forced older families... of social
prominence to develop new more formal mechanisms to protect
their social positions."[9] While Blatzell's findings mark a significant
contribution to the understanding of social structure in pre-industrial America, one must qualify his argument by considering other
factors which influenced the ordering of society throughout this
period. Given the absence of the deeply-rooted and traditional
European views of property, occupation, and social roles in America, a relatively open social structure prevailed. Many argue that
this situation was critical for encouraging industrial development.
Peter George, for example, writes that "hardened patterns of social
stratification and well-defined functions for individuals did not
exist," and that "the absence of hereditary privilege and prestige"
was especially important for the emergence of the industrial entrepreneur.[10] John Ingham, on the other hand, asserts that social
structure varied between cities according to their age, size, and
historical function. As a result, older cities which had developed
more fully prior to industrialization — particularly those in New
England — maintained a more established and thus closed system
of social stratification. In these cities, the new industrial elite would
be closely tied to the established mercantile order.[11]

    While historians argue that North America presented a society
which was conducive to social mobility, they also emphasize, in the
American case, that belief in Puritanism and Lockeian individualism with its doctrine of Social Darwinism was conducive to
entrepreneurial development. Indeed, for Cochran, Americans
held an optimistic view of the opportunities that enhanced their
material welfare. For Peter George, "success was up to the indi-

[9] E. Digby Blatzell, *Philadelphia Gentlemen: The Making of a National Upper Class*
    (Chicago, 1971), p. 12.
[10] George, *Industrial America*, p. 59.
[11] John Ingham, "Rags to Riches Revisited: The Effect of City Size and Related
    Factors on the Recruitment of Business Leaders," *Journal of American History*, 63
    (1976), pp. 615-37.

vidual. . . . These tenets — individualism, competition and mobility, achieved rather than ascribed on hereditary status . . . — all tended to stimulate the emergence of creative and aggressive entrepreneurship."[12]

Did opportunities really exist, as the Cochran thesis implies, for the common man to offer leadership in the transition to an industrial economy? In recent years, two opposing viewpoints have emerged regarding the social origins of the industrial elite and the "rags-to-riches" thesis. Representing one view is Herbert Gutman, who argues that a new, radically different social and economic group moved into control as industrialization took place. In his study of Paterson, New Jersey's locomotive, iron, and machinery manufacturing, Gutman reached an important conclusion. Many of those who successfully participated in the city's transition to an industrial economy were recent immigrants to Paterson; they were not members of the traditional, pre-industrial elite. In fact, the vast majority of Paterson's industrialists were of humble social origins who, "by ability, chance and hard work, had dramatically risen to the top of the pyramid."[13] In essence, Gutman stressed the formation of a new social order, whereby the industrialists represented a group which was alienated from the pre-established social order. Thus, despite their economic prominence, the industrial elite remained separate from the mercantile elite who continued to maintain a high social status and a strong political position within Paterson's society.[14]

The opposing view — for mercantile-industrial continuity — has been stressed most prominently by Stephan Thernstrom and John Ingham. Both contend that the new industrialism remained under the control of those entrepreneurs who dominated a town's economy and society in the pre-industrial era. In his study of Newburyport, Massachusetts, Thernstrom found that few members of the labour-

---

[12] George, *Industrial America*, p. 59.

[13] Herbert Gutman, "The Reality of the Rags-to-Riches 'Myth'," in idem, *Work, Culture and Society* (New York, 1977), pp. 211-33.

[14] Gutman further argues that "the industrial town was too new at the start for the industrialist to command . . . prestige and to hold . . . authority. . . . As a new class . . . the industrialists [were] the owners of disruptive and radical innovations — power driven machinery, the factory and the large corporation. . . . Paterson is a good illustration of the frustrating search by the industrialist for status and unchallenged authority." See Herbert Gutman, "Class, Status and Community Power in Nineteenth-Century American Industrial Cities," in idem, *Work, Culture and Society* (New York, 1977), p. 237.

ing class were able to accumulate anything approaching real
wealth. While acknowledging the achievement of "material improvements (property mobility) and occupational mobility (from
unskilled to semi-skilled and semi-skilled to skilled occupations),"
he contends that "the most common form of social advancement
was upward mobility *within* the working class." He thus recognizes
the improved circumstances of many during the period of his study
(1850-1880), but notes that no one experienced sufficient change to
meet the criteria of the rags-to-riches hypothesis. Thernstrom also
suggests that the nineteenth century society was characterized by
high geographic mobility — of people on the move. Yet, unlike
Gutman, he concludes that migrants were most often the individuals who were least skilled and less likely to gain leadership, and
were often forced to travel from city to city in search of work.[15]
These propositions of social and geographical mobility will be
tested in our study.

Ingham also argues for greater stability in the social order of
industrializing cities, but he tempers this point on the basis of other
factors shaping social mobility. In a comparative analysis of six
American steelmaking cities — Philadelphia, Pittsburgh, Cleveland,
Youngstown, Bethlehem and Wheeling — Ingham studies the influence of both non-social factors, such as city size, age, historical
function and location, and the effects of social elements, such as
kinship, marriage patterns, and membership in social institutions.
From these investigations, he concluded that a distinctive pattern
of mobility may be traced on the basis of several factors. Generally,
the older and larger the city, and the more established its social
structure, fewer opportunities for social mobility were likely to be
present. Cities with well-developed social structures in the pre-
industrial period, such as the old mercantile centres of New
England, often maintained a system of social differentiation which
was closed to penetration by outsiders. Members of the entrepreneurial elite were frequently affiliated with specific social clubs
or organizations, and moreover, by family bonds derived from
immediate kinship or achieved by marriage. Younger cities, on the
other hand, tended to lack this cultural stamp, but maintained
more open systems of recruitment for the industrial economy.
These newer places, Ingham argues, appeared to be "more amen-

---

[15] Stephan Thernstrom, *Poverty and Progress: Social Mobility in a Nineteenth-Century City*
(New York, 1974), pp. 157-65.

able to the rise of men from working class origins to elite status."[16] Ingham also suggests that social and economic autonomy are significant factors in determining mobility. Cities which fall under the orbit of larger centres are often dominated by outsiders. There tended to be a great deal of mobility in these places, but job promotion beyond a certain level often coincided with a transfer to a larger, controlling centre. These larger cities offered opportunities for the promotion of men from the ranks of the working classes and from dissimilar ethnic or religious backgrounds.

Thus, the importance of Ingham's contribution should not be underestimated. Although he concluded that the iron and steel manufacturers were not "alien men operating on alien soil," but came from the leading families of their communities, he also recognized that the recruitment of industrial leaders in the nineteenth century was more complex than previously considered. By expanding the contextual framework traditionally applied through the rags-to-riches thesis, he forces us to consider more cultural conditions, such as kinship and political activity within a place, which cannot help but play an influential role in shaping industrial development.

Although an American literature exists in support of both Gutman's argument for high mobility and the Thernstrom-Ingham hypothesis of social stability and continuity, the majority of studies have favoured the latter viewpoint.[17] From a Canadian perspective, the Horatio Alger experience does not seem to have prevailed. Rather, as historian T. W. Acheson concludes, most industrial entrepreneurs were either directly or indirectly connected to the pre-industrial or mercantile elite. Acheson further emphasizes the importance of social institutions such as family, religion, and community in influencing mobility and the recruitment of the new industrial elite.[18] Even where new or instant cities were created in

---

[16] Ingham, "Rags to Riches Revisited," p. 636.

[17] Other studies which discount the "rags-to-riches" thesis include: C. Wright Mills, "The American Business Elite: A Collective Portrait," in Irving Horowitz, ed., *Power, Politics and People: The Collected Essays of C. Wright Mills* (New York, 1962), pp. 110-39; and Frances W. Gregory and Irene D. Neu, "The American Industrial Elite in the 1870s: Their Social Origins," in W. Miller, ed., *Men in Business: Essays on the Historical Role of the Entrepreneur* (New York, 1962), pp. 193-211.

[18] T. W. Acheson, "The Social Origins of the Canadian Industrial Elite, 1880-1885," in D. MacMillan, ed., *Canadian Business History* (Toronto, 1972), pp. 144-74; and idem, "Changing Social Origins of the Canadian Industrial Elite 1880-1910," *Business History Review*, 47 (1973), pp. 189-217.

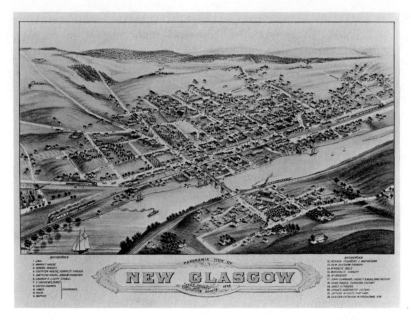

Plate 1. New Glasgow, 1878.   NOVA SCOTIA MUSEUM COLLECTION

late nineteenth-century Canada — such as Winnipeg, Calgary or Vancouver — links to an established business community were essential for success.[19]

What was the path followed in New Glasgow, Nova Scotia? Determining the forces which shaped industrial development in this small town, be they cultural or environmental, helps to expose the nature of available opportunities for upward mobility, and tells us much about the emergence of an entrepreneurial class. Of course, New Glasgow was only one of many towns in the Maritimes to undergo the transition from a mercantile to an industrial economy; and its particular path cannot represent exactly the experiences of other places. Indeed, the success of New Glasgow's industrial development exceeded most Maritime and even many Canadian urban industrial economies of the period. Despite this, New Glasgow's transformation illustrates well the process of recruiting a new industrial elite.

[19] See, for example, Paul Voisey, "In Search of Wealth and Status: An Economic and Social Study of Entrepreneurs in Early Calgary," in A. W. Rasporich and H. Klassen, eds., *Frontier Calgary* (Calgary, 1975), pp. 221-41.

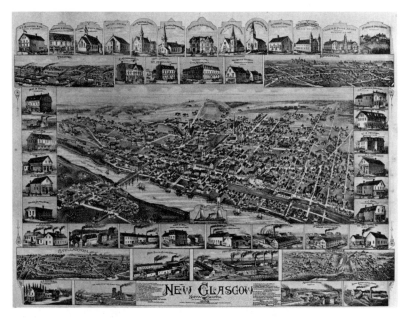

Plate 2. New Glasgow, 1889.   NOVA SCOTIA MUSEUM COLLECTION

The transformation of New Glasgow to become by the late 1870s "a place of no ordinary importance"[20] shows itself readily in a number of ways: the evolving landscape of the town, changes in the business make-up and labour force composition, and the geographical mobility of its population. Fortunately, New Glasgow was well served by nineteenth-century viewmakers who recorded the character of the growing industrial town in 1878 and again in 1889 (Plates 1 and 2). Situated on the East River of Pictou, about 10 km from Pictou Harbour, the town stretched for about 2 km along the eastern bank of the river, extending only briefly across to the river's western side. Shipbuilding yards had always been a prominent feature on the riverfront, but by 1889 the large Carmichael yard and other facilities were closed. In fact, industrial activities — especially the dominant metal-working firms — had become more prominent, occupying sites adjacent to the Intercolonial railway line which had penetrated the business district in the late 1860s to link New Glasgow to neighbouring Trenton and faraway Cape

---

[20] *Teare's Directory of Pictou County* (Pictou, 1879), p. 92.

Breton. Trenton, in fact, was the focus of the Nova Scotia Steel Company's newly established steel-making operations in 1883. These same bird's-eye views reveal the increasing density and outward expansion of the residential areas, the addition of several churches amidst new neighbourhoods, and a more prominent business district along Provost Street.

Such landscape changes were responses to the town's growing population, from 1,676 in 1871 to 3,776 in 1891, with its accompanying demands for new housing, services, and amenities. The incorporation of New Glasgow in 1875 ensured better municipal services, especially water, after the shortcomings of the community's existing services were demonstrated by a disastrous fire in 1874 that gutted much of the downtown area.[21] Not only was there population growth, but also considerable geographical mobility or turnover — as high as nearly 55 percent between 1871 and 1881, and even slightly higher at 57 percent from 1881 to 1891.[22] But despite such visible change in the landscape and the considerable movement of its people, there was remarkable stability in principal elements of the town's social structure. New Glasgow was Scottish in character, through and through. The year 1881 can be used as an example, for the 1871 or 1891 censuses show similar traits. Even if its townspeople were born in Nova Scotia, nearly 80 percent were still of Scottish origin. A similar proportion were members of either the Presbyterian or Church of Scotland religious institutions. The Scottishness of the place was further reinforced by business connections with Scotland and Scottish educational practices, customs, and celebrations such as Hogmanay, or New Year's.

Such elements of stability are all the more remarkable considering the changes in the structure of the business community and the make-up of the labour force. New Glasgow had shared in the early staple trades of Pictou County, particularly the export of timber to British and West Indian markets, foodstuffs to the New Brunswick and Newfoundland colonies, and through its shipping interests, coal to American customers.[23] Shipbuilding, closely

---

[21] "New Glasgow," MG 2, vol. 1244, no. 14, Public Archives of Nova Scotia [hereafter P.A.N.S.]

[22] These rates of population turnover are based on an analysis of the nominal manuscript censuses of 1871, 1881, and 1891 for the New Glasgow census sub-district.

[23] For an overview of the industrial development of Pictou County, see R. M. Guy, "Industrial Development and Urbanization of Pictou County to 1900," unpub-

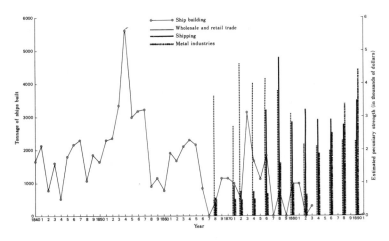

FIGURE 1. THE CHANGING ECONOMY OF NINETEENTH CEN-
TURY NEW GLASGOW.

linked to the staple trades and the shipping industry, was the
mainstay of New Glasgow's economy in the immediate pre-Con-
federation era (Figure 1). Ships built by Thomas Graham, George
McKenzie, and James W. Carmichael employed sometimes over
250 men at their East River yards. Following a peak in the mid-
1850s — associated with Reciprocity and the coal trade with the
United States — shipbuilding suffered a general downturn there-
after, eventually collapsing in the early 1880s.

The demise of shipbuilding and the shipping industry itself is
associated with many factors, not least with the rise of a landward
economy. What forces propelled this mercantile-industrial transition? The breakdown of the General Mining Association's coal
monopoly in 1857 was particularly significant in stimulating a shift
away from the "seaward" economy to "landward" development.[24]
New opportunities for coal mining that attracted Quebec, American,
and Belgian investors were augmented by the construction of a
regional railway system during the 1860s and 1870s, reciprocity
with the United States (1854-1866), and expansion of the St.

lished M.A. thesis, Acadia University, 1962; J. M. Cameron, *Industrial History of the
New Glasgow District* (New Glasgow, 1970); idem, *The Pictonian Colliers* (Kentville,
1974); and McCann, "The Mercantile-Industrial Transition."

24 Rosemary Ommer, "Anticipating the Trend: The Pictou Ship Register, 1840-
1889," *Acadiensis*, 10 (1980), pp. 61-89.

Lawrence industrial market. The political climate, manifested most clearly in the National Policy (1879) of economic incentives — particularly protective tariffs, preferential freight rates, and bounties on iron and steel production — gave promise for industrial opportunities in which Maritime manufacturers could play a vital role.[25] Pictou County's coal and iron ore resources created an environmental context for this new industrialism, but as Thomas Cochran and Burton Folsom would argue, the success or failure of the New Glasgow industrial economy would be determined by "the existing culture of its society," including the ability of its local residents to mobilize capital, new technologies, and a skilled labour force.

Such a transformation was indeed realized, as various economic indicators charted in Figure 1 clearly reveal. Data extracted from the *Mercantile Agency Reference Books* published by Dun, Wiman and Company and R. G. Dun and Company for the period 1868-1890 record the shift from an import-export economy to one based substantially on the metal-making and metal-working sectors. Labour force statistics compiled from the nominal manuscript censuses for 1861, 1871, and 1881 identify the same pattern. Ship carpenters declined from 57 to 31 between 1861 and 1881, while industrial labourers were increasing nearly fivefold, from 14 to 69. The leading sector of the transformation was the rise of the iron and steel industry, a story already told and one which need not be repeated here in any detail.[26] What bears repeating, however, is the fact the community as a whole — and particularly the merchant elite — supported the transformation.

But who were the ironmasters? Did they possess particular social traits? How was leadership attained? Were they members of Ingham's first families? Or were they newcomers and participants in the type of mobility hypothesized by Herbert Gutman? To answer these questions, we first examine the social order of New Glasgow in 1881, differentiating two classes of people — the merchant and manufacturing elite and the metal-working labour pool — within the context of the town's total population (Table 1). The merchant-manufacturing elite have ownership and financial status possessing capital assets of more than $7500; the metal

---

[25] For a further discussion of the National Policy and its impact on the Maritimes, see T. W. Acheson, "The National Policy and the Industrialization of the Maritimes, 1880-1910," *Acadiensis*, 1 (1972), pp. 3-28.

[26] See McCann, "The Mercantile-Industrial Transition."

Table 1

Social Characteristics of New Glasgow's Population in 1881

Category	Total Population (Head of Households) Number	%	Merchant and Manufacturing Elite[1] Number	%	Workers Employed in Metal Industries Number	%
Occupation						
High White Collar	17	3.2	1	4.5		
Major Proprietor	69	12.8	21	95.5	4	8.3
Low White Collar	9	1.7				
Semi-Professionals	1	.2				
Petty Proprietor	46	8.6				
Skilled	186	34.5			43	89.6
Semi-Skilled	26	4.8				
Unskilled	59	11.0				
Farmer	24	4.5				
Miner	5	.9				
Unspecified	96	17.8			1	2.1
Birthplace						
Nova Scotia	411	76.4	20	90.9	38	79.1
New Brunswick	5	.9			2	4.2
Prince Edward Island	8	1.5			1	2.1
Ontario	1	.2				
Quebec	1	.2				
England	27	5.0			1	2.1
Ireland	10	1.9				
Scotland	67	12.4	2	9.1	4	8.3
Other British	1	.2				
French	2	.4				
German	1	.2				
United States	4	.7			2	4.2
Origin						
African	5	.9				
English	60	11.2	1	4.5	5	10.4
French	4	.7			1	2.1
German	3	.6			1	2.1
Indian	3	.6				
Irish	36	6.7			3	6.3
Scottish	426	79.2	20	90.9	38	79.1
American	1	.2	1	4.5		
Religion						
Baptist	11	2.0				
Catholic	70	13.0			5	10.4
Anglican	38	7.0			5	10.4
Methodist	3	.6			2	4.2

Category	Total Population (Head of Households)		Merchant and Manufacturing Elite[1]		Workers Employed in Metal Industries	
	Number	%	Number	%	Number	%
Religion cont'd						
Ch. of Scotland	152	28.3	4	18.2	18	37.5
Presbyterian	263	48.9	18	81.8	17	35.4
Other	1	.2			1	2.1
Present in 1871						
No	292	54.3	10	45.5	26	54.2
Yes	236	43.9	11	50.0	21	43.7
Unknown	10	1.8	1	4.5	1	2.1
Total	538		22		48	

Source: Data have been compiled from the nominal manuscripts of the *Census of Canada*, 1881.

[1] Those listed under the category of "Merchant and Manufacturing Elite" were selected on the basis of their ownership of a business having an estimated pecuniary strength of $7,500 or more in Dun, Wiman and Company, *Mercantile Reference Book*, 1882.

workers, only their labouring skills offering the potential of entry into the ranks of the industrialist. Beyond differences in occupational status, there is little to distinguish these groups from each other. True, there is greater diversity amongst the metal workers, but this is of a minor order. What is striking are their broad similarities: Nova Scotia-born, of Scottish origin, and length of residency in the town. They differ significantly in religious affiliation, with the elite being overwhelmingly Presbyterians — suggesting a break from traditional ways — compared to the greater adherence to the established Church of Scotland by the working class.

Within this social order, is there opportunity for social mobility amongst newcomers, or is the social order closed? To explore this issue, the 1881 residents of New Glasgow were checked for their 1871 presence in Pictou County. Of some 538 heads of households, 230 were present in both 1871 and 1881. Of these, 147 were resident in New Glasgow in 1871; 83 were from other Pictou County locations. Such a division allows us to examine the opportunities for occupational advancement of both natives and newcomers. As Tables 2 and 3 show, newcomers were able to advance very little in comparison to the native group. Of the skilled newcomers, most (75 percent) remained stable in the same broad occupational category, but no one in this category became a major proprietor. A few newcomers did, including those who had brought such status with them, but these were exceptions to the general pattern of limited upward mobility for outsiders. Opportunities for advancement were greater for those people who had lived in the town in 1871. At least 10 people advanced to the ranks of the major proprietor group. When we examine the social characteristics of all these people (the data are available upon request), there is little to differentiate them from others, except their longer-established residency in the town.

New Glasgow's social structure was clearly one that John Ingham would describe as pre-established and distinctly ordered. There was an identifiable class of leaders who controlled the means of production, as well as a large pool of skilled metal workers. Despite the degree of social homogeneity marking the town, mobility to the ranks of the elite was restricted, particularly for newcomers. Because many studies that illustrate limited mobility show considerable ethnic diversity, the fact that homogeneity in New Glasgow's case did not facilitate mobility forces us to seek out other cultural factors that affected the opportunity to rise and prosper as an

Table 2

Occupational Mobility of Native New Glasgow Residents, 1871-1881

Occupation at start of decade[1] (1871)	Occupation at end of decade (percent)						Number of Cases
	Major Proprietor	Other White Collar	Skilled	Semi-Skilled and Unskilled	Farmers	Unspecified	
Major proprietor	76.5	11.8	5.9	—	5.9	—	17
Other white collar	21.4	78.6	—	—	—	—	14
Skilled	6.3	6.3	75.0	3.1	6.3	3.1	64
Semi-skilled and unskilled	14.3	14.3	—	42.9	14.3	14.3	7
Farmers	—	16.7	16.7	16.7	50.0	—	6
Unspecified	5.1	7.7	10.3	12.8	—	64.1	39
							147

Source: Data are compiled from the nominal manuscript censuses of 1871 and 1881.

[1] Occupational categories are derived from S. Thernstrom, *The Other Bostonians* (Cambridge, Mass., 1975).

industrial leader. This can be determined by a biographical study of the leaders of the new industrialism.[27]

New Glasgow's initial round of industrialization was almost completely financed by the local shipping and mercantile elite, principally the Carmichael and McGregor families. As two of the town's oldest established families, both were extensively involved in a variety of economic ventures. James William Carmichael, son of New Glasgow's first general store owner, J. C. Carmichael, was an entrepreneurial pluralist; he was a merchant, shipping owner, banker, sawmill operator, tanner, and shipbuilder, as well as politician. The McGregors were also among the first to establish sizeable mercantile operations in New Glasgow. As the sons of James D. McGregor (the town's first Presbyterian minister), Roderick and James, and in turn their sons, developed a variety of interests in the retail and wholesale trades, shipping, and manufacturing. Other leading shipping and merchant families included the Walkers (Andrew), the McColls (Jeffrey), and to a lesser extent, Angus Chisholm, Thomas Fraser, David Patterson, Harvey Graham, and George Underwood, to name only a few. Most of these families supported the financing of the Nova Scotia Steel Company in 1882,[28] and the personal account book of James W. Carmichael for the years 1870-93 demonstrates how James W. provided cash and credit to all of the above mentioned families.[29] The flow of capital between these families was no doubt facilitated — perhaps even guaranteed — because all were related through marriage and kinship relations. The relationship between the mercantile leaders of New Glasgow's social elite — and its economy — may be defined as an extended family. The inter-marriage between these families and their collective domination of the town's social and service

[27] Biographical information was obtained chiefly from the following sources: J. M. Cameron, "The Scotia Steelmasters," *Collections of the Nova Scotia Historical Society*, 40 (1980), pp. 31-56; H. C. Ritchie, "Genealogical Records," unpublished typescript, New Glasgow Regional Library, 1952; and the nominal manuscript census records for 1851, 1861, 1871, 1881 and 1891, amongst other sources.

[28] "Prospectus of the Nova Scotia Steel Company" and "Letters Patent Incorporating the Nova Scotia Steel Company, Limited," Hawker Siddeley Papers, MS 4-106, Dalhousie University Archives. See also McCann, "Mercantile-Industrial Transition," pp. 42-44.

[29] "Personal Account Book of James W. Carmichael," MG 2, vol. 360, pp. 24-77, P.A.N.S.

Table 3

Occupational Mobility of Newcomers to New Glasgow, 1871-1881

Occupation at start of decade[1] (1871)	Occupation at end of decade (percent)						Number of Cases
	Major Proprietor	Other White Collar	Skilled	Semi-Skilled and Unskilled	Farmers	Unspecified	
Major proprietor	100.0	—	—	—	—	—	4
Other white collar	—	100.0	—	—	—	—	2
Skilled	—	6.9	75.9	6.9	6.9	3.4	29
Semi-skilled and ⁻unskilled	—	—	20.0	60.0	20.0	—	5
Farmers	—	13.0	21.7	26.1	26.1	13.0	23
Unspecified	10.0	25.0	20.0	5.0	—	40.0	20
							83

Source: See Table 2.

institutions resemble greatly the scenario described by Ingham in his study of closed social structures in industrializing cities.[30]

Marriage is also the principal factor propelling skilled artisans to the ranks of the mercantile-industrial elite. Virtually all who achieved mobility maintained a connection to New Glasgow's long-established families. Those who did not advance were recent migrants. Insights as to why the "rags-to-riches" thesis does not apply can be drawn from biographical information of several important ironmasters who achieved success: Graham Fraser,

[30] A general survey of community participation in New Glasgow's public institutions, clubs, and politics is found in James Cameron, *More About New Glasgow* (Kentville, 1974). Cameron described the Y.M.C.A. as the most popular of New Glasgow's clubs. Prominent members included: Roderick McGregor and his son, Peter McGregor; Isaac Matheson and his son William; John Stewart, who sat on its executive; and Harvey Graham, who was to be a leader of the "Y" locally, provincially, and internationally. James W. Carmichael was highly instrumental in establishing the town's first hospital in 1896 and sat on the Aberdeen Hospital Board for much of the rest of his life. His daughter, Caroline, initiated the Ladies' Auxiliary to the Aberdeen and served as its president off and on for many subsequent years. Many officers of the Ladies' Auxiliary were wives and daughters of James D. McGregor, James C. McGregor, George Underwood, Jeffrey McColl, John Stewart, Graham Fraser and Harvey Graham. Finally, Mayors and councillors of New Glasgow between 1876 and 1890 included Jeffrey McColl, James D. McGregor, Peter McGregor, Harvey Graham, George Underwood and James M. Carmichael, to name only a few.

George Forrest McKay, William Matheson, John Stewart and
W. P. McNeil. Fraser and McKay were leaders in the rise of the
company that eventually became Scotia Steel. Skilled and innovative blacksmiths, both came from modest homes. Fraser, born in
1848, obtained his training at the Rhode Island Locomotive
Company and after a short work experience in a Maitland, Nova
Scotia shipyard, returned to ply his trade in James W. Carmichael's
New Glasgow shipyard. Soon after, in 1869, he set up his own
smithing business by convincing Carmichael to let him "iron" his
ships. Fraser then teamed with Forrest McKay to form the Hope
Iron Works in 1872, which prospered to become, in turn, the Nova
Scotia Forge Company (1874) and later the Nova Scotia Steel
Company (1882). Securing additional funds for these ventures was
no doubt aided by the marriage links of both men, but was done
cautiously in a steady progression of market testing and prudent
investment decisions. There was none of Cochran's risk-taking in
the initial development of Scotia Steel.[31] Fraser had married the
daughter of a Pictou shipbuilder and McKay was paired with
Mary Jane Walker, sister of merchant and shipper Andrew Walker.
Through this connection, McKay became indirectly related to
both the Carmichaels, McKenzies, and McGregors. Another obvious connection between the merchants and the industrialists was
William Matheson, son of Isaac. William, who studied engineering
at the University of New Brunswick and apprenticed in Dundee,
Scotland, married James W. Carmichael's daughter. Isaac Matheson was married to James W.'s sister.

The career paths of John Stewart and W. P. McNeil lack these
prominent connections, and help to explain why both, while
enjoying success, never grew to the extent of the larger firms. Both
moved to New Glasgow in the 1860s and soon began the manufacture of agricultural implements; and later, both engaged in iron
bridge construction. But like other metal-working firms, such as
W. Fraser, Bailey Harrow Company and Robert Brown, Stewart
and McNeil never truly entered the ranks of the industrial elite.
This status was reserved for those who, beyond their Scottishness,
were linked together by family ties. Leading roles in the social
order and structure of New Glasgow during the transition to the
new industrialism were clearly closed to most outsiders. This is not

---

[31] On the cautious development of Scotia Steel, see McCann, "The Mercantile-
Industrial Transition."

to suggest that the abilities of the industrialists were unimportant. On the contrary, the connections existing within the community, combined with personal qualities, promising circumstances, and basic good timing, all enhanced the chances to experience social mobility.

New Glasgow's social structure on the eve of the new industrialism was shaped by the organization of the town's mercantile economy. Distinctive classes existed, including a small elite group of proprietors, shippers, and merchants and the majority working class of ship carpenters and labourers, amongst others. Beyond these traits, the ethnic and religious make-up of the community was strikingly uniform in its Scottish character. The precise effects of this homogeneity on mobility are difficult to gauge, but because social and ethnic diversity usually bear negatively on mobility, it is possible that uniformity in New Glasgow's population facilitated the process of social advancement. But other cultural factors loom larger in significance. In fact, the social structure of New Glasgow shows that the town fits rather well John Ingham's model of a closed social order. Very few migrants broke the ranks of the mercantile-industrial elite. It is also clear that the recruitment of industrialists into the elite classes was largely a subjective but nevertheless strongly predicated process. While many hopeful entrepreneurs had necessary skills and ambition, only a few were accepted into the ranks of the new industrial elite. There can be little question that the factors of marriage, kinship, and length of family presence in the community were of paramount importance for success. Cultural factors are critical, as Thomas Cochran argued, but the context of change is related to a closed rather than an open frontier. As John Ingham concluded, the industrial revolution, whatever the changes it wrought in the economic and technological spheres, did little "to disturb the hegemony of the social upper classes over economic affairs."[32] This was the experience of New Glasgow in the late nineteenth century.

[32] John Ingham, "Rags to Riches Revisited," p. 37.

CARRIE MacMILLAN

Seaward Vision and Sense of Place: The Maritime Novel, 1880-1920 [1]

THE LATE NINETEENTH AND EARLY TWENTIETH century was a time of remarkable literary activity in Canada — one in which Maritime writers played a prominent part. During the 1880s and 1890s, the first generation to be raised Canadian reached maturity, many of them caught up in the promise of Confederation and the spirit of imperialism, which, as Carl Berger has argued, was a form of nationalism. [2] Another contributor to the burgeoning of literature was technological change which resulted in the cheaper production of books, including paperbacks, and created a demand for more material, as did an increasingly educated, leisured, and culture-minded, reading public. [3]

As is well documented by Robert Craig Brown and Ramsay Cook in *Canada, 1896-1921: A Nation Transformed*, [4] this was a time of social transition, of the metamorphosis of Canada from a country of farms and small towns to a more urbanized society, of a change in the manufacturing base from wood to steel. These changes were reflected in Maritime communities, particularly those along the railway lines. The industrialization of parts of the Maritimes was tempered, however, by the precarious nature of the post-Confederation economy. Traditional trade with Great Britain

---

[1] I wish to acknowledge with gratitude the support of the Social Sciences and Humanities Research Council of Canada which enabled me to carry out this study and to express my thanks to Cheryl Bell, a former honours English student at Mount Allison University, who assisted me in the project.

[2] Carl Berger, *The Sense of Power: Studies in the Ideas of Canadian Imperialism 1867-1919* (Toronto, 1970).

[3] Gordon Roper, "New Forces: New Fiction 1880-1920," in Carl F. Klink, ed., *Literary History of Canada* (Toronto, 1965), pp. 260-83, documents the dramatic increase in Canadian fiction during the period.

[4] R. C. Brown and R. Cook, *Canada, 1896-1921: A Nation Transformed* (Toronto, 1974).

and the West Indies declined, and the region failed in its competition with central Canada for the lucrative western markets. Thus, the Maritimes experienced, simultaneously, both the rise of manufacturing towns and the periodic takeovers or closures of industry that resulted in waves of emigration.

A study of the literature of the period by Maritime writers may tell us something about the concerns and values of Maritime society as it responded to this erratic and tentative industrialization with its accompanying social changes. Scholars have looked at the more significant poetry of the period — that of Sir Charles G. D. Roberts, Bliss Carman, and Francis Sherman. Influenced by the English Romantic and Victorian traditions and by New England Transcendentalism, their writing is introspective, a record of the poets' spiritual musings in the world of nature. Little is seen of society. But what of the fiction? It has received very little critical attention.

There are several reasons why this substantial body of fiction has been neglected. Literary critics of the period, with few exceptions, tended to see Canadian literature in general, and Canadian fiction in particular, as immative and inferior. They considered fiction, furthermore, to be of a lesser artistic and moral order than poetry and not to merit the same kind of serious attention. Perhaps most important, many of the writers of fiction were women, writing for a female audience. Recent feminist criticism has pointed out that there is a relationship in the period between gender and judgement; women writers were not taken as seriously as men. In the modern period this fiction has suffered, too, as a result of a general reaction against sentimentalism and romance. The works of only a few writers — Charles G. D. Roberts, whose animal stories were very popular until the Second World War, and Margaret Marshall Saunders and Lucy Maud Montogomery, who wrote classics that have kept their names alive — continue to be read. For all these reasons, as well as Canada's general cultural insecurity in the first half of the twentieth century, a considerable number of Maritime Canadian writers have passed into oblivion, except for cataloguing in such compendiums as Watters' *A Checklist of Canadian Literature* (1959), or brief mention in the *Literary History of Canada* (1965). This is so despite the fact that some (Carrie Jenkins Harris, Alice Jones, Susan Carleton Jones, Frederick William Wallace) wrote a respectable half dozen novels, some (Basil King, Hiram Cody) as many as twenty novels, and some (James MacDonald Oxley) about thirty.

For the most part, these writers of fiction came from, or soon gravitated to, the larger Maritime cities — Halifax, Fredericton, Charlottetown — although they may have been born in Douglas or Cody's in the Annapolis Valley. And, in almost all cases, they had a connection with church and university: King (Anglican minister and King's College, Windsor); Cody (Anglican minister and King's College, Windsor); Roberts (son of Anglican minister and University of New Brunswick and King's College, Windsor); Saunders (daughter of Baptist minister and Dalhousie University and Boston University); and Montgomery (married to Presbyterian minister and Dalhousie University. Travelling and living outside the Maritimes was also the norm after a literary career had been decided upon. The writers found it convenient or even imperative to be near other writers, their publishers, and the larger American or English audience; and they responded to the spirit of internationalism that was in the air. Some of the places they lived include: Roberts (New York and London); Saunders (Boston); Fytche (London); King (Cambridge, Massachusetts); and the Jones sisters (France). Some writers, such as Cody and Montgomery, left the Maritimes to live in other parts of Canada. Most of the writers returned to Canada, although not necessarily to the Maritimes, towards the end of their writing careers.

Admittedly, much of the fiction is not of the first rank. At its best it does stand up to the fiction of American writers of the period, such as W. D. Howells, who do have a place in a literary tradition. For the most part, the novels are romantic; their themes, love and adventure. Most portray life in rather idealized terms, present wholly good or wholly bad characters, are sentimental, and are directed at a popular audience. No doubt many novelists felt the temptation to conform to popular taste, but the lure must have been particularly strong for writers from Canada who published outside the country. There would have been little encouragement from a New York or Boston publisher for a writer who submitted a novel that dealt in depth with regional life in an obscure area — Beaver Harbour, New Brunswick, or Guysborough County, Nova Scotia, for example.

Evidence to support this view comes from the publishing career of Margaret Marshall Saunders, who constantly courted her American audience in the choice of her settings and characters. Her study of small-town life, *Deficient Saints: A Tale of Maine* (Boston: Page, 1899) is set, not in the Annapolis Valley or Halifax

J. MacDonald Oxley's *Fife and Drum at Louisburg* (Boston: Little, Brown, 1899); Edward Payson Tenny's *Constance of Acadia* (Boston: Roberts Brothers, 1886); and Arthur James McLeod's *The Notary of Grand Pré* (Boston: Author, 1901). Indeed, it would seem that if Maritime writers wanted to seize the attention of their audience, local or American, they needed only to write a book that incorporated in its title some hint of Acadie. Even works with a contemporary setting might exploit the popularity of the Acadian theme with titles like Margaret Marshall Saunders' *Rose à Charlitte: An Acadian Romance*, Grace Dean (McLeod) Rogers' *Stories of the Land of Evangeline* (Boston: Lothrop, 1891); and Carrie Jenkins Harris' *A Modern Evangeline* (Windsor, Nova Scotia: Anslow, 1896).

There is a certain amount of irony in the fact that the central myth of the region was first made famous by an American. Further, most of the novels of this kind are little better than costume dramas with stereotyped separated lovers and black abbés; they offer little serious analysis (although some writers, like Fytche, did extensive historical research in an attempt at accuracy). However, even if Evangeline did foster a lot of mediocre writing, she allowed Maritime writers the opportunity to look at themselves, to "populate [their] imagination," however superficially, with their own place and history. Also, the large quantity of "Evangeline fiction" —of historical novels set during the French-English wars—suggests the extent to which Maritime writers and society responded to history and also, during the vulnerable post-Confederation period, valued the stability that tradition provides. The fascination with Evangeline represents a tendency to take refuge in romantic conservatism, to turn back in time to a more "noble" and exciting era, as a release from social change and economic uncertainty. Indeed, it might not be entirely inaccurate to claim that Evangeline provides a myth of tragic proportions commensurate with the decline of the age of sail and of the Maritime region after Confederation.

A second kind of fiction that responds to Maritime experience is the "going down the road" or international novel which follows the life of a character who leaves the region. This kind of novel is a response to several things. It reflects the vulnerable social and economic condition of the Maritimes during the period, when many people had to leave the area to find employment. It represents, too, the authors' responses to the pressure of publishers to use settings familiar to an American or English audience. In some cases it represents the authors' interest in the international novel popular at the time. An advantage of the international novel for Canadian writers was that they could use a Canadian character who travels to a foreign setting, usually the United States or Britain, and could define the Canadian type in relation to other regional or national types. In this manner they could write, however indirectly, about their own country.

While one might deplore the pressures that resulted in so much of the fiction's being set outside the region — for superficiality of treatment of both setting and character often resulted — these novels have some redeeming qualities. In the first place, many of them reflect a powerful Maritime reality: "going down the road" in search of a livelihood. Moreover, rather than suggesting a deferential attitude to the rest of the world, the novels present the Maritimes in a very positive light. This is achieved by the authors' portraying Maritime characters who prove themselves and take their place in the larger world. Indeed the novels often present the outside world as displaying shortcomings with which the Maritime character must contend, often in almost heroic terms. This is achieved by the authors' stressing moral themes. While they concede that the larger world (Britain, Europe, or America) possesses greater wealth, a richer cultural tradition, or more brilliant society, the Canadian Maritime character is more innocent, has a stronger sense of right, greater vigour and promise, and is less artificial and corrupt than his or her counterparts from other countries. In other words, the "myth of the north," which scholars have found in other Canadian writing of the period, and which is a product of its nationalism and imperialism, is very evident in the Maritime novel.[8]

One thinks in the national sphere of the novels of Sara Jeannette Duncan, perhaps the strongest novelist of the period, which derive so much of their piquancy from foreign travel and cultural contrast. Duncan's observations made during her own travels in the United States, England, and India helped to provide her with the clear vision of Canada and Canadians presented in her finest novels, *The Imperialist* (Toronto: Copp Clark, 1904) and *Cousin Cinderella* (Toronto: MacMillan, 1908). Of the Maritime novelists, Basil King

---

[8] See Carl Ballstadt, *The Search for English-Canadian Literature* (Toronto, 1975), which contains excerpts from contemporary nationalistic writing that illustrate this concept.

which shapes the character of the Canadian heroine. The European setting is the Mediterranean shore, bleached, dry, and glaring. An aging, calculating, and artificial European woman, the mistress of the Canadian woman's father, presides there. The Canadian girl resists her father's desire to have her make a brilliant European society marriage and chooses instead to marry a robust Canadian — for love.

Susan Carleton Jones, the sister of Alice Jones, sketches an interesting variation in her novel *A Detached Pirate*, although it is very shallow and not well written. In it, Canada becomes a refuge for the heroine, an English woman who has suffered the trauma of an unhappy marriage and divorce in London. In that city she has felt stifled and constrained by the limited freedom of movement and experience for women.[9] Her ocean voyage to Halifax, the social life she finds there, and rustic excursions into the surrounding countryside — where she stays in log cabins and sleeps on spruce boughs — all have a restorative effect. When her past catches up with her, she moves on to New York, where she is reunited with her husband. The change of venue and the wholesome period in Nova Scotia make it easier for the two to talk honestly and openly of their feelings and to realize there have been misunderstandings that led to the separation.

Susan Carleton Jones' *A Girl of the North: A Story of London and Canada* (London: Greening, 1900) is a better written novel. In it, the archetypal Canadian couple, wholesome and nature-loving, fall in love. However, the woman overhears gossip that he has fathered a child by another woman. Because her ideal of him is shattered and because she thinks that women have to support one another, she leaves him and Canada to rebuild her life in England. There she finds a very sophisticated and cynical society of unfaithful marriage partners, ennui relieved by love affairs, tarnished reputations, and "modern" ideas of marriage, such as living apart. Disappointed in love herself, the heroine accepts this society and also a marriage proposal from a titled aristocrat. Just before the marriage, the man she loves arrives from Canada, and she learns it was not he, but his cousin, who fathered the child. Ashamed of her actions, she breaks her engagement and returns secretly to Canada. Her Canadian lover follows her on snowshoes to her home in the woods, "Solitude," and amid the purifying cold and snow they

[9] See note 6 above.

agree to marry. At the end of the novel, the heroine says to her lover: "I am glad we are 'born Canadian,' aren't you?"

In Maria Amelia Fytche's *Kerchiefs to Hunt Souls* (Boston: Arena, 1895),[10] a Nova Scotia woman gives up her successful girls' school and goes to Europe in search of romance. She finds instead very hard conditions for the working woman and a degenerate aristocracy that catches her in a web of deceit. After she is duped into a marriage that is not recognized in France and after the convenient death of her bohemian, aristocratic husband, she moves to England with an honourable suitor to start a home for dispossessed and needy women. Fytche's novel is studded with social criticism of Europe, its employment agencies, homes for working women, and the exploitation of women as governesses. Her Maritime character is an agent for exposing injustice and a figure of redemption.

All of the novels of Carrie Jenkins Harris focus on characters from the Maritimes.[11] Separation from family and loved ones, and the tension and misunderstandings that result, provide their interest. Usually the outside world lures her travellers into some form of unfaithfulness to their origins, but eventually they see the error of their ways and atone. In *Mr. Perkins of Nova Scotia*, for example, the members of a Nova Scotia family make their fortune and decide to send their son on a continental tour to complete his education. The son becomes a snob in Europe, keeping only the "best" society and hiding his "colonial" origins. However, in Europe he is preyed upon by a gang of fortune hunters and returns home, penniless, humbled, and with an acquired respect for the simple life and wholesome values of rural and small town Nova Scotia.

A fourth Maritime writer whose work sheds light on central regional motifs through an exploration of the international thesis is Frederick William Wallace. His novel *Blue Water: A Tale of the Deep Sea Fishermen* (Toronto: Musson, 1935), in which the central character is a lad from a Bay of Fundy fishing community who goes off to Boston to join the schooners that fish off the Grand Banks, shares elements of both the international novel and the regional idyll. Wallace proudly presents his young hero as an outstanding

---

[10] Also published in the Mount Allison University Maritime reprint series (Sackville, New Brunswick, 1980) with an introduction by Carrie MacMillan.

[11] *Cyril Whyman's Mistake* (Toronto: Bryce, 1894); *Faith and Friends* (Windsor, Nova Scotia: Anslow, 1895); *A Modern Evangeline* (Windsor, Nova Scotia: Anslow, 1896); *Mr. Perkins of Nova Scotia* (Windsor, Nova Scotia: Anslow, 1891); *A Romantic Romance* (Windsor, Nova Scotia: Anslow, 1893).

Larry Strangways, a former tutor in the Brokenshire home. In a
burst of clarity, Alex realizes that she does indeed love Strangways
—that she had thought she loved Hugh (or should love Hugh)
because he had been the one member of the family to acknowledge
her and to be kind to her.

By the last chapter, Alex has married Larry Strangways and is
living on the South Shore of Nova Scotia in a modest frame home
very different from the splendid estates they have recently known
on the Atlantic to the south. They have returned from service as
soldier and nurse in Britain and Europe. Alex's reflections on this
pure, early spring morning reveal her peace of mind and happiness:

I am writing in the dawn of a May morning in 1917. Before me lies a sickle
of white beach some four or five miles in curve. Beyond that is the
Atlantic, a mirror of leaden gray. Woods and fields bank themselves
inland; here a dewy pasture, there a stretch of plowed earth recently sown
and harrowed; elsewhere a grove of fir or maple or hazel copse. . . . In the
woods round me the birds, which have only just arrived from Florida,
from the West Indies, from Brazil, are chirruping sleepily. They will doze
again presently, to awake with the sunrise into the chorus of full song. . . .

In this room my baby is sleeping in his little bassinet. It is not the bassinet
of my dreams, nor is this the white enameled nursery, nor am I wearing a
delicate lace peignoir. It is all much more beautiful than that, because it is
as it is. (*The High Heart*, p. 406)

The simple, wholesome images of rural life and the hopeful,
regenerative images of the baby and the spring contrast strongly
with the artificial, overly sumptuous, and very unhappy images of
American society that have prevailed throughout the novel.

The High Heart is a very good novel, marred only at times by a
strident moral tone, no doubt influenced by its having been written
during the war. Narrated in the first person by the very strong and
attractive Alex Adare, and using to advantage contrasting characters and settings, as well as the moral touchstone of the First
World War, it defines the Canadian sensibility at this time.
Ignored or considered of little or no consequence in America and
England, the young Canadian demands recognition. In the end,
although she has proven herself in the American establishment, she
goes her own way, remaining true, through service in the war and a
return to Nova Scotia, to her history and tradition. The novel also
offers a sympathetic, convincing, and memorable study of the
working woman, for Alex is surely representative of those myriads
of Maritime women who went off to the "Boston States" to make
something of themselves.

A third kind of novel that defines a distinct place and tradition is the novel set in the Maritimes, almost inevitably in a small town. These are the novels of the regional idyll. These attempt to record the day-to-day activities, values, and vision of the region. Although they usually comprise a contrived plot and some stereotyped or sentimentalized characters, the writing tends to be, on the whole, realistic. Novels of this kind are much rarer than those belonging to the other two categories. Apparently there was a relatively small market for this kind of novel; publishers tended to favour more exotic settings and idealized characterization. It would appear, then, that these novels are labours of love, novels in which their authors present a world for which they have affection and respect.

The best — indeed almost the only — representatives of the regional idyll are Charles G. D. Roberts' *The Heart That Knows* (Boston: Page, 1906), set in Westcock, New Brunswick; Frederick William Wallace's *Blue Water: A Tale of the Deep Sea Fishermen* (Toronto: Musson, 1907), set partly in a fishing community on the Bay of Fundy; and, as mentioned earlier, Margaret Marshall Saunders' *Rose à Charlitte: An Acadian Romance*, set around the turn of the century in the Clare District of Nova Scotia. All three novels portray small, traditional, rural or seafaring communities whose inhabitants enjoy a simple, quiet existence in tune with the seasons and the sea. But there are also images of social and technological change and of interaction with the outside world. In Roberts' novel, seafaring takes the hero away from the heroine and creates a tragic situation; the sympathetic treatment of the heroine, an unwed mother, is a measure of the novel's liberal approach.[12] Wallace introduces modern fishing methods, including a processing plant, in his novel; and Saunders portrays changing images of Acadians — women in particular — as well as the strong cultural links and social movement between Nova Scotia and New England.

Roberts' *The Heart That Knows* is a tribute to Westcock, New Brunswick, where he was born and spent his first fourteen years. The setting and people are delineated in detail and with a beauty that conveys nostalgia, respect, and affection. Here is Roberts' Tantramar landscape: the warm, upland fields, the wind-blown marshes, the tide-washed and dyke-lined coast, and the romantic prospect of Beausejour and Minudie. Here, too, is the generally

---

[12] Roberts is not the only Canadian novelist of the period to treat unwed motherhood sympathetically. See also Joanna E. Wood, *The Untempered Wind* (New York: Tait, 1894).

reminiscent in this, and in its New England beginning, of Haw-
thorne.

Vesper's voyage by sea and train to western Nova Scotia is one of
initiation, of symbolic death, and of rebirth into larger understanding. The train deposits him in a dark forest in Clare from
which he makes his way to an Acadian inn. Not long after he
arrives and begins to sympathize with the people and their tragic
past, he becomes ill and remains so for several weeks. He is aided in
his quest by Rose à Charlitte, the saintly, long-suffering Evangeline
character who thinks her husband Charlitte, an older man and a
ne'er-do-well who has been more a father than a husband, is dead,
but later learns he is living with another woman in Louisiana.
Vesper is aided in his quest also by Rose's cousin, a self-taught
Acadian scholar embittered by his people's treatment by the
English.

Vesper falls in love with Rose, who nurses him back to health,
but he must wait several years, until Charlitte dies, before he can
claim her. In the meantime, Vesper atones for his ancestor's sins by
befriending and helping two members of the Acadian community
— Rose's son, who forms an intuitive, mystical bond with him, and
the young girl Bidiane, who, he discovers, is the only remaining
descendant of the wronged eighteenth-century Acadian. Vesper
introduces Bidiane, whom he finds living in poverty and ashamed
of her French blood, to Paris where she is gradually educated into
her magnificent French heritage and a better way of life. When she
returns to Clare, she is happy to claim her people. After the passage
of several more years and the death of Charlitte (again one notes
the Evangeline pattern), Vesper returns to Clare and claims Rose.

If Rose represents the long-suffering past of the Acadians,
Bidiane represents the emergent new woman and new society. On
her way back to Clare from Paris, she overhears in a Halifax hotel
an English Nova Scotian talking critically of the Acadians. Later,
in Clare, she discovers to her horror that this same man is none
other than the representative for Clare in the provincial legislature. Not one to let something like this go by, the resourceful and
strong Bidiane organizes with the other women what she calls a
"feminine electioneering campaign" which she takes up and down
the Clare coast (and which includes distribution from her cellar of
"spirits" — Saunders knew her Maritime politics well). Of course,
the women do not have the vote, so they exercise their influence on

the menfolk and are successful in getting elected as their representative an Acadian, Rose's cousin, the erstwhile bitter historian.

Throughout the novel, the terrain — lake and forest — is animated by Acadian myth and legend. Saunders takes us into Acadian homes and captures examples of folk humour through pranks and jokes. She also adds to the local flavour and tradition by sprinkling her text with poetic quotations from the Nova Scotia poets J. F. Herbin and Cornelius O'Brien, Roman Catholic Archbishop of Halifax. She uses local material to heighten her important themes. When one considers the unsympathetic reception of her novel in the United States and observes the direction of her publishing career after the rebuff of her early attempts at social realism, one is filled with a sense of near tragic loss for Maritime Canadian literature.

Although it might not have been easy for Saunders or other Maritime novelists of the day to write about their own society, it is apparent that the Maritime novels discussed here provide evidence of strategies for literary survival. In the historical romance or "Evangeline" novel, the international or "going down the road" novel, and the regional idyll set in the Maritimes, Maritime novelists found ways of defining themselves, of creating a sense of place, of articulating an identity. They rarely described the effects of industrial and social change, except for that of emigration. Instead, they remained true to the traditional verities within the region of land and sea, and the people who lived in relation to them. They did this while maintaining a dual vision — one that reached inward to embrace a sense of all that had shaped them and which they held true, and outward to the distant places dictated by necessity.

PART TWO

The Passing
of
Traditional Society

JOHN G. REID

Health, Education, Economy: Philanthropic Foundations in the Atlantic Region in the 1920s and 1930s

T HE EXPERIENCE OF THE CARNEGIE CORPORATION of New York in the Maritime Provinces and Newfoundland during the period between the two World Wars was unorthodox. Or at least that was the feeling of Morse A. Cartwright, Director of the American Association for Adult Education, when he wrote to Carnegie Corporation president F. P. Keppel in 1936 to thank Keppel for showing him copies of letters received from the president of St. Dunstan's College. Cartwright, a frequent adviser of the Corporation in its programmes of support for adult education, went on to elaborate his view in some detail:

I have one comment to make, namely, that most of the adult education from that part of the world (due no doubt to the success of the Antigonish experiments) seems to be confused as to objective. It seems quite impossible to separate the educational and the economic goals. Perhaps in a pioneer and poverty-stricken country it is not desirable that they be separated and hence my comment is not one of criticism but merely of notation. It does not shock me in the least that oyster culture and religion and art in the home should all be combined in one program as they are on Prince Edward Island, but on the other hand I think that this mixture is in a sense evidence that the Maritime Provinces and Newfoundland are exceptional and quite unlike the situations that ordinarily would be met in the United States. The economic urge is exceedingly strong and I am not at all sure that the interest manifested in education is not largely a reflection of the enlightened self-interest of the people translated into terms of bettering themselves materially.[1]

[1] Morse A. Cartwright to F. P. Keppel, 24 April 1936, St. Dunstan's College File, Carnegie Corporation Archives [C.C.A.] New York. The author wishes to thank the Carnegie Corporation of New York and the Rockefeller Archive Center for providing access to archival material.

Cartwright's perception of the Maritimes and Newfoundland as "a pioneer and poverty-stricken country" was one that was at times reflected in the views of officials of the other major United States philanthropic foundation that was active in these areas during the 1920s and 1930s — the Rockefeller Foundation. When, for example, the Rockefeller Foundation voted in 1929 to co-operate with the government of Newfoundland in the launching of a public health scheme, it cited the scattered distribution of population and the absence of organized local governments as factors that complicated a health situation characterized by high rates of tuberculosis, nutritional diseases, and high infant and maternal mortality rates.[2] When assessed in worldwide terms, moreover, the Rockefeller Foundation's public health initiatives in the Maritimes and Newfoundland were considered to lend themselves to comparisons with similar projects undertaken far from North American shores. A 1939 report on the foundation's public health activities in Nova Scotia, for example, commented that "the Nova Scotia project represents a type of service that the Foundation has often been called upon to undertake in . . . Brazil and other countries of South America, in Czechoslovakia and other countries of Europe, in India and other lands of the Orient. . . ."[3]

Yet, if in some respects the interventions of the two philanthropic foundations in the Maritime provinces and Newfoundland were perceived as excursions into underdeveloped areas, in other ways these regions were treated as part of the North American mainstream. Both foundations made substantial grants to higher education institutions for purposes of endowment. In the field of medical education, for example — and notably in the case of the $500,000 granted in 1920 to the Dalhousie University medical school — the Maritimes and Newfoundland were expressly put in a North American context by the Rockefeller Foundation. Following the setting aside of $5 million earlier in 1920, at the request of J. D. Rockefeller, for the promotion of medical education in Canada, the foundation had set about formulating "a Dominion-wide policy," including support for strategically-placed medical schools. Dalhousie, concluded the foundation's Division of Medical Educa-

[2] Proposal for Aid to Newfoundland, 1929, RG2, Series 427, Box 26, Folder 212, Rockefeller Foundation Archives [R.F.A.] Rockefeller Archive Center, North Tarrytown, N.Y.

[3] Report on Public Health Progress in Nova Scotia, 1939, RG1.1, Series 427, Box 23, Folder 218, R.F.A.

Table 1

*Grants Approved by Rockefeller Foundation for Maritime
Provinces and Newfoundland, 1918-1940*

Recipient	Year(s)	Purpose	Amount
Dalhousie University	1920	Medical school development	$500.00
	1921	Medical school development	50,000
	1928	Teaching in Department of Hygiene	10,000
	1933-38	Teaching of public health	65,400
		LESS unspent balance in 1940	(5,528)
	1936	Institute of Public Affairs	61,200
		LESS unspent balance in 1940	(7,799)
	1937-38	Institute of Public Affairs, morbidity studies[1]	10,000
			683,543
New Brunswick	1923-24	Rural health programme	45,000
			45,000
Nova Scotia	1934	Department of Health sanitary engineering	8,500
	1936	Department of health, local health district	33,400
		LESS unspent balance in 1940	(16,597)
	1937	Department of Health, division of vital statistics	8,160
		LESS unspent balance in 1940	(5,675)
			27,788
Prince Edward Island	1938	Public health laboratory	15,300
		LESS unspent balance in 1940	(15,300)
Total			$756,331

Source: Rockefeller Foundation, *Annual Reports*, 1918-1940.

[1] These grants were not separately listed in the *Annual Reports* of the Foundation, but were taken from a fund designated for "grants-in-aid, social sciences, social security." See Minutes, 5 August 1937 and 30 June 1938, RG 1.1., Series 427, Box 32, Folder 341, R.F.A.

tion in recommending the grant, "is the medical centre of the Maritime Provinces . . . and includes in its territory Newfoundland. The nearest medical schools are McGill to the west and Dartmouth, Portland and Vermont to the south."[4]

Each of these different perceptions contributed to the reasons that prompted the Carnegie Corporation and the Rockefeller

[4] Records of Development of Medical Education in Canada. 1919-1925, pp. 2, 4-6, RG1.1, Series 427, Box 4, Folder 33; and History of Rockefeller Involvement with Dalhousie Medical School, 1919-1927, pp. 8-10, RG1.1, Series 427, Box 4, Folder 34, R.F.A.

Foundation to spend a combined total of more than $4 million in
the Maritimes and Newfoundland between 1918 and 1940. Indeed,
when the two perceptions are considered together, a strong case
could be made for regarding these regions as an ideal testing
ground for new ventures. Of the Carnegie Corporation's involvement in the establishment of Memorial University College in
Newfoundland, for example, Morse Cartwright wrote in 1927 that
"the whole Newfoundland venture is a most interesting adult
education (as well as a regularized education) experiment in a
peculiarly pioneer field." Similarly, in recommending Rockefeller
Foundation support for the founding of the Institute of Public
Affairs at Dalhousie University in 1936, the foundation official
Stacy May saw the project as "a control experiment against which
to measure experiments supported in the United States," involving
"sufficient variables... to serve as an interesting contrast and not
so many (as in Europe) as to make the experiment irrelevant."[5] Yet
whether informed by one or the other perception, or the combination of both, the actions of the two foundations also depended upon
the policies and methods which they had evolved since being
established earlier in the century.

When the Carnegie Corporation became, in 1911, the latest of
several philanthropic trusts established by Andrew Carnegie, its
aims were avowedly educational: "to promote the advancement
and diffusion of knowledge among the people of the United
States." Shortly afterwards, the corporation was empowered by
Carnegie to appropriate part of its annual income for similar
purposes in Canada and in British overseas territories.[6] The aims of
the Rockefeller Foundation, formally established in 1913, had
been enunciated by Rockefeller as early as 1901: "to promote the
well-being and to advance the civilization of the peoples of the
United States and its territories and possessions and of foreign

---

[5] Morse A. Cartwright to F. P. Keppel, 4 March 1927, Memorial University of
Newfoundland File, C.C.A.; and Stacy May, Notes on Dalhousie Project, 3 May
1936, RG1.1, Series 427, Box 33, Folder 345, R.F.A. For breakdown of the total
grants by the two foundations, see Tables 1 and 2. These figures may be put in an
overall Canadian context by reference to Robin S. Harris, *A History of Higher
Education in Canada, 1663-1960* (Toronto, 1976), pp. 343-48.

[6] Robert M. Lester, *Forty Years of Carnegie Giving: A Summary of the Benefactions of
Andrew Carnegie and of the Work of Philanthropic Trusts Which He Created* (New York,
1941), pp. 57-58; Howard J. Savage, *Fruit of an Impulse: Forty-five Years of the Carnegie
Foundation, 1905-1950* (New York, 1953), pp. 27-28; and Stephen H. Stackpole,
Carnegie Corporation: Commonwealth Program, 1911-1961 (New York, 1963), pp. 3-4.

lands in the acquisition and dissemination of knowledge, in the prevention and relief of suffering, and in the promotion of any and all of the elements of human progress." Although this declaration was phrased generally, the specialization of the foundation in health-related activities was quickly established under the influence of Rockefeller's close adviser, the Baptist minister Frederick T. Gates.[7] As philanthropic agencies, therefore, the chief interests of the Carnegie Corporation and the Rockefeller Foundation diverged. More minor differences also emerged over time. The Rockefeller Foundation, according to the opinion expressed in 1930 by F. P. Keppel, tended to have a larger full-time professional staff; Keppel attributed the difference to Andrew Carnegie's original business practice of working with a small staff, as opposed to Rockefeller's continuous reliance on expert advisers and organizers.[8]

[7] Raymond B. Fosdick, *The Story of the Rockefeller Foundation* (New York, 1952), pp. 14-21.

[8] F. P. Keppel, *The Foundation: Its Place in American Life* (New York, 1930), pp. 69-70.

Table 2

Grants Approved by Carnegie Corporation of New York for Maritime Provinces and Newfoundland, 1918-1940

Recipient	Year(s)	Purpose	Amount
Acadia University	1920-29	Endowment	$275,000
	1927	Arts teaching material	5,000
	1928	Adult education	5,000
	1932	Emergency support	10,000
	1932	Purchase of books for library	15,000
	1933	Music study material	2,500
	1934	Development of fine arts	200
	1934-40	Fine arts work	11,000
	1940	Research in mathematics	5,000
			328,700
Central Advisory Committee on Education in the Atlantic Provinces	1924-40	Expenses of meetings[1]	19,771
			19,771

Recipient	Year(s)	Purpose	Amount
Dalhousie University	1918-19	Repairs following Halifax Explosion	20,626
	1920	Endowment in medicine	500,000
	1921	Hospital teaching facilities	50,000
	1924	Payment of deficits	190,000
	1926	Arts teaching material	5,000
	1929	Books for dental school library	2,000
	1929	Endowment	400,000
	1932	Books for library	9,000
	1933	Endowment in geology	125,000
	1934	Professorship of German	8,000
	1934	Department of pathology	4,000
	1934	Research on pleochroic haloes	1,500
	1937	Medical school library development	50,000
			1,365,126
Halifax Ladies College	1936	Music study material	1,475
			1,475
Jubilee Guilds of Newfoundland	1935	Administrative expenses	4,000
			4,000
Memorial University College	1924	Establishment of junior college	75,000
	1926	Library service for isolated areas	5,000
	1927	Summer session	4,000
	1928-37	Support	185,000
	1930	Additional equipment	7,500
	1930	Scholarship fund	7,500
	1932	Arts teaching material	5,000
	1932	Books for library	3,000
	1938	Music study material	1,325
			293,325
Mount Allison University	1932	Support	10,000
	1932	Books for library	4,500
	1933	Arts teaching material	5,000
	1933	Endowment in chemistry	125,000
	1936	Music study material	2,550
	1937	Professorship of Germanic Studies	5,000
			152,050

Recipient	Year(s)	Purpose	Amount
New Brunswick Museum	1934	Educational Programme	9,000
			9,000
Newfoundland Adult Education Association	1931-34	Support	18,500
	1937	Experiment in adult education	1,000
			19,500
Newfoundland Public Libraries Board	1940	Books for travelling library programme[2]	2,000
			2,000
Nova Scotia Regional Libraries Commission	1940	Purchase of books[3]	10,000
			10,000
Prince Edward Island, Government of	1933-55	Demonstrations of library services	95,000
			95,000
Prince Edward Island Libraries	1939	Arts teaching material	2,000
			2,000
Prince of Wales College	1932	Books for library	4,500
	1933	Endowment in economics and sociology	75,000
			79,500
Public Archives of Nova Scotia	1934	Educational programme	1,500
			1,500
St. Dunstan's University	1932	Books for library	1,800
			1,800

Recipient	Year(s)	Purpose	Amount
St. Francis Xavier University	1919	Endowment in French	50,000
	1932	Support	10,000
	1932	Books for library	4,500
	1932-40	Extension activities[4]	65,000
			129,500
St. Joseph's University	1933	Books for library	1,000
			1,000
Study by Learned and Sills	1921-24	Expenses	5,575
			5,575
University of King's College	1922	Current Expenses	40,000
	1923	Institutional co-operation in Halifax	52,500
	1923	Endowment	600,000
	1925-27	Support	105,000
	1932	Books for library	3,000
			800,500
University of New Brunswick	1932	Books for library	4,500
			4,500
Total			3,325,822

Sources: Robert M. Lester, *Review of Grants in the Maritime Provinces of Canada and in Newfoundland,* 1911-1933 (New York, 1934), pp. 31-33; Stephen Stackpole, *Carnegie Corporation commonwealth Program,* 1911-1961 (New York, 1963), pp. 39-49.

[1] Payments on behalf of the Central Advisory Committee to 1940 are calculated from the figure for 1924-42 in Stackpole, *Commonwealth Program,* by subtracting amoungs paid after 1940. See R. M. Lester to G. J. Trueman, 5 August 1941, 2 December 1941, Trueman to Lester, 23 December 1941, Lester to Trueman, 10 May 1942, Trueman Papers, 7837-134, 7837-147, Mount Allison University Archives.

[2] Of this grant of $10,000 spread over five years, $2,000 was payable in 1940. See W. M. Woods to F. P. Keppel, 5 April 1940, Newfoundland Public Libraries Board Files, C.C.A.

[3] Of this grant of $50,000 spread over five years, $10,000 was payable in 1940. See [H. F. Munro] to F. P. Keppel, 23 January 1941, J. J. Tompkins Papers, MG10-2, 5 (c), Beaton Institute, University College of Cape Breton.

[4] In addition to Stackpole, *Commonwealth Program,* see also [R. M. Lester] to R. B. Fosdick, 28 February 1938, St. Francis Xavier University Extension Department Files, C.C.A.

The Rockefeller Foundation also had closer and more frequent contacts with public authorities than did the Carnegie Corporation, largely because its public health work necessarily included cooperation with governments.[9]

Despite these differences between the two foundations, the characteristics that they had in common were more striking. Both depended for their endowments upon the wealth gathered by their founders during the late nineteenth century period of industrialization in the United States. Both were profoundly influenced by the "gospel of wealth" propounded by Andrew Carnegie in an essay in the *North American Review* of 1889. For Carnegie, any effort to reverse or to subvert through revolution the achievements of capitalist society constituted an attack on "the foundation upon which civilization itself rests." Yet the concentration of wealth in the hands of a few successful industrialists presented a moral and political difficulty if such wealth were selfishly used. Rather, argued Carnegie, wealth was to be regarded as a trust, and the wealthy individual as "the mere trustee and agent for his poorer brethren."[10] Both foundations had then had their high motivations publicly challenged in 1915 by the Congressional Commission on Industrial Relations, on the ground that they were essentially tools of corporate interests from which they sprang, and were able through their grants of funding to exercise a dangerous and irresponsible influence in such important areas as education and social services.[11] Both had responded in later years by recognizing the obligation of foundations as tax-exempt bodies to allow public scrutiny of their finances and activities, by denying that they wielded power other than a power to assist progressive causes, and ultimately by reaffirming a faith in the progress of human civilization regardless of class conflicts. In 1922, for example, the acting president of the Carnegie Corporation, Henry S. Pritchett, commented in his annual report that "the method that the founder

[9] *Ibid.*, pp. 43-4.

[10] Andrew Carnegie, "The Gospel of Wealth," in Carnegie, *The Gospel of Wealth and Other Timely Essays*, ed. by Edward C. Kirkland (Cambridge, Mass., 1962), pp. 14-49. On the influence of Carnegie on Rockefeller, see Fosdick, *Rockefeller Foundation*, pp. 14-21; and Keppel, *The Foundation*, pp. 20-21.

[11] *U.S. Commission on Industrial Relations: Final Report and Testimony*, Vol. I, pp. 80ff., U.S. 64th Congress, 1st Session, Senate Documents, No. 415; and Keppel, *The Foundation*, pp. 26-29. On the work of the commission, see also Graham Adams, Jr., *Age of Industrial Violence, 1910-15: The Activities and Findings of the United States Commission on Industrial Relations* (New York, 1966).

emphasized is not that of the establishment and support of agencies operated under the direction of the trustees, but rather the intelligent and discriminating assistance of such causes and forces in the social order as seem to promise effective service . . . [in any] direction that ministers to the advancement of civilization."[12]

The Carnegie Corporation and the Rockefeller Foundation can be closely compared not only in the general matter of their origins, but also in the origins of their interest in the Maritime Provinces and Newfoundland. The 1920 plan of assistance to the Dalhousie medical school was in effect a joint project of the two foundations. As early as 1910, the Carnegie Foundation for the Advancement of Teaching — a separate agency from the Carnegie Corporation, but closely related — had intervened vigorously in the current debates over the future of medical education in North America by publishing an exhaustive study of the subject that it had commissioned from Abraham Flexner. Flexner's report had made sweeping recommendations for rationalization of medical education along lines that emphasized scientific medicine, and henceforth this was one area where the interests of the Carnegie Corporation and the Rockefeller Foundation overlapped.[13] Thus, by the time the Rockefeller Foundation voted its $500,000 to Dalhousie on 26 May 1920, the Carnegie Corporation had resolved to contribute a further $500,000 conditional on the provision of the same amount by the Rockefeller Foundation. Dalhousie would thus provide a strong central medical school for the Maritimes and Newfoundland, just as — so the relevant minute of the Rockefeller Foundation implied — Dalhousie as a university might ultimately be a central institution at least for all Nova Scotia: "although it [Dalhousie] is non-denominational it receives no state aid . . . on account of the jealousies of the other colleges of Nova Scotia, all of which are practically denominational. It has made every effort to be considered the Provincial University but for the reason stated, thus far without success."[14]

[12] Carnegie Corporation of New York, *Report of the Acting President* (New York, 1922), pp. 7-8. For further discussion of Pritchett's concept of social progress, see Ellen Condliffe Lagemann, *Private Power for the Public Good: A History of the Carnegie Foundation for the Advancement of Teaching* (Middletown, Conn., 1983), pp. 21-36.

[13] Savage, *Fruit of an Impulse*, pp. 105-07; and E. Richard Brown, *Rockefeller Medicine Men: Medicine and Capitalism in America* (Berkeley, 1979), pp. 142-56.

[14] History of Rockefeller Involvement with Dalhousie Medical School, 1919-1927, p. 8, RG1.1, Series 427, Box 4, Folder 34, R.F.A.; H. S. Pritchett to R. M. Pearce, 21 May 1920, Dalhousie University File, C.C.A.

The funding of the Dalhousie medical school was not the first involvement of either foundation in the Atlantic region. The Rockefeller Foundation had responded to an appeal for assistance at the time of the 1914 Newfoundland sealing disaster by recommending that a personal donation be made by Rockefeller; the foundation had also been involved in an advisory capacity in relief work following the Halifax Explosion and in the ensuing public health work of the Massachusetts-Halifax Health Commission.[15] The Carnegie Corporation, meanwhile, had already made grants to Dalhousie University amounting to some $45,000, and had also in 1919 granted $50,000 to St. Francis Xavier University for the endowment of a professorship in French, at the behest of the university's vice-president, J. J. Tompkins.[16] Nevertheless, the large grants to the Dalhousie medical school were for both foundations by far their most important interventions, and furthermore established centralizing principles that were once again to be brought forward by the Carnegie Corporation in the following year.

It was in May 1921 that the Carnegie Corporation approved the sending of a small commission "to examine and report upon the educational situation in Newfoundland and the Maritime Provinces of Canada, in order that the Corporation may have reliable data upon which to base any action looking toward appropriations for educational institutions in the region mentioned."[17] The president of the corporation, J. R. Angell, was not sure that the Maritimes and Newfoundland did in fact constitute a single region; in Newfoundland, he believed, the corporation itself might well intervene directly to institute a system of higher education, whereas in the Maritimes the existing institutions could be supported, provided they could be encouraged to adopt "any practicable forms of co-operation."[18] In the event, the commission — consist-

---

[15] E. H. Outerbridge to S. J. Murphy, 20 April 1914, RG1.1, Series 427, Box 3, Folder 25, R.F.A.; Jerome D. Greene to J. D. Rockefeller, Jr., 27 April 1914, *ibid.*; on the Rockefeller Foundation's involvement in Halifax relief work and the Massachusetts-Halifax Health Commission, see the extensive files in RG1.1, Series 427, Box 2, Folders 14-21, R.F.A.

[16] Robert M. Lester, *Review of Grants in the Maritime Provinces of Canada and Newfoundland, 1911-1933* (New York, 1934), pp. 31-34, J. J. Tompkins to J. Bertram, 3 December 1919, St. Francis Xavier University File, C.C.A.

[17] Lester, *Review of Grants*, p. 8.

[18] J. R. Angell to H. S. Pritchett, 10 August 1921, Maritime Provinces Educational Federation File, C.C.A.

ing of W. S. Learned of the Carnegie Foundation for the Advancement of Teaching, and K.C.M. Sills, Nova Scotia-born president of Bowdoin College, Maine — directed its recommendations chiefly at the Maritimes. The Maritime colleges, they recommended, should be centralized in a federation located in Halifax. They envisaged, too, that the new institution, supplemented by a junior college in St. John's, would draw students from Newfoundland, and would "furnish this remote population the best of service."[19]

Thus far, the interventions of the Carnegie Corporation and the Rockefeller Foundation in the Maritimes and Newfoundland had been closely comparable. Remote and backward as these regions might be considered to be, the two foundations were convinced that large-scale centralizing schemes aimed at the modernization of medical education and of higher education as a whole were capable of bringing standards into conformity with those prevailing elsewhere in North America. Nevertheless, the roles played by the respective foundations were to differ in the ensuing years, for reasons that lay chiefly in the diversity of perceptions within the provinces themselves as to their needs. The Carnegie Corporation and the Rockefeller Foundation ultimately established their closest contacts with, and drew their most influential advice from, different groups within the social and intellectual milieu of the Maritimes and Newfoundland.

The Rockefeller Foundation was the simpler case, for its activities in the Maritimes and Newfoundland continued to be directed at the development of health-related programmes at Dalhousie University, and at working with provincial governments in the field of public health.[20] For the Foundation, these were conventional lines of operation, and in the case of the relationship with Dalhousie they proceeded smoothly and successfully. The original grants of 1920 were supplemented in 1921 by a further allocation of $50,000 from the Rockefeller Foundation (matched by a similar grant from the Carnegie Corporation) to enable the Salvation Army to complete the construction of its Grace Maternity Hospital in Halifax, which was to serve as part of the clinical facilities of the

---

[19] William S. Learned and Kenneth C. M. Sills, *Education in the Maritime Provinces of Canada* (New York, 1922), p. 48 and passim.

[20] Not included here are the substantial personal gifts of John D. Rockefeller, Jr., to Acadia College; see the correspondence in J. D. Rockefeller, Jr., Papers, RG2, Educational Interests, Acadia University, Folders 123, 124, R.A.C.

medical school. Smaller grants of $5,000 were made in 1928 and 1929 to supplement the teaching staff in the Department of Hygiene, and then in 1933 an allocation of $44,000 was made to be used over a five-year period for teaching in public health and preventive medicine. This grant was supplemented by a further $21,400, voted in 1938 to be payable over three years.[21] Finally, in a venture that went outside the confines of the medical school, although still retaining a connection with public health, the Rockefeller Foundation agreed in 1936 to fund a programme of training and research in the field of public administration. Leading to the establishment of the Institute of Public Affairs at Dalhousie, this was the first initiative of the foundation in the public administration field outside of the United States.[22] The programme not only led, according to Dalhousie president Carleton Stanley, to immediate success in "breaking down the artificial barriers between department and department and faculty and faculty," but also to sponsorship of province-wide conferences and courses in areas such as industrial relations and municipal administration.[23] The continuing connection with the field of public health was reaffirmed in 1937 and 1938 when major studies were initiated of death rates and the availability of medical services in Cape Breton and in Yarmouth.[24]

Appraisals by the Rockefeller Foundation of the results of its grants to Dalhousie University were consistently favourable. The programme of teaching in the field of public health, with the establishment at the university of a Public Health Centre, was singled out for special praise. "With Foundation aid," read an internal report of the foundation in 1938, "the [Dalhousie Medical] School has been singularly successful in establishing itself and the Center as part of the community;" it was, the report continued,

---

[21] History of Rockefeller Involvement with Dalhousie Medical School, 1919-1927, pp. 13, 144, Box 4, Folder 34, Minutes on Dalhousie University: Public Health and Preventive Medicine, [1938] Box 5, Folder 43, Series 427, RG1.1, R.F.A.

[22] Stacy May, Notes on Dalhousie Project, 3 May 1936, RG1.1, Series 427, Box 33, Folder 345, R.F.A. See also the other relevant material in this folder.

[23] Carleton Stanley to Donald Mainland, DAL/MS/1/3, Institute of Public Affairs, Dalhousie University Archives [D.U.A.]. See also the documentation in the related files, Institute of Public Affairs-Dalhousie Bureau of Industrial Relations, and Institute of Public Affairs-Municipal Consulting Bureau.

[24] Minutes on Dalhousie University Morbidity Studies, 5 August 1937 and 30 June 1938, RG1.1, Series 427, Box 32, Folder 341, R.F.A.

"the only medical school in the four Maritime provinces — Nova
Scotia, Newfoundland, New Brunswick and Prince Edward Island."[25]
The achievement recognized, therefore, was the provision of modern, professionalized medicine on a central basis to a region
perceived as comprising the Maritime provinces and Newfoundland. Efforts to work individually with the provincial governments
in the generation of public health programmes were regarded as
less uniformly successful. In accordance with normal foundation
policies, the intervention of the Foundation was directed at launch0
ing programmes which would eventually be carried on by governments out of their own resources. Grants for the establishment of a
new sanitary engineering organization within the Nova Scotia
Department of Health in 1934, and for the setting up of a model
public health district in Cape Breton in 1936, were favourably
appraised in 1939. So successful was the first public health district
that the province had subsequently decided to establish a second
district centred on Yarmouth.[26]

Other efforts met greater difficulties, or were conceived on a
lesser scale. The early success of the Massachusetts-Halifax Health
Commission in using the Halifax-Dartmouth area to give a "demonstration of what the introduction of public health methods could do
for a community" — a venture with which the Rockefeller Foundation was closely connected in giving advice and recommending
personnel, though it did not contribute funds — was not long
sustained after the commission phased out its work during the mid-
1920s. Hopes that the cities of Halifax and Dartmouth, and the
province, would provide for its continuation were never entirely
fulfilled, and many trained public health workers thereupon left
for the United States.[27] In New Brunswick, a Rockefeller Foundation grant of $27,000 voted in 1922 "for the purpose of carrying
out a rural health program" was hindered by lack of investment by

[25] Minutes on Dalhousie University: Public Health and Preventive Medicine, [1938]
RG1.1, Series 427, Box 5, Folder 43, R.F.A.

[26] Minutes on Nova Scotia Bureau of Sanitary Engineering, 27 October 1934, Box 23,
Folder 21; Minutes on Nova Scotia Local Health District, 19 September 1936,
Box 19, Folder 176; Report on Public Health Progress in Nova Scotia, Box 23,
Folder 218, Series 427, RG1.1, R.F.A.

[27] Minutes of Massachusetts-Halifax Health Commission, 23 March 1928, MG20,
Vol. 197, Public Archives of Nova Scotia [P.A.N.S.]; G. F. Pearson to V. G. Heiser,
RG1.1, Series 427, Box 2, Folder 20, R.F.A.; and Kathryn M. McPherson, "Nurses
and Nursing in Early Twentieth-Century Halifax," unpublished M.A. thesis, Dalhousie University, 1982, pp. 17, 98-101, and 110-11.

the provincial government, although a further efort was made in 1928.[28] In 1929, after correspondence with Sir Wilfred Grenfell, as well as with the government of Newfoundland, the Foundation resolved to cooperate in a public health initiative with the Board of Health in St. John's, but this project apparently failed to get underway.[29] On Prince Edward Island, meanwhile, the Foundation's first initiative was a small vote of $15,300 over a five-year period, 1939-43, for support of a public health laboratory.[30]

In giving support to Dalhousie University, and in efforts to promote public health schemes in the Atlantic region, the Rockefeller Foundation was following its customary practices. This is not to say that these interventions were unimportant, or that their success or failure did not influence prevailing standards of education and health. Yet they were transactions largely governed by a commitment to the professionalization of health care and were arranged in consultation with government and university officials or health professionals whose assumptions did not essentially vary from those of the officials to the Foundation.[31]

In the case of the initiatives launched by the Carnegie Corporation, however, this was not necessarily true. Undoubtedly, the report published by Learned and Sills in 1922 was based upon an intelligent appraisal not only of the situation of education in the Maritime provinces, but also of the political and societal characteristics of the region. The commissioners noted, for example, the sense of injustice that informed the Maritime Rights movement:

In all the provinces, a condition of actual prosperity is translated into a feeling of comparative poverty for the reason that all the other Canadian provinces have inherited great resources thru [sic] the vast extension of their original territory, while for the Maritime Provinces there is no opportunity for expansion. It is thus possible for Ontario to finance an

---

28 See the correspondence of 1922 in RG5, IHB, Series 1, Sub. II, Series 427, Canada 1922, Folder 1865, R.F.A.; W. F. Roberts to F. F. Russell, 11 September 1923, RG5.2, Series 427, Roberts 1923 and 1924, R.F.A.; and G. G. Melvin to C. N. Leach, 31 July 1928, RG1.1, Series 427, Box 24, Folder 227, R.F.A.

29 See the correspondence in RG2, Series 427, Box 26, Folder 212, R.F.A.; and H. M. Mosdell to J. A. Ferrell, 28 April 1930, Box 43, Folder 356, R.F.A.

30 Minutes on P.E.I. Public Health Laboratory, 1936, RG1.1, Series 427, Box 23, Folder 221, R.F.A.

31 On the earlier evolution of the medical profession in the Maritimes, see Colin D. Howell, "Reform and the Monopolistic Impulse: The Professionalization of Medicine in the Maritimes," *Acadiensis*, 11 (1981), pp. 3-22.

elaborate education program without resorting to general taxation, while good schools in the Maritime Provinces must be paid for largely out of the earnings of the people themselves. The adjustment of this inequality is now an issue in Canadian politics, or at least in that aspect of it that especially interests the Maritime Provinces.[32]

Learned and Sills also commented upon the importance of small town and rural societies within the region, which they linked with the strength of organized religion:

Undisturbed by foreign immigration and maintaining a conservative, chiefly small-town and rural life, the people are thoroughly denominationalized, only a small fraction of one per cent of the population giving no specific religious affiliation in the census. Furthermore, these various groups form the best understood and most actively motivated social organizations in a small town regime, and wield relatively much larger influence than in large cities. People, including the men, go to church.[33]

Yet the commissioners did not allow these characteristics to influence significantly their findings or recommendations. For them, the principal justification for the reforms they advocated was that the cause of educational efficiency would be advanced. A by-product would be "an illuminating experiment almost certain to succeed" which would "serve as a model appropriate to many existing American situations."[34] What Learned and Sills did not anticipate was the extent to which support for their plan would be influenced by the notion that economic justice and educational development were directly and inseparably linked, and the extent to which opposition would focus on whether centralization was an appropriate strategy for a rural and small town population struggling to cope with economic dislocation. These two concerns would eventually have an important influence on later schemes supported by the Carnegie Corporation in the Maritimes and in Newfoundland.

The events that led to the ultimate failure of the Learned/Sills university federation scheme are well known and need no repetition here.[35] Whether what Learned privately described in 1925 as "the foolish but tenacious notion of the wicked exposure to tender

---

[32] Learned and Sills, *Education in the Maritime Provinces*, p. 5.

[33] *Ibid.*, p. 14.

[34] *Ibid.*, p. 50.

[35] For one treatment, and a bibliography, see John G. Reid, "Mount Allison College: The Reluctant University," *Acadiensis*, 10 (1980), pp. 35-66.

youth to the wicked influences of a bad city" caused the lack of response by most Maritime colleges and universities to the Carnegie Corporation's expressed willingness to contribute $3 million to support the expenses of implementation, or even the unreasoned opposition of "the poorer and weaker rural brethren," there was no doubt that opposition to centralization was a crucial issue in the debate.[36] At its most rational level, the argument could be made that to force young people to travel long distances to one central institution was not a sound way of attempting to provide educational opportunities given the economic and social circumstances of the day. Yet when Learned called, as he did in writing to the chairman of the Dalhousie board of governors, G. F. Pearson, in July 1922, for "frequent and thorough-going discussions [of] the strictly educational features of the proposed union," he was asking for more than many of the scheme's most vigorous supporters were willing to give. Some advocates of the scheme, such as Presidents A. Stanley Mackenzie of Dalhousie University and T. Stannage Boyle of King's, were evidently influenced by academic, as well as possibly by institutional, motivations; although even Mackenzie was not averse on occasion to linking the federation scheme with Maritime rights, and citing the achievements of the large western universities in the fields of research and extension work.[37] For many of the most vigorous and publicly committed supporters, however, the economic argument was paramount.

For J. J. Tompkins, for example, who waged a constant battle to rally opinion behind the federation scheme even after he had been relieved of his duties at St. Francis Xavier University in late 1922 and sent as parish priest to the outlying port of Canso, the federation scheme represented a final opportunity for the Maritime provinces to regain their prosperity through self-help. His sense of urgency was well expressed in the summer of 1922 in a letter to his ally, the Halifax lawyer and newspaper editor Angus L. Macdonald:

---

[36] Learned to Keppel, 2 March 1925, Maritime Provinces Educational Federation Files, C.C.A.; Learned to G. F. Pearson, 14 July 1922, *ibid.* See also Lester, *Review of Grants*, pp. 11-13. For discussion of the issue of centralization in the wider context of the overall activities of the Carnegie Foundation for the Advancement of Teaching, see Lagemann, *Private Power for the Public Good*, pp. 179-93.

[37] See, for example, A. S. Mackenzie to G. J. Trueman, 26 April 1926, DAL/MS/1/3, Mount Allison University: University Federation, D.U.A.

Get your coat off in good earnest. We have the best case in the world and
no better cause ever was placed before the people of these provinces. . . .
We *ought* to win and it will be *our own fault* if we don't. Failure will spell
disaster for us all. Success will bring a new and glorious era to these
provinces and give our poor people a chance for life in these strenuous
days.[38]

The popular aspects of the scheme, and their relation to socio-
economic issues, were continually stressed by Tompkins. Whether
corresponding with the Cape Breton labour leader J. B. McLachlan in an effort to organize a "Labor College" within the federation,
building on the existing programmes of the Workers' Educational
Club in Glace Bay, or dismissing with near-contempt the inclina-
tion of Mackenzie and Pearson to work through established political channels, Tompkins consistently regarded popular support as
the key to the federation issue. "The Labor idea," he wrote in
September 1922, "is growing like a snowball. It is going to get the
people on the run. . . ."[39]

In his predictions of success for the federation scheme, Tompkins
was over-optimistic. Yet even in defeat, the scheme had important
consequences. One result of the negotiations was the allocation of
substantial grants to individual universities: although Dalhousie
and King's, as participants in the only actual union to result from
the federation scheme, enjoyed the major share of such grants,
Acadia and Mount Allison also benefited.[40] Less obvious than
endowment grants, but also of great significance, was the way in
which the scheme had brought into continuing contact with the
Carnegie Corporation a number of supporters of federation who
put a high priority upon the economic significance of education.
These supporters had favoured the proposal not because of a desire
for centralization *per se*, but because of the opportunities which they
had expected would be offered to small towns and rural communities, as well as to cities, by the existence of the federation. As well as
Tompkins and Angus L. Macdonald, this group included Tompkins'

[38] Tompkins to Macdonald, 30 July 1922, Angus L. Macdonald Papers, MG2,
Cabinet 5, Folder 1348, P.A.N.S.

[39] Tompkins to Learned, 5 October 1922, J. B. McLachlan to Tompkins, 4 October
1922, Tompkins to Learned, 21 February 1923, Maritime Provinces Educational
Federation Files, C.C.A.

[40] See Table 2.

colleague at St. Francis Xavier, M. M. Coady, and the Newfoundland deputy minister of education, Vincent P. Burke.[41]

As the 1920s went on, new proposals were generated in the Maritimes and Newfoundland, based on the assumed linkage between education and economy, and found support from the Carnegie Corporation. The creation of Memorial College in St. John's, influenced by Burke among others, was facilitated by a grant of $75,000 over a five-year period from the Carnegie Corporation, which was voted in 1924. From the beginning, the new institution recognized an obligation to extend study opportunities throughout Newfoundland, and specific grants were made during the early years to provide for a summer school and for extension of library service to "those living in small, isolated settlements." In writing to Keppel in 1928 to request renewal and increase of the corporation's funding of Memorial College, Burke cited the need of young people in Newfoundland "to prepare to take their regular places in the development of those great resources in the midst of which they have always lived but, owing to lack of the necessary educational advantages... very few of them indeed have had the training required."[42] The connection between educational and economic issues was even more explicit in the work of the Extension Department of St. Francis Xavier University, which during the formative years 1931-1937 received the major part of its revenues in the form of grants from the Carnegie Corporation, voted at the urging of Coady and Tompkins in support of the department's main purpose as enunciated by the university's board of governors: "the improvement of the economic, social and religious conditions of the people of Eastern Nova Scotia."[43]

---

[41] See M. M. Coady to A. L. Macdonald, 1 December 1922, Macdonald Papers, MG2, Cabinet 5, Folder 1348, P.A.N.S.; also [A. L. Macdonald] to V. P. Burke, 9 January 1923, Folder 1348A, P.A.N.S.

[42] V. P. Burke, Traveling Library, Second Announcement, September 1928, and Burke to Keppel, 17 May 1928, Memorial University of Newfoundland Files, C.C.A. See also Lester, *Review of Grants*, pp. 23-24.

[43] F. P. Keppel, Notes of Interview with M. M. Coady, 12 April 1929, Keppel, Notes of Interview with Coady, 8 October 1931, J. J. Tompkins to R. M. Lester, 12 November 1931, and Proposal of Extension Department of St. Francis Xavier University, 11 December 1931, St. Francis Xavier University Extension Department File, C.C.A. On the revenues of the Extension Department, see *Mobilizing for Enlightenment: St. Francis Xavier University Goes to the People* (Antigonish, n.d.), Appendix B, copy in St. Francis Xavier University Extension Department File, C.C.A.

In the winning of Carnegie Corporation support for the Antigonish experiment, and for other extension, co-operative, and
travelling library projects in the Maritimes and Newfoundland,
the personal prestige of Tompkins was one important factor.
Tompkins' tireless advocacy of the federation scheme, his fortitude
when exiled to Canso, and his continuing zeal on behalf of the
cause of education in the region were enough to prompt the
normally matter-of-fact president of the corporation, F. P. Keppel,
to declare in a letter of 1939 that "he [Thompkins] is, quite
literally, a saint and he is at the same time one of the most ingenious
and adroit practical men I have ever known."[44] There was more to
the relationship, however, than personal influence. Although a
severe critic of unrestrained capitalism, Tompkins had long advocated a non-Marxist solution to labour-capital conflicts and to
general economic problems in the Maritime region. Study and self-
reliance, he believed, promoted by such educational ventures as
the "people's school" he inaugurated at St. Francis Xavier in early
1921, were the routes to progress for the labour movement and for
all who sought individual or communal self-improvement.[45] This
emphasis was continued in subsequent educational ventures supported or influenced by Tompkins, and it was one that had clear
affinities with the underlying philosophical principles of the philanthropic foundations. The commitment of both the Carnegie
Corporation and the Rockefeller Foundation to human progress
by means other than class struggle, and their insistence that their
own role should be essentially that of a catalyst, agreed well with
the concept of self-help through study and cooperation. In view of
Andrew Carnegie's well-known reluctance to assist denominational
institutions, there was a certain irony in that the Carnegie Corporation's support should so readily be given to projects closely
associated with a Roman Catholic university. Tompkins had
remarked in a letter of 1927 that the time was past "when a good
christian was supposed to make a choice between God and Carnegie." The secretary of the Carnegie Corporation, J. B. Bertram,
expressed support in 1931 for the corporation's funding of the St.

---

[44] [F. P. Keppel] to R. Wilberforce, 11 April 1939, Newfoundland File, C.C.A.
[45] See the article by Tompkins in *The Casket* (Antigonish), 29 July 1920, and the
report of his speech to a regional conference of Rotary Clubs in *The Daily Times*
(Moncton), 17 March 1922. On the "people's school" at Antigonish, see the
documentation in J. J. Tompkins Papers, MG10-2, 5 (a), Beaton Institute, University College of Cape Breton.

Francis Xavier extension programme in terms that showed that he too was untroubled by any such supposed antithesis: "if we can help people to help themselves instead of putting out a life line to the Red Cross or their fellow tax payers' pockets every time they get in a jam, we shall be carrying out the ideas of the Founder."[46]

For Bertram, however, the extension movement at St. Francis Xavier had an even wider significance. "This experiment in the Maritimes," he declared to Keppel, "is of more moment than merely to raise the people there out of their perilous condition; it may well be a demonstration of what is needed in many sections throughout the United States."[47]

During the 1920s and early 1930s, the perception of the Maritimes and Newfoundland in the minds of officials of the Carnegie Corporation had undergone considerable change. Rather than being seen as remote areas that needed an infusion of modern progressive ideas in order to become fully North American, or even as convenient laboratories for carefully-controlled experiments, initiatives such as the Antigonish movement were now regarded as capable of generating their own methods and their own distinctive insights. During the 1930s, Prince Edward Island provided another example: with support from the Carnegie Corporation for public library development and for a chair of sociology and economics at Prince of Wales College, study clubs, cooperatives and credit unions proliferated.[48] To be sure, it would be easy to claim too much for the significance of such projects, either as part of the Carnegie Corporation's overall activities in the Atlantic region or in terms of long-term social and economic significance. The Carnegie Corporation's programmes were by no means entirely given over to projects that directly combined economic and educational impulses, as witness the large sums devoted to more conventional endowment grants to established institutions such as Dalhousie,

---

[46] J. J. Tompkins to H. J. Savage, 3 October 1927, *ibid.*, 6 (a); J. B. Bertram to F. P. Keppel, 31 December 1931, St. Francis Xavier University Extension Department Files, C.C.A. On Tompkins and his relationship with the Antigonish Movement, see Daniel W. MacInnes, "Clerics, Fishermen, Farmers, and Workers: The Antigonish Movement and Identity in Eastern Nova Scotia," unpublished Ph.D. thesis, McMaster University, 1978, pp. 158-70, 187, 216-21.

[47] J. B. Bertram to F. P. Keppel, 31 December 1931, St. Francis Xavier University Extension Department Files, C.C.A.

[48] See J. T. Croteau, *Cradled in the Waves: The Story of a People's Co-operative Achievement in Economic Betterment on Prince Edward Island, Canada* (Toronto, 1951); also J. A. Murphy to F. P. Keppel, 5 July 1937, St. Dunstan's College File, C.C.A.

King's, Acadia and Mount Allison. Furthermore, in retrospect it may seem that to place as much faith as did Tompkins and his associates in the economic value of education was naive, and substituted a simplistic remedy for the complexities of regional underdevelopment. Nevertheless, to a significant extent, the perception of the Maritimes and Newfoundland entertained by officials of the Carnegie Corporation had been reshaped through the influence of advisers within the provinces themselves.

For the Atlantic region, the inter-war period was a time of intractable socio-economic problems that defied easy solutions. The intervention of major philanthropic foundations in areas such as health and education provided one possible avenue to beneficial change. Initially, the definition of the kind of change that would be beneficial was determined in large part by the perceptions that prevailed within the foundations. Insofar as the foundations dealt with officials of existing universities and of governments, little modification of those perceptions was brought about, even though important changes were achieved in the health care and higher education systems. Yet through certain less orthodox ventures, officials of the Carnegie Corporation in particular saw their earlier perceptions refashioned by the influence of their local advisers. At a time when the regional economies were at a low ebb, the result of the dialogues with the Carnegie Corporation was to obtain support for movements that at the least gave evidence of social and intellectual vitality. For the officials who looked on from New York, the result was acceptance if not full understanding. "It seems to me," concluded Cartwright in 1936, "that the end justifies the means. The people there are receiving educational advantages, and far be it from me to enquire into their motives."[49]

---

[49] Cartwright to Keppel, 24 April 1936, *ibid.*

C. MARK DAVIS

Small Town Reformism: The Temperance Issue in Amherst, Nova Scotia[1]

T HE STUDY AND APPRECIATION OF TOWNS, BOTH large and small, within the Canadian context is still very much in its infancy. Scholars from a variety of disciplines have explored the structure of American towns over the last two decades, unearthing a number of intriguing considerations.[2] Investigations of Canadian settlements have largely ignored the town, concentrating instead on either dynamic urban centres or static and vanishing rural agricultural areas.[3] When Canadian towns are examined, usually one of two narrow approaches is utilized. The emphasis is placed upon either the town's structure, institutions and organizations, or specific events such as disasters, strikes and epidemics. A somewhat more sophisticated version of the later approach dwells upon the prime factors which account for the town's creation or decline. In the Maritimes, such topics have included Loyalist migration, the shipbuilding era, mining tragedies, or the coming of the railway.[4]

Both the institutional focus and the event-specific history of towns can be limited in time and restricted in scope. While it may

---

[1] This essay has benefitted from the kind assistance of Peter Latta, then Curator, Cumberland County Museum and Larry McCann, Mount Allison University.

[2] See for example J. A. Jakle, *The American Small Town* (Hamden, Connecticut, 1982); L. E. Atherton, "The Small Town in the Gilded Age," in J. Cary and J. Wernberg, eds., *The Social Fabric* (Boston, 1984), pp. 57-75; R. R. Lingeman, *Small Town America* (New York, 1980); and articles in *Rural Sociology; Agricultural History* and *Demography*, amongst other journals.

[3] See, however, Alan F. J. Artibise, ed., *Town and City* (Regina, 1980); and G. D. Hodge and M. A. Qadeer, *Towns and Villages in Canada* (Toronto, 1983).

[4] See for example Roger Brown, *Blood on the Coal: The Story of the Springhill Mining Disasters* (Hantsport, Nova Scotia, 1976); P. MacLellan, "A Loyalist Crucible: Digby, Nova Scotia 1783- 1792," *Nova Scotia Historical Quarterly*, 3. (1983), pp. 23-38; M. Archibald, *Shelburne Loyalists* (Halifax, 1983); D. E. Stephens, *Truro: A Railway Town* (Hantsport, Nova Scotia, 1981); and M. J. Bird, *The Town That Died: A Chronicle of the Halifax Explosion* (Toronto, 1962).

be unwise to question critically the developing historiography of Canadian towns before the subject has had a chance to experiment and mature, clearly the raising of some other suggestions may encourage new ideas to be incorporated into future studies. Since the history of a number of Maritime towns is presently being undertaken, the developing historiography can only benefit from ideas and perspectives contributed by scholars from a variety of disciplines.

Analyzing the social issues which once commanded the attention of townspeople is a difficult — perhaps unenviable — yet tantalizing task. It is also an essential, even enlightening, one. The examination of social concerns brings important topics under scrutiny, including public health, welfare, education, the role of women and seniors, industrial safety, and the adoption of science and technology. Seldom are social issues time- or place-specific. Examination of their importance should result in a broader town history, in which the concerns, anxieties, and hopes of ordinary people are explored; in which group and class interaction and hostility are examined; and by which part of the town's identity is revealed. Moreover, such a town history allows comparisons to be made with other towns on a provincial, regional, national, and international level.

One particular issue which figured prominently in every Maritime town from the early 1830s to at least 1930, if not beyond, was liquor reform. To drink or not to drink — this was a vexing question upon which nearly everyone held an opinion, and usually very definite ones. Deeply devoted groups and individuals on both sides of the issue took stands, clashed, and regrouped as the temperance and prohibition movement in Maritime Canada rose, progressed, waned, and declined. A case study of prohibitionism in Amherst, Nova Scotia, is therefore both fascinating and revealing. It shows that Amherst was an early and an ardent advocate of the temperance cause over a lengthy period. Temperance and later prohibition were supported for many reasons, be they religious, economic, or political in nature. Amherst was the home of several important provincial anti-liquor leaders, both in the nineteenth and the twentieth centuries. It was a conjunction of interests that sought reform. The influential role of the church and church leaders, particularly the Baptists, was clearly evident; and local business elites actively supported the movement to reform what were perceived as unnecessarily liberal drinking habits.

Unfortunately, the full history of Amherst, Nova Scotia has yet to be written. This Cumberland County town, perched as it is on the agriculturally rich Chignecto Isthmus, strategically guarding the New Brunswick-Nova Scotia border, possesses a deep and exceptionally rich historical past. Largely because of its geographical location, Amherst has long responded to the major economic, social, and religious forces which significantly shaped and defined the Maritime regional experience. The history of early Indian times, the French era, the British conquest, transportation, confederation, nationalization of industries, and Maritime regionalism cannot be written without reference to Amherst.[5] Given this historical record, it is not surprising to discover that Amherst figured prominently in the struggle for liquor reform.

Amherst responded very quickly to the first nineteenth century wave of temperance sentiment that swept the province. On 31 December 1829, Baptist Reverend Charles Tupper of the Amherst First Baptist Church, who was reportedly "the best trained intellectually among the young ministers of that day," established the town's first temperance society in his church's basement.[6] It had twenty supporters. From that small beginning temperance beliefs in Amherst began to grow. In 1831 the Amherst town-led Cumberland County Association Against Intemperance appeared, and in 1848 the American-spawned Sons of Temperance was operating with over one hundred members. Reverend Tupper merged his small Baptist group with the Sons of Temperance and in 1852 hosted in Amherst the Provincial Annual Meeting of the Nova Scotia Sons of Temperance. At that meeting Reverend Tupper's son, Charles Tupper, future Prime Minister of Canada, joined the organization and later served as County Temperance Deputy. In

---

[5] See for example C. R. McKay, "Investors, Government and the CMTR: A Study In Entrepreneurial Failure," *Acadiensis*, 9 (1979), pp. 71-94; G. Wynn, "Late Eighteenth Century Agriculture on the Bay of Fundy Marshlands," *Acadiensis*, 8 (1979), pp. 80-89; E. C. Wright, "Cumberland Township, a Focal Point of Settlement on the Bay of Fundy," *Canadian Historical Review*, 27 (1946); I. McKay, "Strikes In the Maritimes, 1901-1914," *Acadiensis*, 13 (1983), pp. 3-46; N. Reilly, "The General Strike In Amherst, Nova Scotia, 1919," *Acadiensis*, 9 (1980), pp. 56-77; L. D. McCann, "Metropolitanism and Branch Businesses in the Maritimes, 1881-1931," *Acadiensis*, 13 (1983), pp. 112-125; A. R. Lamy, "The Development and Decline of Amherst as an Industrial Center," unpublished B.A. thesis, Mount Allison University, 1930; and M. R. Boyer, "The Amherst Prisoner of War Internment Camp, 1915-1919," unpublished B.A. thesis, Mount Allison University, 1985.

[6] E. M. Saunders, *History of the Baptists of the Maritime Provinces* (Halifax, 1902), p. 247.

1862 at the International Temperance and Prohibition Convention in London, England, Reverend Tupper claimed that "no man has a moral right to injure his fellowman or to follow an occupation injurious to the community. That the liquor traffic is injurious to the community, is certain and therefore ought to be prohibited."[7] In 1877 in Amherst, it was reported that the town had forty-two licensed drinking places and that "violence and disorder prevailed to such an extent that it was not safe for women and children to walk in the streets."[8] Later, when the town was incorporated in 1889 with a population of 3500, there existed several organizations to battle intemperance. They included the Independent Order of Good Templars, the Amherst Branch of the Dominion Prohibitory Alliance, the Sons of Temperance, the Association Against Intemperance, the Women's Christian Temperance Union (hereafter W.C.T.U.), the Liquor Reform Club, the Moral Reform League, the Law and Order Society, and the Royal Templars of Temperance.

From this base of support the Amherst temperance community demanded and obtained a dry town and county. In October of 1883, the 1878 Canada Temperance Act or the Scott Act was adopted in Cumberland County with a 1300 vote majority in which Amherst voted solidly dry.[9] Officially, at least, Amherst was a dry town for the next forty-six years, from 1883 to 1929. In the 1894 Provincial Prohibition Plebiscite, Cumberland County gave the largest county majority for prohibition.[10] In the 1898 National Prohibition Plebiscite, Cumberland totalled a 4000 majority with Amherst voting 10 to 1 for prohibition.[11] The outcome was duplicated in the 1920 Provincial Prohibition Referendum. Only in 1929, after four decades of frustration, did Amherst reject provincial prohibition by 400 votes and endorse Government control with 700 votes.[12]

In the one hundred years of Maritime temperance history, Amherst supplied a remarkable number of important provincial

---

[7] *International Temperance and Prohibition Convention* (London, England, 1863), n.p.

[8] *Amherst Daily News*, 23 April 1910.

[9] *Chignecto Post*, 1 November 1883.

[10] *The Vanguard: A Journal of Moral Reform*, Toronto, May, 1894.

[11] R. Spence, *Prohibition in Canada* (Toronto, 1919), p. 218.

[12] *Presbyterian Witness*, 20 November 1920; and *Journal of the House of Assembly, Nova Scotia*, 1929, Appendix 27, p. 38.

and regional prohibition leaders. Reverend Charles Tupper was one of Nova Scotia's original temperance pioneers. Born in Cornwallis, Nova Scotia in 1794, he became Baptist minister of River Phillip, Westchester, and Amherst in 1819. Between 1819 and 1834, besides preaching in Amherst, he also held pastorates in New Brunswick and Prince Edward Island and is credited with beginning temperance organizations in Sackville and Bedeque. He brought the Sons of Temperance to Amherst in 1848, hosted their provincial meeting in 1852, and even after moving from Amherst to Aylesford, Nova Scotia in 1852, he constantly worked for the temperance cause.[13] He was the British North American representative to the 1862 London International Temperance and Prohibition Convention, and as editor of the *Christian Messenger* and the *Baptist Missionary*, kept the issue squarely before his flock. He indoctrinated both his sons, Dr. Charles Tupper and Dr. Nathan Tupper, to the evils of intemperance and remained a devoted follower and leader till his death in 1881.

There were other temperance activists. In 1887, Amherst was the birth place for the temperance paper, the *Cumberland Voice*, which supported in 1889 the Amherstonian leader of the short-lived Nova Scotia Temperance Party, J. L. Bulmer. In 1888 or 1889 the *Cumberland Voice* was renamed the *Canadian Voice*, and it strove to be a regional temperance paper until it collapsed in 1894.[14] Mr. J. A. Simpson (1858-1923), Keeper of the Amherst Jail, was one of the main provincial leaders of the Independent Order of Good Templars. He joined the organization in 1872, served in several offices including Grand Marshall (1884), Grand Councillor (1887), Grand Chief Templar (1889), Grand Superintendent of Juvenile Work (1893-1920), and was Amherst Temperance Inspector in 1920. In total, he was active in the temperance organizations for some fifty-one years.[15] Perry J. Stackhouse of the Amherst First Baptist Church (1910-1914) was not only an ardent local temperance leader, but also encouraged Baptists to view the liquor question within the context of the social gospel. In 1916 he

---

[13] The first Sons of Temperance was established in Yarmouth, 17 November 1847. For information on Reverend Tupper see *The Canadian Biographical Dictionary* (Toronto, 1881), and *One Hundred Years with the Baptists of Amherst, N. S., 1810-1910* (n.d.)

[14] Spence, *op. cit.*, p. 148.

[15] *Minutes*, Independent Order of Good Templars, 1872-1923.

wrote *The Social Ideals of the Lord's Prayer* in which he claimed that
the Lord's Prayer

presents a glowing picture of the new social order in the coming age. It is
evident that if God's will is to be done on earth as it is in heaven, there is
before us a golden age in which poverty, social injustice, war, class hatred
and all the other great evils which hang like festering sores on the body
politic will have disappeared.

One of the greatest curses of modern civilization is the drink traffic. No
one can thoughtfully study that subject without discovering that economic
causes are responsible for a great deal of drinking. Wages are in many
cases so small that the wage earners are compelled to house themselves in
cheerless and squalid quarters. From such surroundings issues forth every
night an army of men who find a refuge and the gratification of their
social instincts in the saloon.

The test of a church member is no longer his loyalty to a creed, but the
contribution he is making to the welfare of society. The Church is not an
end in itself but a means of bringing in the reign of God in human life.[16]

There were many others who filled secondary provincial temperance offices. R. W. Davis, Manager of the Gem Theater, was
treasurer of the Provincial Royal Templars of Temperance (1898);
Mrs. Botsford Black was Treasurer of the Provincial W.C.T.U.
(1895, 1898, 1899, 1900). Mrs. D. M. Hopper was Recording
Secretary for the Provincial W.C.T.U. (1898). W. A. Fillmore,
coal dealer, cousin of Roscoe Fillmore, an active Maritime socialist
(1887-1968), was Vice-President of the temperance-inclined Nova
Scotia Farmers Association (1926). Finally, J. Bryenton was Trustee
of the Provincial Royal Templars of Temperance (1898).

One of the more interesting features of prohibitionism in Amherst
concerns the influential role played by the Church, which was
easily the town's most dominant social force, leading reforms,
promoting improvements, and directing social activities. Between
1891 and 1931 Cumberland County's population was made up of
Methodists (29 percent), Baptists (23), Presbyterians (18), Roman
Catholics (14), Anglicans (12); and, after 1925, the United Church
component stood at 37 percent. In fact, it was one particular
church, the Baptist, that was the primary driving force behind the
crusade. Beginning with Reverend Tupper, the Baptist ministers of
Amherst carried on the tradition as temperance spokesmen and
spiritual leaders. They included the Reverends Samuel McCully

---

[16] P. J. Stockhouse, *The Social Ideals of the Lord's Prayer* (Philadelphia, 1916), pp. 2, 165.

(minister from 1819-1849); David Allen Steele (1867-1896); J. H. Macdonald (1897-1899); W. E. Bates (1899-1904); P. J. Stackhouse (1910-1914); C. W. Rose (1914-1923); and F. L. Orchard (1923-1935). As the early temperance movement gained force, other denominations became active in the cause. For example, Ira Drysdale of Wallace, a member of the Presbyterian Church, was Worthy Patriarch of the Amherst Sons of Temperance in the 1890s; Methodist Reverend J. L. Batty was Secretary of the 1898 Cumberland County Plebiscite Committee; Methodist Reverend A. M. Angus was Provincial Chaplain of the International Order of Odd Fellows and President of the 1920 Cumberland Provincial Temperance Alliance; and E. E. Hewson, Congregationalist and lawyer, constantly pressured the provincial governments for stricter enforcement throughout the 1920s. Reverends A. M. Angus, C. E. Crowell, and W. J. Dean were active on behalf of the United Church after 1925. But generally the Baptists maintained control, moving out of Church organizations to capture the leadership of secular ones. For example, Reverend Charles Tupper, Charles Tupper, Nathan Tupper, J. A. Simpson, Mrs. Botsford Black, W. A. Filmore, and Mrs. D. M. Hopper all were Baptists. Other prominent local Baptist temperance leaders were M. D. Pride, President of the Sons of Temperance (1876- 1878); C. R. Casey, Scott Act Inspector (1880s); Reverend G. F. Miles, President of the Amherst Dominion Prohibitory Alliance (1884); Mrs. K. Carter, Secretary, Amherst W.C.U.U. (1933-1937); Mrs. D. F. Quigley, President of Amherst W.C.T.U. (1896); Mrs. Charles Christie, President of the Amherst W.C.T.U. (1901); Mrs. Cora Maud Taylor, President of the Amherst W.C.T.U. (1931-1934) and President of the Cumberland County W.C.T.U. (1930-1937); and Mrs. J. A. Simpson, District Secretary of Cumberland County I.O.G.T. (1890s). Baptist men who were honorary members of the Amherst W.C.T.U. in 1897 included Alex Christie, George Christie, F. A. Cates, Mark Curry, C. R. Casey, C. A. Black, Nelson A. Rhodes, Thomas Dunlap, and M. D. Pride.

The firm support temperance and prohibition elicited in late nineteenth and early twentieth century Amherst was not only due to the Baptist presence. Local business and industrial elites also favoured the cause. For the businessman the promise of a dry work place, the increase in work efficiency, and the decline in industrial accidents rendered prohibition a worthy cause. Yet in Amherst, temperance was usually promoted for more than one reason. Many of the business families also held deep religious convictions, particularly with the Baptist faith. Doctors were often businessmen who medically frowned upon drinking. Civic boosterism was also a motivating factor. A sober and hard-working population naturally projected a town image that might encourage more employers to locate in Amherst.

For many, religious beliefs, good business sense, and civic duty fanned temperance sentiment.[17] The Baptist-business-temperance combination was highly evident. For example, the Taylor family was half-owner of the Taylor and Tennant bottling company, established in 1889. The Rhodes and Curry families were founders of the 1877 Rhodes Curry Company which in 1909 became the Canadian Car and Foundry Company, employing some 2000 men. Nathaniel Curry was Mayor of Amherst in 1894, 1895, and 1902, and President of the Amherst Board of Trade from 1896 to 1899. N. A. Rhodes was Amherst Mayor in 1904. The Dunlap family established the Dunlap Brothers Hardware Company in 1865, and Thomas Dunlap became mayor for the first three years after incorporation, 1890 through 1892. C. R. Casey and Sons were manufacturers of leathers and larakins. The Pride and Quigley families founded in 1867 the Amherst Boot and Shoe which amalgamated in 1875 to form the Pride, Quigley and Casey Steam Tannery. M. D. Pride was President of the Amherst Board of Trade from 1899 to 1902.

More examples of the Baptist-business-political alliance are worthy of mention. Mrs. Botsford Black was wife of the manager of the Amherst Laundry and Heating. She and Dr. Charles Allen Black were of the Senator T. R. Black family, who sold real estate, was a director of Rhodes Curry Company, and Cumberland MLA (1884-90, 1894-1901). Dr. Black himself ran a Victoria Street drug store in 1875. F. A. Cates ran Cates Meat Market and W. A. Fillmore was a coal dealer who served as President of the Amherst Board of Trade in 1928 and 1929. George, Alexander and Charles Christie owned Christie Brothers, manufacturers of coffins and caskets. While Kelton Carter and D. M. Hopper did not own a

---

[17] There is not a single source for the bulk of the material reported in the next several paragraphs. It was obtained by searching through the minutes of the various temperance organizations and matching them against Baptist Church records, Amherst business directories, or municipal and Board of Trade records. Some business information is available in *Amherst: Diamond Jubilee 1899-1949* (Amherst, 1949); *The News and Sentinel*, 28 June 1935; and *Chignecto Post*, 10 January, 1884.

business, both worked for Rhodes-Curry. Speculation suggests that the Simpson family's involvement in the prohibition issue stemmed from both their Baptist faith and J. A. Simpson's experiences as Keeper of the Amherst jail. Understanding why Dr. Charles Tupper and Dr. Nathan Tupper joined the temperance crusade is extremely complicated. They were the sons of Baptist Reverend Charles Tupper, who entered the medical profession and owned and operated an Amherst drug store. Charles participated in politics at the local, provincial, and national levels. Thus, it was apparently to his political advantage to support temperance issues.

Other businessmen who were involved in the temperance crusade whose religious affiliation is not clearly known include: R. W. Davis, Manager of Gem Theater; Mrs. T. R. Angus, Secretary, Amherst W.C.T.U. (1931) and grocery store owner; A. D. Ross, editor of the *Amherst Daily News*, Honorary member of the W.C.T.U., and Secretary of the Amherst Board of Trade (1905); E. E. Hewson, lawyer, Congregationalist, insurance broker and of the Hewson Woollen Mills family; and Mrs. Jason Wattling, President, Amherst W.C.T.U. (1937) and wife of a tinsmith. While D. C. Allen was not a business-man, he was a medical doctor and Mayor of Amherst in 1893 and 1898 who worked hard for prohibition in the 1898 plebiscite.

E. L. Dicks, in "From Temperance To Prohibition in Nine-teenth Century Nova Scotia," has claimed that temperance was "the first mass movement in colonial society to control and modify its own behavior with little help from the usual elites."[18] Obviously this does not appear to be the case in Amherst in either colonial or post-colonial times. Indeed, in Amherst, even the repeal move-ment was led by local elites. President of the Amherst Branch of the 1929 Temperance Reform Association for Government Control was David M. Robb, Presbyterian (and son of Alexander Robb who founded Robb Engineering Works in 1848), who eventually became general manager of the family business. Ironically, Robb must have done little to convince Nova Scotia Premier E. N. Rhodes, a Baptist lawyer and son of N. A. Rhodes of the Amherst Rhodes Curry family, that by 1929 provincial prohibition was an "awful flop."

The prohibition era in Amherst, Nova Scotia was a complicated affair, cutting across and even disrupting religious, social, economic,

[18] E. L. Dicks, "From Temperance To Prohibition In Nineteenth Century Nova Scotia," *Dalhousie Review*, 61 (1981), p. 530.

medical, and political lines. While the most prominent Baptist families were often associated with the dry crusade, by so doing they probably alienated other non-Baptist families from taking a more active part. One of the enduring myths of the small town focuses upon their so-called quiet, loyal, friendly, and togetherness nature. In Amherst, however, prohibition was a divisive issue. Certainly there were divisions in Amherst before, during, and after prohibition as Nolan Reilly's work on the 1919 Amherst General Strike ably demonstrates.[19] Prohibition further divided cohesiveness by separating drinkers from non-drinkers, tavern and hotel owners from other entrepreneurs, temperance advocates from prohibitionists, and law enforcers and Scott Act agents such as Inspectors Casey and Latta from the general drinking public, extremist voluntary enforcement groups, and church and municipal authorities. In April of 1887, for example, the Moral Reform League commandeered a fire engine and flushed out an entire restaurant because it was serving liquor.[20] *Daily News* editor A. D. Ross, Presbyterian, was immersed in a perplexing situation during the prohibition era by being a Liberal temperance advocate who through his newspaper was forced to applaud the anti-liquor stance of the provincial Conservatives to satisfy his readership.[21] Referendums and plebiscites were always peak times for such bitterness, antagonism and political commentary.

Towns possess their own dynamic and evolving character. Certainly Amherst does. Yet seldom is the intrinsic nature of conflicts and aspirations revealed in institutional, geneological or event-focused studies of these towns. In the Maritimes, at least, social concerns are usually much older than the institutions and organizations they came to influence. Only by taking a long view of town development and digging beneath the immediate structure will a fuller portrait of a community's milieu and flavour emerge. If this is done, then not only will town histories be more comprehensive in scope and depth, but they will also prove valuable to social history of a regional or national nature.

---

[19] Nolan Reilly, "The General Strike in Amherst, Nova Scotia, 1919," *Acadiensis*, 13 (1983), pp. 112-125.

[20] T. E. Lowther, owner of the Amherst Hotel and member of the Law and Order League, was always suspiciously regarded by his temperance colleagues. *Amherst Daily News*, 4 September 1897; and *Amherst Daily News*, 9 April 1887.

[21] *Amherst Daily News*, 25 April 1907.

GWENDOLYN DAVIES

The Song Fishermen:
A Regional Poetry Celebration

"T HE TWENTIES," NOTED MUNROE BEATTIE IN *The Literary History of Canada*, were "a time of fresh beginnings," a period when the forces of modernism entered Canadian literature from Europe and the United States and hastened the demise of the romantic-Victorian tradition that had so long dominated national writing.[1] Periodicals like *Poetry: A Magazine of Verse* from Chicago; *transition: an international quarterly for creative experiment* from Paris; *The Canadian Forum*, founded in Toronto in 1920; and *The McGill Fortnightly Review*, established in Montreal in 1925, all helped to broaden both the outlook and the outlets for a new generation of Canadian writers. National poetry, noted Leo Kennedy, "sired by Decorum out of Claptrap," could now begin to be emancipated from the "state of amiable mediocrity" and insipidness in which it had been languishing for so long.[2]

While no student of Canadian literary history can deny the excitement of a period that witnessed the birth of *The Canadian Forum*, the emergence of the Group of Seven, the establishment of *The McGill Fortnightly Review*, the formation of the McGill group of poets, and the growing international experience of writers like Morley Callaghan and John Glassco, it would be remiss for such a student to ignore the central Canadian bias of much that has been said about Canadian writing in the 1920s, or to overlook the emphasis it places on modernism as a yardstick of literary excellence. For this reason, regional romance-writers like Frank Parker Day of Nova Scotia or Margaret Duley of Newfoundland have often been overlooked in analyses of our modern literary development. It is also for this reason that the existence of a small but

---

[1] Munro Beattie, "Poetry: 1920-1935," in *The Literary History of Canada*, 2nd ed., II (Toronto: University of Toronto Press, 1976), p. 235.

[2] *Ibid.*, p. 241.

distinctively romantic group of Nova Scotian poets writing con-
temporaneously with the McGill group has gone completely unnoticed in *The Literary History of Canada, The Oxford Companion to
Canadian Literature*, and other standard discussions of Canadian
literary history.

Self-styled "The Song Fishermen," these writers organized
lectures and recitals in Nova Scotia, produced illustrated poetry
broadsheets, kept in touch with Maritime writers living outside the
region, fostered emerging talent (like that of Charles Bruce),
published a memorial to Bliss Carman upon his death, and
between 1928 and 1930 channeled their energies into the creation
of a poetry publication entitled *The Song Fishermen's Song Sheets*.
Including such well-known writers as Charles G. D. Roberts, Bliss
Carman, James D. Gillis, Andrew Merkel, James D. Logan,
Kenneth Leslie, Charles Bruce, and Robert Norwood, as well as a
host of lesser-known versifiers, the Song Fishermen were to represent a Nova Scotian voice in poetry at the very time when rural
values and the oral tradition were being eroded by out-migration,
a changing economy, and the impact of modern media. As attuned
to the developments in modern poetry as were their colleagues in
London, Paris, New York or Montreal, the Song Fishermen
nonetheless turned to traditional ballads, old sea chanteys, and
even Gaelic literary forms in an attempt to evoke what they saw as
the essence of Nova Scotia — to convey in the language of the lyric
and the ballad their affinity for the sea and their joy in the simple
comradeship of the Song Fishermen coterie.

No one who reads the Song Fishermen today can fail to be struck
by the sheer exuberance of many of their poems or by the enormous
sense of camaraderie permeating the correspondence of the Song
Fishermen inner circle. Founded not so much out of a sense of
literary purpose as out of a recognition of mutual literary kinship,
the Fishermen had their genesis long before the song sheets and
broadsheets began to appear in the late 1920s. The key figures from
the beginning were always to be the Reverend Dr. Robert Norwood of St. Bartholomews, New York, one of the most prestigious
Episcopalian churches in America at the time, and Andrew Merkel
of the Canadian Press Office in Halifax. Both men were sons of
rural Anglican rectors who had been companions over the years in
the Maritimes, Maine and New York. After the death of his father,
the young Merkel had even been sent to Hubbards near Halifax to

Three of the Song Fishermen in Halifax. Left to right: Charles G. D. Roberts, Kenneth Leslie, and Bliss Carmen.

PUBLIC ARCHIVES OF NOVA SCOTIA

live with the Norwood family for a period of time.[3] A friendship of
years and a mutual interest in poetry continued to draw Norwood
and Merkel together long after they had embarked on their
separate careers, and it was therefore understandable that whenever Norwood was at his summer home in Hubbards, or whenever
mutual friends of the two crossed paths, literary and social connections were immediately established. Characteristically, it was
Merkel who organized a poetry recital for Norwood in Halifax in
1922, and it was Merkel who in 1923 sent the poetry of Charles
Bruce, a student at Mount Allison University, to Maritime writer,
Annie Campbell Huestis, in Brooklyn.

Huestis showed this poetry to Robert Norwood in New York,[4]
and Norwood subsequently sought out and praised the young poet,
Charles Bruce, when he visited Mount Allison on a recital tour on 2
February 1924. After publicly acknowledging the work of Bruce
from the stage at Mount Allison, Norwood was to conclude further
recitals in his 1924 Maritime tour by reading not only his own new
poem, "The Spinner," but also the verses of his new-found protege
at Mount Allison.[5] A year later when Charles G.D. Roberts,
Norwood's former English Professor at King's, returned to Canada
after living abroad for thirty years, it was only natural that it was to
the Merkel household that he gravitated, and that Merkel should
invite the young Charles Bruce to Halifax from Sackville to meet
Roberts and hear him read at a recital. So pleased was Roberts
with his reception in the city that he urged his cousin, Bliss
Carman, to favour Halifax with a reading as well,[6] and in the next
few years, E.J. Pratt, Wilson MacDonald, Theodore Roberts, and
Robert Norwood all complemented the visits of Roberts and
Carman by making Halifax a stopping-off place in their literary
travels. Their destination invariably included 50 South Park
Street, the hospitable home of Andrew Merkel and his wife Tully,

---

[3] Andrew Merkel, "Life of Robert Norwood, Outstanding Preacher and Poet,
Recalled by Writer," unidentified newspaper clipping, MG 20, vol. 17, 7:3. Public
Archives of Nova Scotia [hereafter P.A.N.S.].

[4] Robert Norwood to "My dear Mr. Bruce," New York, 22 November 1923, Charles
Bruce Papers, Ms. 2, 297, c. 136, Dalhousie University Archives [hereafter D.U.A.].

[5] "Lecture-Recital Was Much Enjoyed," *The Argosy Weekly* (2 February 1924), p. 1,
col. 4; p. 5, col. 1.

[6] H. Pearson Gundy, ed., *Letters of Bliss Carman* (Montreal, 1981), pp. 332 and 363;
and Andrew Merkel, "Nucleus of Poetry Centre Established in Halifax," unidentified newspaper clipping, Hilda Tyler Collection, MG 1, vol. 925A, P.A.N.S.

"a unique institution," according to Thomas Raddall, that became "the core of the literary life in Halifax for a generation." "For thirty years," recalls Raddall, "the Merkels and their hospitality to writers of every sort made this house famous amongst the fraternity of the pen. Here came Charles and Theodore Roberts, Norwood, Carman, Kenneth Leslie and a host of others who made it their headquarters whenever their footsteps turned homeward to Nova Scotia and the sea."[7]

By 1928 when Charles Bruce had joined the Canadian Press in Halifax under Merkel's tutelage, when Norwood had underwritten the costs of Bruce's first poetry collection, *Wild Apples*,[8] and when Norwood and Roberts had returned to Halifax in September to give a poetry recital together, a strongly unified literary coterie had emerged from the readings, public lectures, and social interconnections which Andrew Merkel had helped to generate and support throughout the 1920s. The result of this was that by October of 1928 the group had evolved a dramatic image of themselves as "Fishers of Song," a loosely-connected fellowship of literary fisherfolk who culled from the wind, the sea, and the traditional life style of Nova Scotia the poetic catches that defined their province.

Out of the self-romanticization of the Song Fishermen emerged two different publications in the autumn of 1928. One was to be a short-lived series of broadsheets produced under the rubric *Nova Scotia Catches*. The other was to be a more enduring, if less elegantly-produced, collection of poems and communications appearing under the title, *The Song Fishermen's Song Sheets*. In the case of the broadsheets, only three seem to have been published, the first one containing the poem "The Bluenose to the Wind" by Andrew Merkel; the second, "On the Road to Maccan" by Kenneth Leslie (an early version of "The Shaunachie Man," his tribute to Robert Norwood); and the third, "Ragwort" by Charles Bruce. Handsomely illustrated and tinted by the artist Donald MacKay who had just returned to Canada after studying with Graham Sutherland in London and at the Academie Colorossie in Paris, the broadsheets also introduced to the public the group's newly-established publishing arm, the Abenaki Press. Given this name by Bliss Carman who saw in the ancient tribe of the Abenaki the same

---

[7] Thomas H. Raddall, *In My Time* (Toronto: McClelland and Stewart, 1976), p. 223.

[8] Discussion with Harry Bruce, son of Charles Bruce.

affinity to "water and wind and weeds and the human heart"[9] epitomized by the Song Fishermen's poetry, the press proved to be an unprofitable venture in spite of the elegance of its broadsheet productions and the quality of its poetry.

The Song Fishermen were forced, as a result, to fall back on the second of their publishing ventures for a more sustained system of communication. Thus it was that a series of nondescript but serviceable sheets run off on a mimeograph machine in the Halifax office of the Canadian Press became the vehicle of the newly-formed Song Fishermen in October, 1928. Issued "ever so often"[10] under the editorship of Andrew Merkel and costing a dollar from time to time to cover postage, the publication was to grow from a single sheet of one poem and eleven recipients in the first issue, to twelve sheets and over sixty recipients by the end of its first year. Adding the headnote "Come All Ye" to its masthead in the sixth number (2 December 1928) to signify the oral and balladic root of much of the poetry, the *Song Fishermen's Sheets* also became a vehicle for members' correspondence after the first few issues, affording Bliss Carman, Robert Norwood, Charles G.D. Roberts, and the other non-residents an opportunity to maintain contact with the main Halifax group, as well as to know what was happening to the other members of the coterie scattered from Glace Bay to New York.

From the beginning of the *Song Fishermen's Sheets*, there was a conscious effort on the part of all the participating poets to sustain the marine metaphors and themes which would give focus to an otherwise disparate collection of poetry. The inevitable consequence of this was that a number of the poems seemed to be straining self-consciously for effect rather than to be emerging organically from a central image or idea. The rhetoric of "the catch" (the Song Catches; the "catches are now in the hands of the printer;" "Evelyn Tufts hooks, gaffs, and lands the following")[11] recurred throughout the sheets as a jocular but functional unifying device, and the motif was given further play by Eliza Ritchie and Kenneth Leslie several years later when they decided to call

---

[9] *The Song Fishermen's Song Sheet*, Number 1 (19 October 1928); and, "The Song Fishermen" in Charlie Bruce to "Dear Mrs. Taylor," Toronto, August 23-66, Charles Bruce Papers, D.U.A.

[10] This phrase appeared in the headnote of each *Song Fishermen's Song Sheet*.

[11] See *The Song Fishermen's Song Sheet*, Number 10 (13 April 1929), p. 3; Number 2 (25 October 1928), p. 1; and Number 3 (1 November 1928), p. 1.

prospective poetry collections *Songs of the Maritimes* (1931) and *A Catch of Song* (1933) respectively.[12]

In spite of this self-conscious rhetoric and a large body of verse written just for the sheer fun of it, there emerged in the *Song Fishermen's Sheets* a number of poems that illustrated the strength of talent amongst the writers, all of whom were initially brought together by friendship but continued to write out of an intense commitment to their craft. Kenneth Leslie's broadsheet poem, "On the Road to Maccan," Martha Ann's concrete poem, "Poor Bob," published in December, 1928, Joe Wallace's "The Working Class to Saccho and Vanzetti," in April, 1929, Robert Norwood's "Homeward Oars," in May, 1929, and Kenneth Leslie's "A Memory of James D. Gillis, Teacher," in June, 1929, all illustrate why the *Song Fishermen's Sheets* created excitement amongst critics like Lorne Pierce and John Hanlon Mitchell who were on the mailing list.[13] As well, the group's memorial to Bliss Carman compiled shortly after his death drew deserved praise for the quality of its poetry and the quality of its production. Published in pamphlet form as Number 13 of the Song Sheets, it contained Leslie's vigorously tuneful tribute, "Go, Lank Rover," echoing the Vagabondia rhythms and youthful spirit that Carman had come to represent to the Song Fishermen.

The success of this publication and the increasing publicity the *Song Sheets* were receiving convinced Merkel by the summer of 1929 that the sheets had grown beyond their original intention of generating fun and communication and had, instead, reached a calibre of performance warranting a book-length anthology of Song Fishermen poetry. "After the September number comes out," he noted, "we have half intentions of drying out the year's catch, pressing it into drums, and loading it aboard a three-master for ports unknown, perhaps Demerara; in other words, binding some of our songs into a printed book for more permanent and wider distribution."[14] Thus it was that in Number 15 of the *Sheets*, Merkel came as close to writing an editorial or stating a rationale

---

[12] Eliza Ritchie's *Songs of the Maritimes* was published by McClelland's of Toronto in 1931. Ken Leslie's *A Catch of Song* was being discussed as a publication of The MacMillan Company in 1933 but did not appear. See a letter from MacMillan's to "Dear Mr. Leslie," 15 September 1933, Kenneth Leslie Papers, MG 1, vol. 2201, no. 10. P.A.N.S.

[13] J.H.M., "Novascotiana," *The Halifax Chronicle* (29 December 1929), p. 8.

[14] "Announcement," *The Song Fishermen's Song Sheet*, Number 15 (29 July 1929), p. 1.

for the existence of the group as he was ever to do; and what emerged was a restatement of the traditional values and rural lifestyle which he felt to be the informing principle of the Song Fishermen's philosophy and the Song Fishermen's poems:

We have been writing for fun, and for our own fun. We are rather isolated down here in Nova Scotia. The material and commercial centre of gravity is distant from us, and has drawn many of our people away. The march of progress goes by us on the other side of the hill. It is a march which leaves little time for playing or singing.

There is always plenty of time here, and it is when time is on your hands that you will sing. Ross Bishop, the clockmaker of Bridgetown, locks his shop, hangs a sign on the door, "Gone Fishing," and goes. You cannot do that in Toronto or New York. Ross has plenty of time on his hands. He plays five or six instruments of music. He studies geology. He is an inventor. He loves to sit quiet in the woods and listen to nothing in particular for no definite length of time. The windows of his soul are open. He does a certain amount of mending clocks, but he does not have to punch them as he did that time he worked up in Waltham.

Let us not get too ambitious. Keep your eyes free from the glare of big cities and big reputations. Keep your mind free from the contemporary illusion which names every new thing a good thing, and turns its back on old things which have been proved in many thousand years of human blood and tears.[15]

For any Maritimer familiar with the unemployment and break-up of the region's rural life in the 1920s and 1930s, Merkel's description of small towns seems romanticized and cliched in *Sheet Number 15*. Yet, the Song Fishermen were far too worldly a group not to recognize the forces eroding the idealized Nova Scotia of their poems and of Merkel's editorial. In 1923, Merkel had covered the brutal confrontations between labour and capital in Cape Breton for the Canadian Press, earning the respect of all parties for the fairness of his reporting. His knowledge of historical realities in Cape Breton had intruded even into the *Song Fishermen's Sheets* when, in February 1929, he responded to Stuart McCawley's contribution of "The Yahie Miners" with his own editorial aside:

We are indebted to Stuart McCawley for The Yahie Miners. He writes it was written about 1884 and is still being sung in Cape Breton. "Yahie," he explains, means "uncouth farmer". He might have added that the ballad deals with a condition that is largely responsible for the difficulties

[15] *Ibid.*

that are encountered in the prosecution of the coal industry in Nova
Scotia. Coal mining in Cape Breton is really a seasonal occupation. Before
the entry of the Dominion Coal Company the mines were operated for the
most part during the summer months when the St. Lawrence was free
from ice and there was ready access to an adequate market. A large
proportion of the mine workers were farmers who returned to their homes
in the country when navigation closed in the Fall. Since that time efforts
to operate the mines continuously have failed because of the limited
market offering during the winter months and as a result distress in many
of the communities has become a hardy perennial.[16]

Robert Norwood and the other Song Fishermen had a similar
understanding of the region. Norwood had served in the parishes of
Neil's Harbour, Hubbards, and Springhill before moving to urban
churches outside the Maritimes, and well knew the precariousness
of rural economies. Joe Wallace had already been involved with
the Independent Labour Party and the Workers' Party throughout
the 1920s, and Kenneth Leslie had begun to demonstrate in his
writing that sense of conscience that was to define his later social
and political conduct in New York. It was typical of Leslie that
when he read Joe Wallace's poem 'I brought them forth,' he wrote
to the *Song Sheets* that Wallace's poem was "an arrow in the throat
of despair." For Leslie, Wallace had "spoken the burden of those
who suffer when justice bows to power."[17]

Thus, it was probably inevitable that the *Song Fishermen's Sheets*
would someday change in tone as the "old things" of Merkel's
romanticized Nova Scotia altered, and shades of this had already
appeared in the *Sheets* with the publication of Wallace's "The
Working Class to Saccho and Vanzetti" (13 April 1929) and "The
Giant out of a Job" (23 June 1929). Yet neither Merkel nor the
other Song Fishermen could have anticipated how quickly the *Song
Fishermen's Sheets* were to end. Almost as Merkel wrote of "drying
out the year's catch" and "pressing it into drums," the "material
and commercial sensibility" he so deplored began to assert itself in
a most unexpected form. J.B. Livesay, father of the poet Dorothy
Livesay and General Manager of the Canadian Press, had, ac-

[16] For Merkel's response to the Cape Breton situation, see John Mellon, *The Company
Store: James Bryson McLachlan and the Cape Breton Coal Miners, 1900-1925* (Toronto,
1983), pp. 205-6; and *The Song Fishermen's Song Sheet* Number 8 (14 February 1929),
p. 8.
[17] "Kenneth Leslie writes," *The Song Fishermen's Song Sheet*, Number 11 (2 May 1929),
p. 1.

cording to Merkel, "many excellent qualities, including a love for poetry, but Livesay decided the Song Sheet, issued not more than once a month and entirely made up to contributions, was taking too much of the time of his Atlantic Superintendent. So he instructed me to dispense with it forthwith."[18]

Deprived of a publishing arm because of Livesay's decision, Merkel and the Song Fishermen coterie decided to proceed with a previously discussed Song Fishermen's picnic as a "climax" to their years of conviviality and poeticizing.[19] Thus, they began to organize an elaborately festive marine excursion befitting their nautical metaphor and outrivalling anything concocted by Stephen Leacock in his famous expedition of the Mariposa Belle.[20] Already embarked on a poetry contest in the *Song Sheets* based on a challenge in one of James D. Gillis's paragraphs in *The Cape Breton Giant*,[21] the Song Fishermen arranged for Gillis to judge the anonymous entries, select a winner, and journey down to Halifax from his home at Melrose Hill in Inverness County to be present at the marine excursion and the coronation of a Song Fishermen's Song King. Gillis, a poet, Gaelic singer, and original speaker of the English language, who in the words of Merkel, "just missed being an honest-to-goodness genius,"[22] had been drawn into the Song Fishermen circle in 1928 when some of the coterie had journeyed to Cape Breton to introduce themselves to him. His colourful style in letters to the group had enlivened many a *Song Sheet* correspondence page, and his judgments on the poems in the *Song Fishermen's Sheets* were always original: "Your literature is absolutely pure and safe and will eventually tend to uplift the people more profoundly than forseen, and in agreeable ways."[23]

The two-day celebration to which Gillis journeyed on the 12th and 13th of September, 1929, began in Halifax on the Thursday evening with a quartet of sea chanteys and a lecture by Robert

---

18 Andrew Merkel, "Nucleus of Poetry Centre Established in Halifax," unidentified newspaper clipping, Hilda Tyler Collection, MG 1, vol. 925A, no. 14. P.A.N.S.

19 *Ibid.*

20 Stephen Leacock, "The Sinking of the Mariposa Belle," in idem, *Sunshine Sketches of a Little Town* (Toronto, 1931; 1969).

21 "All Hands On Deck," *The Song Fishermen's Song Sheet*, Number 11 (2 May 1929), pp. 8-10.

22 Merkel, "Nucleus of Poetry Circle Established in Halifax."

23 "The following letter has been received from James D. Gillis," *The Song Fishermen's Song Sheet*, Number 10 (13 April 1929), p. 1.

James D. Gillis, Melrose Hill, Inverness County, Cape Breton.
                              PUBLIC ARCHIVES OF NOVA SCOTIA

Norwood on "Poetry and Nova Scotia." The evening's proceedings left an impression on Gillis, who afterwards recalled the event
in *The Song Fishermen's Song Sheet*:

I attended the Song Fishermen's Picnic, whose grace note was a Lecture
by Dr. Norwood, of New York City. This Lecture was delivered on the
night before the Picnic. The subject was the Modern Poets of N.S. Dr.
Norwood is a widely known scholar, theologian, thinker and poet and
now refreshed and replenished by a trip to Palestine. I think I am within
my rights to say that the Lecture was not often if ever surpassed. He
shouldered the most untried and heavy problems, explained the function
of mind and its expression in deeds, prose, and poetry — giving special
attention to the poets and poetry of Nova Scotia.[24]

The next morning, some thirty Songsters met at the statue of
Robbie Burns opposite the Halifax Public Gardens, were piped to
a waiting motorcade, boarded a schooner named "The Drama" at
Shad Bay (accompanied again by the sound of pipes), and under a
sharply snapping Nova Scotia flag, sailed down the coast to East
Dover. Here, the "dry-footed"[25] went ashore to visit the school, the
church, and the unique rock formation known as Dover Castle,
while the true fishermen set sail to capture the catch of the day, two
large pollack. By two o'clock the entire body had reassembled on
shore for fish chowder, and then settled down for the real business
of the event — the crowning of Stuart McCawley of Glace Bay as
the King of the Song Fishermen. Bob Leslie, whose free verse
offended Judge James D. Gillis ("If I must read it in seclusion it is
wicked or no good."),[26] received a consolation prize of a rhyming
dictionary. Stuart McCawley was solemnly crowned by Robert
Norwood with a diadem of dulse. James D. Gillis piped and sang in
Gaelic, Patricia McGrath gave an exhibition of Highland dancing,
and Kenneth Leslie played the violin and sang his own composition, "Bluenose Blues." "The said lyric," Gillis was to note later,
"with the music should be generally known. It is most innocent,
unobtrusive, almost pathetic. At the same time it plainly shows the
best attitude for a young Nova Scotian in the chaos of inevitable

[24] "A Word From J. D. Gillis," *The Song Fishermen's Song Sheet*, Number 16 (4 April
1930),p. 2.

[25] This expression was one used by Charles Bruce to designate those who preferred the
land to the sea. It appears in his poem "Biography" in *The Mulgrave Road* (Toronto,
1951), p. 5.

[26] "The Entertaining Steersman," *The Song Fishermen's Song Sheet*, Number 14 (23 June
1929), p. 1.

opposition if he wants to triumph in the end."[27] The celebration —
as did the group — ended in a clasping of hands, a singing of Auld
Lang Syne, and a skirl of pipes. Lovers of tradition to the end, the
Song Fishermen concluded their poetic lovefest with the same
sense of unity and panache that had marked their entire career.

Following the publication of the last *Song Fishermen's Sheet* in the
spring of 1930, attempts were made to sustain the output of the
group. Theodore Goodridge Roberts had already expressed his
admiration for the Song Sheets in the Saint John *Telegraph Journal*
of 14 December 1929, and he now offered the Fishermen an outlet
in a new journal he was founding. A notice sent to the Song
Fishermen participants announced: "*The Song Fishermen's Song
Sheet* has found a permanent home, through the courtesy of
Theodore Goodridge Roberts, in ACADIE, a semi-monthly magazine which will appear for the first time on April 15, the birthday of
Bliss Carman, Canada's best-loved poet."[28] After representative
offerings of The Fishermen had appeared in *Acadie*, however, the
idea was dropped. There were some who thought that Robert
Norwood might infuse new life into the *Song Sheets*, and in his
correspondence with intimate friends like Kenneth Leslie he explored that possibility:

You are right about the Song Sheet. It must be reborn, and I hope the day
will come when I will be in a position to do something definite for it in the
way of financial help. And you are quite right about "Acadie." It won't
last, but the Song Sheet was a big venture. I learned from Ethel Butler
that I am guilty of having killed Cock Robin. She beat me black and blue
this summer. I tried to make her see that it was not easy for me that
evening to do better than I did, because I, too, was a Song Sheet
fisherman, and that what she thought was my levity was really a way of
concealing my brooding love for the whole group. I must have blundered,
but I certainly put myself into it. Anyway, it is hard for me to function
according to program. But that is past, and one day, I hope to prove to the
bunch that I have my arms around them all. They are very dear to me.[29]

Even with the best will of Norwood directed toward the publication, however, there were too many forces distracting the group
to make it possible for them to reorganize their energies in a

[27] "A Word from J. D. Gillis," p. 2.
[28] "Announcement," Kenneth Leslie Papers, MG 1, vol. 2201, no. 7, 1929. P.A.N.S.
[29] Bob to "Beloved Ken," 6 September 1930, Kenneth Leslie Papers, MG 1, vol. 2196, folder 10, no. 7. P.A.N.S.

coherent way. The Depression of the 1930s was upon people. Ken
Leslie was typical of many of the fishermen in moving away. And
within two years, Robert Norwood was dead, struck down pre-
maturely by a coronary thrombosis. His death, like that of Carman,
took from the group a spiritual and symbolic centre. The Song
Fishermen and their *Song Sheets* therefore slipped into the nirvana
of memory, recalled nostalgically by Merkel, Bruce, Leslie, and
company over the succeeding years, but forgotten by literary
historians and by the province once mythologized by their vision of
its rural and nautical character.

Only in the subsequent poems of Kenneth Leslie's *By Stubborn
Stars* (1938) and Charles Bruce's *The Mulgrave Road* (1951) did
something of the Song Fishermen flavour survive the Song Fishermen group. In "Words are Never Enough," Bruce recalled the
"salt in the blood," the "soundless well of knowing, / That sea, in
the flesh and nerves and the puzzling mind / Of children born to
the long grip of its tide"[30] that characterized many of the Song
Fishermen's poems. Yet in the end, the inimitable James D. Gillis
had the last word on the world "on the other side of the hill"
described by Merkel in his editorial of July, 1929. In that world,
"the march of progress" went on. It was that "progress" that James
D. Gillis first noticed when he arrived in Halifax in 1929. "Such
discipline of offending travellers has turned multitudes away to
auto cars, and pilgrims to more congenial haunts," he noted in the
Song Sheets after his visit; "But Halifax City is simply a condensed
population claiming no prescience or inspiration."[31] In rural life,
James D. Gillis and the Song Fishermen found inspiration. In the
modern city, they found no prescience — nothing to celebrate
when "we have been writing for fun, and for our own fun."[32]

---

[30] Charles Bruce, "Words are Never Enough" in *The Mulgrave Road* (Toronto, 1951),
p. 26-27.

[31] "A Word From J. D. Gillis," p. 2.

[32] "Announcement," *The Song Fishermen's Song Sheet*, Number 15 (29 July 1929), p. 1.

THADDEUS HOLOWNIA

The Gas Station: Corner Stone of Rural and Small Town Architecture

THE DOMINANT MACHINE IN MODERN NORTH American society is the automobile. Those of us who live in rural areas rely on the automobile to get us to and from work and, in the Maritimes especially, most trips to any recreational area or rural locale depend on personal rather than public transportation.

We tend to take the highway and its surrounds for granted. Since Henry Ford rolled his first iron horse out of the factory, service stations have proliferated across the landscape and have continued to take up sentinel positions at crossroads and major intersections. Not until the oil crisis of the mid-1970s was there a break in the expanding numbers of service stations. We have progressed a long way from the stagecoach and the inn: the 1980s have produced a new direction in roadside architecture. Tight monetary conditions make pumping just gasoline no longer a profitable venture. No longer do gas stations serve communities in traditional ways. Specialized technologies and a dramatic influx of import cars have made even the survival of the small independent mechanic very difficult.

With these economic changes, the styles of gas station architecture have also changed. Quickly fading are the one- and two-bay buildings. Those multi-turret, Disneyesque-styled stations are also being replaced by the box-like convenience store and self-service gas bar. No longer do you automatically have your oil, tires, and water checked. However, you can pick up your ice, favorite video tapes, and night-time snack while your spouse fills up the tank.

The photographs reproduced here are architectural examples of the historical gas station styles built by the Maritimes' predominant gas dealer — Irving. Irving gas stations are to be found at most major intersections east of Québec City.

Some styles are quickly disappearing and I have attempted to preserve many of these on film in the documentary style of Walter Evans and Roy Stryker.

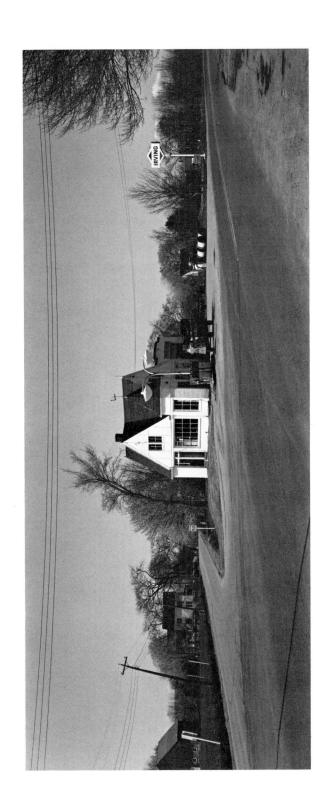

ERIC ROSS

The Rise and Fall of Pictou Island[1]

"DRIFTING UP FROM THE HARBOUR ON THE stillness of the evening air, you could hear the sobbing voices of the folk crowded aboard the sailing ships below: they knew that never again would they breathe the beauty of the lochs and the hills and that the hand-shake of the ship's side was the hand-shake of the deathbed." So whispered an elderly man of Mull, a few years ago, as he stood in the silence of the setting sun, high above the snug harbour of Tobermory, Scotland. He was speaking of the early years of the nineteenth century when thousands of migrants from Mull and the nearby Highlands and Isles carried their ancient language and customs to the distant shores of New Zealand, Australia, Africa and the Americas. Here, we will look at just one small group who, for a century and a half, kept alive the old ways on a tiny speck of land called Pictou Island.

You will need a good map to find Pictou Island: it is only about four and one half miles long, one and a quarter miles wide and of low elevation. Eyes accustomed to Mull and the other Hebrides must have found it very flat, indeed. From the southern side of the island, where they made their homes, the people could look out across the Northumberland Strait to the blue hills of Nova Scotia, a

[1] This study is based largely on interviews with present and former Pictou Island residents, on field observations, on census data, and on items from *The Pictou Advocate* (1895-1975). Most of the interviews were conducted in the summers of 1975, 1976, 1984, and 1985. Grateful acknowledgement is accorded to the following interviewees: the late Howard MacLean, the late Andy MacCallum and Mrs. MacCallum, Alfred Maclean, Carl MacCallum, Mr. and Mrs. Earnie Rankin, Jack "Happy" MacDonald and the late Mrs. MacDonald, Barry Mack, Billy MacMillan, Ken Banks, the late Mr. and Mrs. Campbell MacCallum, Mr. and Mrs. Chris Stafford, David Harding, Beth Munroe, Charlie Munroe, Florence MacMaster, Calvin MacCallum, Mr. and Mrs. Roy MacCallum, Ona Glover, Ruth Munroe, the late John Malcolm MacCallum, and Mr. and Mrs. Parker Lewis.

somewhat modest reminder of home. Along the foot of the hills and
dotting the shoreline, were the tiny houses of their fellow Highlanders of Pictou County. On the other side of the island was the
low horizon on Prince Edward Island where many another Highland heart beat strong. In summer, the shallow waters of the strait
could be remarkably pleasant and warm, allowing for easy communication with the neighboring shores; in winter, they were
choked with ice for months at a time, isolating the Islanders from
virtually all contact with the outside world. This was a time of
retreat and seclusion when the Island became the world, a time
when the Islanders were knitted into one big family, a time of
music, story telling and dancing, of weaving, hooking rugs and
making lobster pots, a time of enjoyment and of preservation of the
old ways. Summer brought contact with a wider world but it, too,
was largely Scottish and did little to change the ways of the
Islanders. Their world may have been limited in space but it was
rich in time; it was a world where the past, the present and the
future lived side by side, a world of ghost ships and of tales of people
and of happenings long ago, of the events of the present day, and of
forerunners telling of future occurrences, particularly of death.

Although Pictou Island was well known to the Micmac Indians,
it was not settled until the arrival of four Irish families in 1814, or
soon after. In 1819, they were followed by the first of the Highlanders.
The newcomers apparently feuded with the Irish who soon moved
on, but before they left, most of the forest on the Island was
consumed in a fire said to have been set by one of the Irish wives.
More Highland settlers followed during the 1820s and 1830s from
the islands of Mull and Tiree and from the mainland of Ross and
Argyll with the last of them arriving in the early 1840s. A century of
census data record the contours of population change. By 1838,
there were 17 families in a vigorous young community of 119 souls.
No family was without children still at home and thirteen of them
shared a total of 58 children under 14. Among the 17 heads of
family — all of whom were male — were two carpenters and a
blacksmith; the rest were farmers. Since land on the tiny island was
limited and such a small community could support few tradesmen,
most of the children eventually would be forced to leave. Thus, by
1858 the population had reached a plateau of 158 in 25 households,
and remained at that level, with minor variations, until the end of
the century when it was still only 159, although the number of
households had climbed to 36. During the first two decades of the

twentieth century, fishing, particularly lobsters, became an important means of support, allowing the population to grow rapidly, to reach a high of 227 in 37 households in 1921. By that time, there were already problems in the fisheries and soon the population began to decline as rapidly as it had risen and, by 1951, had dropped through the old plateau. Since then, it has continued to plummet until today only a handful live on the Island year around.

The Island's shape — much like an elongated oatmeal loaf — allowed for an easy settlement pattern: the land was simply cut into 32 slices — each encompassing from 50 to 150 acres. All of the lots were long and narrow except for those toward the two "heels" which were sliced somewhat thicker to compensate for the narrowing of the island. As the population increased, some lots were cut into still thinner slices. All houses were constructed in a line a short distance from the south shore. This, along with the narrowness of the lots, meant that neighbours were much closer to one another than was common in other pioneering communities (Figure 1).

Clearing the land was a heroic task — especially for men from the open glens of Scotland — and it is still remembered today in tales passed down about the "old boys" who farmed all day and then pulled stumps at night and burned them so there would be enough light to pull more stumps. In time, the whole southern half of the Island was swept clean of virtually every tree. Hardly a twig was left to shelter the farms from winter's blast: it seems the settlers preferred taking their chances with the fury of the wind to risking a torn up tree crashing through their roofs. The northern half of the Island was left in forest, thus providing each farm with an extensive woodlot from which to draw fuel, lumber, and materials for making boats, lobster-pots and dyes. Each farm also had its "back fence" which marked the boundary between cleared and uncleared land. All of these fences were joined to form a continuous line from one end of the Island to the other. In the spring, each farmer drove his animals — except milking cows — through the "back fence gate" into the woods where they foraged together much as they might have done on common land at the head of some Scottish glen. With the animals safely out of the way, the fields could be planted without fear of marauding mouths and hooves. To forget to close the back gate was one of the worst sins a child could commit, and could result in his not being able to sit comfortably for several days. After the harvest was gathered in the fall, the gates were opened and soon most of the animals found the way back to

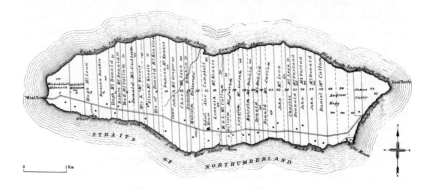

FIGURE 1. PICTOU ISLAND, 1878 (from *Illustrated Atlas of Pictou County, Nova Scotia, 1879*).

The first Scottish settlers on Pictou Island took up land along the southern shore. Soon afterward, the Island was surveyed into long-lots, and all existing holdings were made to conform to the new settlement pattern. Later, when the original road following along the shore was moved inland to higher and drier ground on orders from the county, the reluctant Islanders were forced to make another adjustment. Several families now found their homes too far from the road. In time, as new houses were built and old ones replaced, the centre of Island life gradually shifted to the new road and away from the shore.

their home farms. Any mixups were easily sorted out through the animals having been marked before they were sent off into the woods.

The absence of a harbour — or even a bay — along the smooth coastline of the island meant that there was no shelter for boats. Near the west end, there was a small wharf but it was too exposed for boats to be left there in safety. For these reasons, only small boats which could easily be hauled up were practicable. Without larger craft, fishing was restricted mostly to the shallow waters near the Island and for many years was regarded merely as a seasonal adjunct to farming. Most of the modest catch was for home consumption or was spread on the fields as fertilizer. Outside markets were impractical, given the technology of the times. Lobsters were very plentiful; so plentiful, in fact, that they were held in low regard as a food. It took an American firm, Shedd and Knox of Boston, to realize their worth and to provide a means for getting them to distant markets where they were appreciated. In the later 1870s, Shedd and Knox established a factory at the east end of the island to can lobsters. In 1881, they moved to the mainland but it was not long before others followed their lead and built factories on the Island until, by the early 1900s, there were no fewer than five canneries in operation at the same time. For some Islanders, fishing became more important than agriculture and for the first time, there were those who began to regard themselves as fishermen rather than farmers.

The lobster fishery contributed much to the Island's heyday between 1900 and 1950, but it did not do so alone. Potatoes, grains, beef, eggs, wool and even milk also made their contributions. The community was then in its prime and old timers, now living out their years in exile on the mainland, remember it in a warm haze of sepia-washed nostalgia.

Each year began and ended with the Scottish rituals of New Year and Hogmanay. During the evening of the day before New Year's, or Hogmanay, people would gather at certain houses to sing Gaelic songs and to dance — preferably to the skirl of the bagpipe. There were probably never more than one or two Islanders who could play the pipes, but pipers came over for special occasions from the mainland or from Prince Edward Island. After singing and dancing until the "peeping of the dawn," the more gregarious set out with flasks of whisky to wish their neighbours a happy New Year. The flasks were done up in straw and came from

Halifax packed in barrels. Those who still had the ancient tongue — or by that time thought they had — would tap on the door and "say a whole bunch of Gaelic." On at least one door step, the family still got out a broom and in Gaelic would say, "sweep out the old year and sweep in the new."

New Year's usually marked the end of easy communication with the mainland. The "hard" winter generally set in at about that time and for several months the Island remained icebound — sometimes well into May. During the first decades of the twentieth century, signal fires of blazing straw were still the only means of communication with the mainland. Like the telegram, by then long in use elsewhere in Canada, their message was all too often one of serious illness or death. A fire set on the mainland in January 1920 provides a typical case in point. When the Islanders saw it, a crew set off over the ice. It was 45 hours before they returned to their anxious relatives with the news of the death of a resident of the Island in the town of Pictou. As on many other occasions, the crossing provided Islanders with opportunities for acts of heroism. It was said that there was not a man who would not risk his life to go for medical aid. In some years, an ice bridge formed and it was possible to walk across. Occasionally, as in March 1932, it was possible to go by horse and sleigh all the way to Pictou, but normally the way was blocked by open stretches of water and by 30 feet piles of pack ice. Dog teams were not used for fear that the animals would drown or be crushed in the ice. Instead, the Islanders resorted to dory-like hulls with runners. These could be both manhandled across the ice or rowed through open stretches of water. Often the ice-boats would leave the Island in the morning and not reach Pictou until five or six o'clock that evening. Sometimes they would be carried by the tide far from their intended landing place. Occasionally, a boat would be trapped in the ice for many hours at a time as it inched through the chilled darkness towards the blazing shoreline beacon which had been set as a guide.

The boats were intended primarily for bringing over the mail. Passengers, if able-bodied, were expected to help the two or three crewmen in working the craft. Sometimes, the passenger was too ill or badly injured to help and was on his way to the doctor or to the Pictou Cottage Hospital; sometimes, as in January 1926, the passenger was a doctor on his way to visit his patients on the Island; and sometimes, as in the winter of 1932, the passenger was the stiff-frozen corpse of an Islander on its way home for burial. Three of the iceboats in use after January 1926 were veterans from the Canadian National Railways' Cape Tormentine crossing to Prince Edward Island.

Some Pictou Islanders made the hazardous crossing to be with family members who had moved to the nearby mainland — there were 25 to 35 of these in 1920 — and, not surprisingly, they were among those who were especially anxious to see improvement in communication. Several pleas were made for an underwater telephone cable, including a petition to the Dominion Government in 1918. However, it was not until 1921, that a cable was finally laid. It was not an unqualified success since it was out of commission for weeks and even months at a time. Part of the problem was ice. In 1932, it was replaced by a new cable. A radio link was also established in the same year. This was fortunate since the cable was again damaged by ice in 1948. However, by that time, planes were flying back and forth several times a day, fulfilling a dream for communication by air expressed in the *Pictou Advocate* as far back as 1928.

There was never an airstrip on the island. In the early days, the small planes landed in a farmer's field; later, they dodged the telephone poles to land on the narrow, dusty surface of the Island's only road. The mail plane came twice a week — either from Prince Edward Island or from Trenton/New Glasgow depending on who had the contract.

In spite of the isolation — or perhaps because of it — winter was the favourite season. Days began at five-thirty or six with a brisk sortie to the barns to milk the cows and do other chores. Only afterwards came the warmth of the kitchen stove and the homely smells of burning hardwood, of fresh bread being toasted over glowing coals, and of the faintly acrid smoke of the oil lamp's chimney as it cast its mellow circle over the breakfast table — over the shorts porridge, the sliced pork, the oat cakes, the raisin loaf, the jams, the molasses and the tea. Pork was an inevitable part of every meal of the day whether breakfast, dinner, supper or lunch. Lunch was taken at bedtime and could be quite heavy with biscuits, bannock, molasses and tea. Biscuits and bannock were part of nearly every meal and it was said that not to have had bannock on the table would have been grounds for divorce.

After breakfast, children went off to school, women got down to making bread and other household tasks, and the men set out to walk a mile or two back into the woods to get on with the pleasant task of cutting the year's supply of firewood. They loved the fresh air, the scent of the spruce, and the ring of the axe. (Far too often an axe missed its mark and resulted in dangerous injuries — usually to the foot.) Children looked forward to the days when they could go with their fathers to watch the trees bounce as they hit the snow covered ground with their frozen branches snapping off like so many giant wishbones. At that time of the year, the woods were safe: the bulls and steers of summer were at home in the barn, if they had not already been slaughtered. Then came the best part of the day, the ride home on top of the wood behind the twitching, steaming flanks of the horses and the rhythmic jingle of the bells. (Oxen were once used as well, but later Islanders knew of them only through the large wooden yokes that lay, half-forgotten, in some corner of the barn.) For the child, there was a wonderful feeling of security; there was no threat whatsoever. Like his father, his mind was concentrated on the Island. He had found his own entertainment and he had his own people to attend to and to help out. When they got home, it might be getting dark but there was still the night wood to be cut and carried in before supper.

With snow on the ground, the darkness was never complete and both young and old were tempted to go out skating after supper if the ice on the pond was good. The younger fellows enjoyed playing hockey. One year they had a teacher who not only helped them with the game, but took them out into the woods and taught them how to cut their own hockey sticks. The first opportunity to play on a real rink came in February 1922 when they crossed to Pictou and defeated a church team by three goals to two. The victors returned triumphantly to the Island where they were entertained in at least two different homes.

Hockey and skating were not alone in drawing people out in the evenings: there were house parties with singing, dancing and cards; there were pie socials to raise money for the church and for other causes; and there were Saturday night frolics in the Community Hall with step-dancing, lancers, strip-the-willow, and four-hand and eight-hand reels. The music was supplied by Islanders playing the piano, fiddles, accordions, banjos and guitars. Most of the musicians learned to play by ear from their parents and so much of the music was rooted in the past. Saturday night could be rowdy with a great deal of drinking, but it was also a time of preparation for the Sabbath — a Sabbath which differed little from the Sabbath back in the Highlands.

Everything possible was done on Saturday night — there were those who would not even bring in a bucket of water on Sunday let alone lift a pair of scissors. Only in summer was there a minister. In winter, church was conducted by the elders who held services Sunday morning and evening, with Sunday School in the afternoon. Everyone got out to church — probably as much through habit as from conviction. The evening service was largely a prayer meeting where anyone who was capable might read from the Scriptures, or perhaps a Bible story from the *Nova Scotian*. Another prayer meeting was held on Wednesday night — it provided the young fellow with a place to take his girl friend. There were also young people's groups which met in the Community Hall and a Women's Missionary Society (W.M.S.) which provided glimpses of distant lands such as India and Japan.

The active meetings of the W.M.S. typified many of the winter activities. Pleasure came from working together whether it was raising money for famine relief in India or sewing clothing for the needy in a Maritime mining town. The same could be said of the "old-fashioned chopping frolics" which were still being held in the mid-1930s. These, of course, were for the men. Women's activities were almost all indoors and provided an important antidote to cabin fever during the long winter. Spinning, dying, and weaving were still being carried on in the early years of this century. The dyes were made from materials gathered in the woods and from stale urine saved for that purpose. Newly woven blankets required "beating." This was done to the rhythm of traditional Gaelic songs. Quilting, knitting, and hooking rugs (using Rosenbergs) provided other opportunities for the women to get out of the house. Meanwhile, the men were busy chopping fence posts, cutting ice for the icehouses, and preparing for the fishing season. When the lobster factories were still functioning a great deal of wood was required for cooking the meat. This all had to be chopped and hauled to the factories in winter. There was also wood for trap-gear to be cut, new lobster pots to be made, old ones to be repaired and head-nets to be knitted. Some men worked on their own gear, others made traps for sale to the factories or to other fishermen.

The fishing season came on the heels of winter and so everything — even much of the boat-building and repair — had to be done by spring. The Island could provide all the wood that went into building a boat — including the keel, stem and stern-post which the builder, himself, selected in the woods before construction began. Sawing was done by whipsaws in the early days. These were operated by two men — one on a platform above, the other lying on his back below. One pulled the saw up, the other, down. In time, the whipsaw gave way to a rotary saw operated by a horse-powered treadmill. The horses, in turn, were displaced by gasoline engines during the second decade of the twentieth century. Although the early nails were forge-made, their manufacture was beyond the skill of the Island blacksmiths. Thus, they had to be imported from the mainland — the only part of the ship not from the Island. The boats were small and were intended only for local fishing — the largest built on the Island was thirty feet long.

There was never a tavern on the Island, but in the years when there was a store operating, it became a favourite gathering place. It was there that the older folks gathered to swap stories after dark. Unheard (and almost unseen) in the darkened corners, silent children listened and absorbed tales and lore which stretched back to the beginning of the Island and even across the ocean into the mists of the Highlands of long ago. Many of the tales touched on death and the gifted story-teller could fill the room with a cosy aura of delicious gloom, seasoned here and there with quick flashes of black humour. To the children, it must have seemed that the oldtimers were never happier than when they were miserable. Most of the stories were set on Pictou Island, yet, had the children been able to journey to the land of their ancestors, they would have been amazed at how similar were the stories told there — stories of rattling chains, of ghosts, of second sight and of forerunners prophesying death. For some reason — perhaps it was his simple life close to nature — the Highlander was more attuned than most to the nudgings of the forerunner.

There were people on the Island who could tell a week before-hand if the hand of death was coming. They might see a hearse coming through the gate; they might hear chains rattling or a persistent knocking on the window; they might dream of being lost or in a fire, or of a boat up on land; or they might see on the road someone who had left the Island years before. Like other Islanders, they also knew that if the horse pulling the hearse stopped on the way to the cemetery, there would soon be another death. Was the body in the hearse responsible for stopping the horse? The folks back on Mull might have thought so. There, the last person buried had the task of guarding the graveyard until the next person arrived. No doubt he would be anxious to be relieved of his duties as soon as possible. Unnatural death could result in a restless ghost and there were tales of this house or that house, of this hill or that hill. They were very real to the Islanders — so real, in fact, that certain places were avoided and at least two houses were said to have been burned because they were haunted.

Many Islanders had witnessed the phantom ship which appeared from time to time sailing to the eastward between the Island and the Mainland. It was an old fashioned sailing ship with its rigging and sails on fire, and would stay in view for an hour or so before seemingly drifting off with the tide. As it went away, it seemed to retain the same shape and size. There were several versions of the origin of the phantom: one had it that it was an old pirate ship whose crew had mutinied and had set it afire; another said that it was a ship bound for Cape Horn which had burned off the southeast end of the Island.

Bordering on the supernatural were stories told of the "grannies" or healing women. They were the last in a line of women who had been more numerous in the days before the rise of the medical profession and the accompanying shift from female to male of those who delivered the babies and cared for the sick. From generation to generation, the grannies had passed on the mysteries of their healing arts, an essential element of which was the "charm" — the secret word or words which helped in the healing process. For example, if the grannie were told that someone had something in his eye, as long as it could move, she could take it out (even if the person were some distance away on the Island) provided she had his full name and baptism, and knew which eye it was in. This was done by taking a special bowl to the spring where the charm was repeated and the water was dipped three times. No matter where the person was, the offending object would leave his eye. This charm had come from Scotland. It was probably Gaelic but since secrecy was essential for the efficacy of a charm, nobody but the grannie would know this for certain. If the illness were serious, the grannie would turn her patient over to the doctor who would be summoned from the mainland by the lighting of a smokefire on the shore. Unfortunately, the charm — handed down from generation to generation — was lost when the last grannie died, over on the mainland, before she could pass it on to a successor who also had "the gift."

Illness and isolation loomed large in people's minds — especially in winter. When the telephone rang in the night, it was always assumed that someone was ill. People would get up and listen in on the party line and then, as likely as not, get dressed and go over to the sick person. Tending the sick was a familiar part of life and perhaps it was not surprising that a number of girls went away to places like Montreal, Boston and Concord, New Hampshire, to train as nurses. Only one seems to have returned to the Island to work, but she served for over forty years, caring for the sick, delivering babies, and even serving as undertaker. Whenever possible, the more seriously ill were taken over to the Cottage Hospital and, later, to the Sutherland Memorial Hospital in Pictou. Those requiring special treatment were sent to Halifax.

Isolation may have intensified the fear of illness, but it also probably spared the Islanders some of the regular epidemics of communicable diseases such as measles. It did not, however, protect them from the worldwide epidemic of Spanish influenza in 1918-1919 — it was responsible for shutting down the church and the school — nor from occasional bouts of typhoid, scarlet fever, and diphtheria, or from pleurisy, pneumonia, and tuberculosis. All in all, the Islanders were probably as healthy as any other people of the time. Certainly there were many who lived into extreme old age — a fact considered worthy of comment by an Island visitor as far back as 1907. Like other small isolated communities, there was one problem almost too delicate for discussion — close intermarriage. Perhaps one of the oldtimers put it best when he said that he had "seen a few mistakes . . . they should have read their Bibles."

The most important source of new blood came with the lobster industry. The Island factories required more workers than the Island could provide and so outsiders were drawn in at "fishing time." A few were fishermen, but most were women employed in packing the lobster meat in cans. Some were from Prince Edward Island and, with similar Highland backgrounds, had much in common with the Pictou Islanders. Nevertheless, they were not liked by all of the Islanders and were the butt of some of their jokes. The remainder were mostly from the Cape Bald (Cap Pelé) area of New Brunswick and were of Acadian French origin.

The arrival of as many as 50 or 60 girls each spring caused great excitement among the young men of Pictou Island. Evenings were spent in coltish pursuit and it was usually midnight before they got home to bed. No sooner were they asleep — or so it seemed — than their fathers were calling them to get up to go fishing again. Some found wives among the Prince Edward Islanders and occasionally one of the Prince Edward Island fishermen took home a Pictou Island bride, but there were almost no marriages with the Acadians. They were fun to go out with but you did not marry them. Part of the reason may have been a difference in religion: the Islanders were Protestant, the Acadians Roman Catholic.

Pictou Islanders regarded their wedding as something very special. Indeed, they were the main events or entertainments of the year. The ceremony, itself, was almost always held on the mainland — probably because there was seldom an ordained minister on the Island. After the service, the wedding party would return to the Island for a supper at the bride's home that "would stagger fourteen billy-goats" and a dance in the Community Hall that would go on "until the rooster'd crow." It was "nothing to see a fellow sitting on the side of the road playing a violin and a couple of fellows dancing on the bridge, after daylight." People loved the bagpipes and a piper usually came over with the wedding party. Weddings not only joined a couple but united the whole community.

Spring came late to Pictou Island — later than to the nearby mainland. The delay was caused by cold water and ice in the strait and helped give Pictou Island a climate more like that of Prince Edward Island than the mainland. The lobster fishery opened at various dates between April 20 and the first of May. However, there were years when the ice prevented the setting of the traps until well into May. The season lasted for two months and so closed between June 20 and June 30. This was the most hectic time of the year since most Islanders were involved in both fishing and farming. The short growing season meant that planting time corresponded with the fishing season; by the end of June, there was also the hay to be cut.

July and August were easier months. There was now time for box socials, picnics on the north shore, and for suppers and candy sales. A special treat was a feast of ice cream brought over from the dairy in Scotsburn. Since there was no way of keeping it cold, the ice cream had to be consumed at once and thus thrift provided a justification for gluttony. Deep in his Highland soul the Islander knew that every pleasure had its price. Along with the candy sales and the ice cream came the summer visits of the dentist who, of necessity, went about his work without the benefit of electric drills or lights. In some years, there were excursions to the mainland to see the Orange Parade on the Glorious Twelfth. There were other occasions when mainlanders made excursions to the Island to attend picnics or church suppers, and at least one mainland baseball team — from Caribou — played a team from the Island.

Summer was the time of the year when visitors from nearby Pictou and far off upper Canada and the "Boston States" came home to the Island. In later years, some drove back from the states in a "cawr," even though they had left only a year earlier in a "car." Once home, they would comment on the "hosses" still being used to repair the Island's only road. They knew that the men holding the road contract would be either Liberal or Conservative, depending upon which party had won the last provincial election. Each summer they would see a new house or two being built as the older storey-and-a-half peak-roofed dwellings gave way to modern bungalows.

Early in May, the summer minister or catechist arrived. He was usually a student studying for the ministry. Sometime in August he was joined for a day by "the reverend" from the mainland who came over to give communion. Very occasionally — it happened in 1927 — there was a service in Gaelic and "all the old people that could get there was there with their ears wide open." As was so often the case among peoples who had migrated to the new world, the church was the institution most responsible for preserving the language and the old ways. This was especially true when the population was both homogeneous and isolated as was the case on Pictou Island. Most of the people were Presbyterian. For many years they met in the school house but, in 1910, a minister named Sutherland encouraged them to build the fine little church which still stands near the centre of the Island. In the early 1920s, members of the congregation found themselves caught between the pull of their Scottish past and the draw of the emerging United Church of Canada. The 1925 vote on whether to join the United Church split the congregation almost evenly with a slight majority favouring continuing as Presbyterians. The Presbyterians held on to the church building and the others formed a new congregation which met in the school house. Once in a while, they would bring a United Church minister over from the mainland. In time, the

Presbyterians found they could no longer keep up the church and a neat accommodation was reached with the United congregation. Both bodies would worship together in the church but the minister would alternate between Presbyterian one year and United the next. Once again the community was united.

About the time the summer minister was leaving in the fall, the teacher was arriving for the winter. Both were birds of passage who seldom returned more than once or twice — if at all. The teacher was usually young, female, and just out of normal school, although a few were male and some had had no formal teacher's training. Unless the teacher happened to marry an Islander, she usually stayed only one year — in spite of an isolation allowance. Upon her departure, there would be a party, a gift, and words of thanks. Hers had not been an easy year — although probably no more difficult than that of teachers in similar one-room schools elsewhere in Canada. Depending upon the year, the enrolment ranged from 20 to 50 in up to 10 grades. Attendance was quite sporadic, especially during periods when the children were needed at home or in the spring when many left to work in the lobster canneries during the time when they were still operating on the Island. Probably the children's labour was required; yet, education does not seem to have been highly valued and one would have been hard pressed to find the local equivalent of the shepherd composing Latin sonnets, so beloved in Highland mythology. Pupils ranged in age from 5 to 15. As they grew older, they became increasingly aware that they were "becoming too big to go to school" and were subjected to withering remarks like "you're not still going to school?" Nevertheless, there were always some students who persisted and took advantage of whatever schooling was available on the Island and then went on for more education or training on the mainland.

The school teacher provided a glimpse of the outside world. True, her background may not have been all that different from that of the Islanders but still, she was from another community and brought a somewhat different view of the world, and often created in her pupils an awareness of possibilities other than farming and fishing. If she had special talents or training in music, art, or games, these were made freely available to the community — especially at the time of the annual Christmas party in the Community Hall. Organized by the teacher, the party was one of the main events of the year, and drew in almost everyone for an evening of costumes, acting, recitations, and singing. In the corner, there was always a

Christmas tree surrounded with gifts awaiting the arrival of Santa Claus, late in the evening, to give them out. Not long after the party, the teacher might escape to the mainland for a holiday at home — and possibly a small measure of privacy. On the Island, she was never out of sight: her every move was watched. Her only choice had been to stay with one of the families who took turns in "boarding the teacher." Frequently, the family had children going to the school; there was no reprieve.

Movement to and from the Island in the Fall was by no means confined to the teacher and the minister. In later years, there were fishermen returning from the lobster season at Cape Tormentine, potato pickers returning from back-breaking work on Prince Edward Island and, sometimes, as many as a half-dozen Islanders coming back from the annual harvest excursion to the wheat fields of the far-off Prairies. At the beginning of winter, there was another small exodus as some men left for the lumber woods of the neighbouring mainland. Late fall was thus one of the few times of the year when most of the men were at home.

November and December were busy months at the Island dock: there were daily landings and shippings of potatoes, grain, fish, lumber, flour, livestock, and cranberries. This was also the time when people got in their winter supplies — everything for six months, including groceries, clothing, and Christmas presents. If they ran out later, they knew they were out of luck. A list was kept from year to year. Things had to be used frugally. For instance, when the molasses was through running, the head was knocked out of the barrel to get at the sugar on the bottom. Nothing was wasted.

After the grain was threshed, the miller came over from Balmoral Mills near Tatamagouche. A bit later, some of the two hundred head of cattle were slaughtered. Meanwhile, seaweed (mostly kelp) was gathered for banking the houses against the winter's cold and for adding to the manure piles where it eventually became part of the fertilizer added to the fields. In the days when the factories were still operating, lobster bodies were also spread to enrich the soils.

Each fall there were 60 horses to be shod. The blacksmith made the shoes and did about six horses a day. When conditions were right, the new shoes could be tried during winter horseraces on the ice. In the early 1930s, a schooner loaded with coal was wrecked on the Island. The captain allowed the blacksmith to fill his cellar with coal for the smithy.

Another coal ship had been wrecked back in 1916, but neither ship caused anything like the excitement aroused by the fleeing rum-runner which smashed onto the reef in 1934. The rum was in five gallon barrels which floated ashore. These were spirited off by the Islanders who stashed them away in hiding places where they became fair game for anyone who could find them. That rum saw the Island through a whole long winter.

Each year ended as it began with the Scottish rituals of Hogmanay and New Year's. Among them was the custom of shaking hands on the first encounter in the new year. This marked a fresh beginning and let neighbours know that the past was past and the slate was clean. Once again, the annual cycle could commence.

The strong sense of community grew out of a long tradition of sharing the work, the pleasures and the suffering of this world — a tradition which had been successfully transplanted from Scotland and nurtured in the isolation of Pictou Island. It was a community that was largely self-sufficient: the few necessities not supplied by the Island were met through trade with the nearby mainland and with Prince Edward Island or through seasonable labour in those places. With the coming of the twentieth century, economic and social ties with the outside world became stronger. At first, these seemed to benefit the Island, but later, especially after World War II, every structural change in the Canadian economy, every advance in technology and every piece of social legislation seemed to have an adverse effect on the community as a whole — although individuals did benefit — whether one is speaking of the impact of the changing scale and centralization of marketing, the coming of radio and television, the automation of the lighthouses, the consolidation of the school system, or the impact of unemployment insurance cheques.

In a hundred little ways, the Islanders found themselves forming links with the mainland which distanced them from one another. For instance, the coming of the gasoline engine for boats meant the end of the teamwork which had been necessary with sailing craft. One man could operate the "putt putt" engine whose fuel had to be bought on the mainland. Similarly, with the introduction of propane for cooking later on, the need for chopping frolics was diminished and dependence upon the mainland was increased.

There was remarkably little resistance to change. Most innovations were willingly adopted in the spirit of new world optimism. However, other changes, like the consolidation of the schools, which robbed the Islanders of their children, were accepted with a sense of fatalism born long ago in the Highlands of Scotland.

Fishing proved to have the greatest success in surviving and, occasionally, benefiting from the many changes taking place. Even today, it attracts many former residents back to the Island during "fishing time." Few traces remain of the old Island factories — they have long since moved to the mainland to be near the railway and to take advantage of the availability of electricity — and it has been many years since they provided not only seasonable jobs but also a market for fuelwood, eggs and other foodstuffs from the Island which were used to feed the workers. From the factories, in turn, came the vast quantities of lobster bodies which had been spread as fertilizer on the fields — the lime from the shells helping to sweeten the acidic soils. Goods taken to the company store were paid for in credit — not cash — which could be exchanged for items like sugar, prunes, raisins or tea.

All canning on the Island was done by hand. First the lobster was cooked using wood stoves. Then it was shelled and placed in cans which were sealed in a process using muriatic (hydrocloric) acid — much to the distress of the workers' fingers. The cans were then boiled for one-and-a-quarter hours in a bath also fired with wood. After removal from the bath, a small mallet was used to prick a hole in the lid to let the air out — not to mention much of the goodness of the lobster. Finally, the hole was soldered and, the following morning, was tested for leaks — which often occurred.

At first, the company owned the fishing gear and paid the fishermen for operating it. The more lobsters caught, the higher the income. Later, the boats, engines and traps were sold to the fishermen at a reduced price. Those without sufficient money found themselves immediately in debt to the company. Others also got behind when a poor season forced them to ask the company to carry them over to the next year. Aid was in the form of money (rather than goods) although the companies continued to operate stores. The system does not appear to have been excessively exploitive since the goods were sold at the going rate and no interest was charged on the loans. Indeed, some fishermen borrowed money which they did not need and put it in the bank for the interest it would earn.

No one really understood what went on in the secret world of the lobster at the bottom of the sea or why their numbers fluctuated from year to year for no apparent reason. One year, there might be scarcely enough for the fishermen's own tables, yet the next year, they would be "back strong" and there would be a good season. When the numbers were down there was talk of over-fishing and in more recent years, some of the blame has fallen on the scallop draggers whom the fishermen accuse of dragging the bottom when the lobsters are shelling. Today, scientists working both in the laboratory and at sea are beginning to unlock the mysteries of the lobster's life. As part of their study, lobsters are captured, dyed and released to learn just where they go.

"Fishing time" still beckons the Islander no matter where he might be living today, and important events like death and marriage are still remembered as having happened during fishing time. Some Islanders still manage to get back each year for a "spell of fishing" — opening the old farmstead with its familiar odour of mice and mustiness and the sound of buzzing flies racing to the tops of the windows only to drop down and start again. For a few weeks, there is a glimpse into the past, into the good old days; doors are once again open to anyone passing by, but the welcoming food on the table is from the sterile supermarkets of the mainland rather than from the farm.

Fields remembered by old men as gardens of Eden (nourished with lobster bodies) have been invaded by evergreens — advanced guards from the forest. They, in turn, are now being threatened by alders which are creeping from the cover of low-lying ditches towards the farm buildings themselves. Apart from a few kitchen gardens and a number of beef cattle and sheep, agriculture belongs to the past. The land, which had drawn the Islanders from Scotland so long ago and which had always been regarded as a sacred trust to be preserved in the family, is today slipping into the hands of strangers — to back-to-the-landers, to cottagers and to absentee speculators.

Why have the farms been let go? The reasons are many: the closing of lobster factories meant an end to the Island market for foodstuffs and for cordwood; the introduction of the Wood Island-Caribou ferry allowed Prince Edward Island producers to flood Pictou Island's traditional potato market on the nearby mainland; the closing of easily accessible grist-mills discouraged the production of grains; the mechanization of forestry meant that oats — traditionally the largest crop — were no longer needed for horses in the woods; tighter governmental regulations and transport difficulties spelled the end of dairying; raising chickens — fed on Island wheat — became less practical after foxes invaded the Island, apparently crossing on the ice in winter; and beef entering the local market from western Canada provided stiff competition for Island producers. No wonder Islanders felt buffeted by forces over which they had little control. Even an attempt to raise silver foxes went under after prostitutes in distant London diminished the fur's social cachet by flaunting foxes as a badge of office.

In the nineteenth century, before the coming of the railway and the settling of the west, Canada was very much a maritime country. Even in Ontario and Quebec, water was the favoured means of transport. Hundreds of boats plied inland rivers and lakes as well as the coastlines of the maritime provinces. Railways and, later, highways filled with cars and trucks led to the collapse of internal water transport until, by the 1950s, the only domestic water routes remaining were those providing links in the highway and rail systems. The very mentality of the country veered from water to land, leaving the Islanders isolated in another era. They could not fully enter into a life where people went shopping in cars for goods that had come from far away on a train or truck. Nor could they any longer sell their small — and varying — amounts of produce to local stores and wholesalers who now found it more convenient to buy from larger and more dependable sources elsewhere.

Without a harbour and (depending upon the period) with only one or two small wharves — and they were often in poor condition — the Island could not take boats of any size. In an earlier period, it was on the route of the small ferries plying between New Glasgow, Nova Scotia and Murray Harbour, Prince Edward Island. However, the modern car ferries between Caribou, Nova Scotia and Wood Island, Prince Edward Island bypass the Island to the west. Probably few of the passengers even notice that the Island is there.

Near the Caribou Ferry terminal, another ferry — really just a small fishing boat — can be seen setting-off for the Island early in the morning three times a week during the open season. There are usually only a few passengers on board — returning Islanders, cottagers, and the occasional tourist. Others reach the Island by air on the twice weekly, summer and winter, mail plane from Trenton. Provided it is not too loaded with groceries, it can take one or two passengers. Landing and taking off from the Island's narrow road is an adventure some Islanders try to avoid by closing their eyes. Helicopters are also available for emergencies and have been used to take patients to hospitals on the mainland. However, knowing that they can now leave the Island in time of sickness has not been enough to deter older residents from moving to the mainland to be nearer medical services.

In the old days, travel on the Island was by horse. Before the wharves were built, new horses from Prince Edward Island or the mainland were made to swim ashore from the ships bringing them over. Horses were much loved by the Islander — not only for getting around but for working the farms and for racing. At one time, there was one horse for every four Islanders. However, this ratio began to change in 1923 when the first car arrived — perched precariously on top of a small gasoline operated fishing boat. Then, as later, there were only five miles of road but the owner justified his purchase by pointing out that he lived at the far end of the Island. Despite the Island's small size, cars became common — partly because they were not licensed or inspected and were fueled with inexpensive coloured gasoline intended for farm use. Many were old wrecks when they arrived — cars which could not pass inspection on the mainland. After being driven "into the ground" on the Island, they were disposed of by being pushed over a cliff where they continue to rust away as eyesores. One man claimed that he had run his truck 80,000 miles on the five mile road. Tractors also became common and horses gradually went out of use altogether: the equine era ended ignominiously when the last horse backed into a well and drowned. Horses were fed oats and hay grown on the Island and, of course, produced offspring to share their tasks and to take over after they were gone; cars and tractors depended upon fuel and parts from the mainland and, in the absence of reproduction, had to be replaced. Unlike the horse, they supplied no fertilizer to enrich the fields. The old self-sufficiency and harmony with nature was being disrupted as dependence upon the outside world increased. Life speeded-up and the tiny Island became ever smaller. Even the dead were being whisked off to the cemetery in the back of the old horse drawn hearse now set on the back of a truck.

In a different way, changes in the telephone system also strengthened the connection with the outside world and weakened the bonds among the residents of the Island. In 1969, a microwave link replaced the cable to the mainland. Seven years later, the old crank phones were replaced by a dial system which provided more privacy since there were fewer people on each line and no operator.

However, this also lessened the sense of togetherness in a community which had always accepted that anyone could listen in.

Occasionally, eavesdroppers on the telephone were frustrated by older residents using Gaelic. Islanders "with the Gaelic" had learned it at home from parents who had made a point of not using English with their children. English was to be picked up later at school. Since the teachers were from the outside, few, if any, would have known Gaelic. English was the language of education. Yet as late as 1920 — a century after the Island was first settled — six of the 37 families still had Gaelic-speaking children. The school was a link with the future and was destructive of the ancient language and the old ways — unlike the church, which was a link with the past and a guardian of the old customs; by conducting services in Gaelic from time to time, it helped to keep the language alive. In the time of early settlement, when it was still widely used, Gaelic had helped to shelter the community from the full intrusion of the larger world but, as English became dominant, outside influences became stronger and much of the music, poetry and song which had been carried over from Scotland was lost. Even so, children from the Island who attended the West Pictou High School at Lyons Brook in the early 1970s, discovered that they spoke differently from the other students and were still dancing half-time and square sets when everyone else was into the twist. Perhaps this was surprising since the students had already been exposed to the outside world through television, radio and recordings before leaving the Island.

Recorded music had been around for a long time — since 1921, at least, when a man from Pictou brought over his new Edison phonograph and put on a musical entertainment in the Community Hall for a "large and appreciative" audience. It may have been the first time that the Islanders sat listening to a machine instead of making music themselves. The first radio came to Pictou Island in 1930. Like all radios of the time, it was battery-operated. By 1935, there were nine sets as the popularity of radio continued to increase. Television transmission began in the Maritimes in the late 1950s and it was not long before several Island households installed little gasoline electric generators so that they could operate television sets. There seemed to have been little interest in using the power source for lights and some owners regretted having bought the generators after battery-operated black and white televisions became available. (Colour television required on-line power and so has not been available on the Island. In recent years, it has become one more pull drawing people to the mainland.) During quiet winter evenings in the 1960s, one could hear the generators up and down the Island as people gathered to watch "Hockey Night in Canada" instead of going to the traditional Saturday night party and dance. Probably no force has been more destructive of the old ways than television — except for the consolidation of the schools.

As elsewhere in Canada, Nova Scotian schools were consolidated in order that students — especially at the senior level — could have access to better facilities and teaching than was possible in smaller schools. For these reasons it was decided that Island students reaching high school would be sent to the West Pictou School at Lyon's Brook, the closest regional school on the mainland. Rather than sending their children over to board, some parents preferred to keep the family together by moving to the mainland. If there were also younger children, they, of course, went along as well. Soon, there were too few children left to justify keeping the Island school going and, in 1971, it was closed — forcing the remaining parents with young children to follow the others to the mainland.

As individuals, the students probably benefited from being sent to Lyon's Brook. They gained from the science laboratories, the sports facilities, and an opportunity to form a wider circle of friends which helped them to overcome the shyness inherent in members of a tight little community. They learned to adjust to the values of the outside world — a necessary step before taking a job demanding regular habits and placing one's own interests, and those of the employers, above those of the community. Fishing and farming were looked down upon in the school. New skills were acquired, and goals were set that could not be achieved on the Island. In the end, few students found that they could ever go home again. As individuals, they were better able to cope with the wider world but the community which had nourished them had been destroyed.

Young Pictou Islanders have blended into life on the mainland and work at a variety of occupations in many different locations. For their parents, settling into regular jobs has not been as easy and there has been a strong tendency for them to quit work and go back to the Island during fishing time; they are still tied to the older rhythm of the seasons and the freedom of the fishing boat and the farm, rather than to the relentless ticking of the clock on the confining walls of the factory and office.

Thanks to old age pensions and other social services, those

reaching retirement now have a choice of either staying with family or retaining their independence and living on their own. In the days before social benefits became common, political patronage provided one of the few means for "getting something out of the government." At election time, several jobs were at stake — postmaster, lighthouse keeper, looking after the road, and working the lifeboats — so it was important to end up on the winning side. Jobs with pensions were the most sought after. Elections were thus times of great excitement — not to say of entertainment. Political allegiances were said to run in families, with wives and children taking their stance from the head of the household. Nevertheless, there were floating voters to be wooed, if not bought — a pint of rum or whisky was the going rate for a vote.

No social benefit has had a greater impact on the Island than the unemployment insurance cheque. Set up under a federal Act proclaimed in 1949, unemployment insurance at first had little effect on the Island since most of its population consisted to self-employed farmers and fishermen who were not eligible to receive benefits. However, in the 1950s, benefits were extended to fishermen who had worked so many weeks in the year — the number of weeks varied from time to time. This led Islanders to concentrate on fishing and to give up on farming rather than combine fishing, farming and, perhaps, another activity such as working in the woods or picking potatoes on Prince Edward Island, as had been done formerly. Since the lobster season was in late spring and early summer, the most convenient arrangement was to spend the winter on the mainland — especially if there were children in school — and the spring and summer on the Island. Unemployment insurance thus combined with poor markets for agricultural produce and the consolidation of the schools to depopulate the Island for much of the year. The Unemployment Insurance Commission also required that applicants for benefits be readily available for employment and not off on a remote Island. Ironically, the Unemployment Insurance Commission — born out of the modern industrial state — has helped perpetuate the old rhythm of seasonable activities by replacing part of the annual cycle of work with an insurance cheque sent through the mail.

Unemployment Insurance helped some members of a recent group of settlers to establish themselves on Pictou Islands. Misnamed "hippies" by the old community, they were part of the back-to-the-land movement which swept the industrial world in the 1960s and 1970s and resulted in a sprouting of "communes" from Hokkaido to the Isle of Mull. In spite of coming from many different geographical regions, the back-to-the-landers, or neopioneers, had a great deal in common and felt an international bond of fellowship. Within North America, there was a great deal of movement among the communes whether they were in California, the Maritimes, British Columbia or New England. Communes could be almost anywhere but preferred locations were on remote islands or on "the dirt road off the dirt road." Old, often abandoned, farms were favoured choices. The first sign neighbours might have that the neopioneers had settled among them could be simply a window patched with cardboard, or a poncho hung on the line, or it might be the beginning of a complete "restoration" of the house beyond anything ever imagined by its builder. Sagging roofs were straightened, aluminum doors were discarded, beams were exposed, old brick, tiny window-panes and barn-boards were added, and old, desiccated furniture was stripped bare. Such dwellings reflected the newcomers' fantasy of the local way of life, a way of life they were soon striving to preserve from the pressures of government, developers and, indeed, from the locals themselves. Parked beside the house might be a Volvo with university parking permits on the windshield, or a faded Volkswagen van with bumper-stickers bearing slogans of the latest causes of other places and other years.

Many of the commune dwellers were the products of homes where children instinctively jumped into open car doors to be delivered to little leagues, ballet or music. They knew about summer camps — horses, canoes, and leathercraft — and about all of the things they had been sent to camp to avoid. Without commitment, they had gone on to university and had heard about sociology and psychology before abandoning the ivory tower for the real world where they clumped together to discover themselves as individuals — in exactly the same sort of way. For them, never again the tyranny of middle-class suburbs, high-rise offices, or international corporations. They had gone back to the land. They were the neopioneers.

The neopioneers of the sixties and seventies came to the land with very different skills from the original pioneers of the early nineteenth century. They often knew little about farming, but unemployment insurance, tax laws, and welfare systems held few mysteries for them, and they were quite at ease in the whole alphabet of government granting agencies. In the back of their vans, along with recordings of yesterday's protest songs, were *Whole Earth Catalogues, Foxfire, Harrowsmith,* and a range of "where to" and "how to" books. In time, they came to admire the descendents of the original settlers among whom they had settled. They seemed like "real people." Through the windows of half-ton trucks stopped in the middle of the road, the newcomers learned the local lore about weather and crops, about hunting and fishing, and about things that went bump in the night. Half-assimilated local expressions slipped into their speech, and jeans, granny-dresses, and overalls were adjusted to the local scene. Imitation might be flattering but the caricatures it sometimes begot could be quite bizarre.

When a small group of neopioneers arrived on Pictou Island in the early 1970s, there was resentment — both against the new-comers and against the man whose land and barn had been sold to them through speculators. They were known as "the hippies" and were the butt of snide remarks and jokes. In a matter of days, however, the fishing season opened and they were out in the boats sharing the work with the Islanders. Acceptance came rapidly and the hippy label was dropped. They became known as "the people at the barn" and then as individuals with first names like every-body else. Their way of life was not approved of and there was a genuine concern for the welfare of "the girl," but the newcomers were sensitive to the feelings of the Islanders and did not confront them with their differing ways. From the Islanders, they learned much about fishing, farming and cutting the winter's wood. In return, they were good neighbours, repairing tractors, helping with the hay and even digging a grave. Most of the Islanders are now glad that they were there — "helping to keep the Island alive."

The old settlers had brought from Scotland a way of life which had evolved over generations of living in an environment not that dissimilar from Pictou Island. True, the winters were colder and the summers were warmer on Pictou Island and, instead of cutting peat for fuel, wood had to be chopped. Yet, in most essential ways, the old life could be carried on in the new land: the same crops could be grown and the same animals raised; wool could still be spun and woven into cloth; kelp could still be gathered for the fields; and even the same fish could be found in the sea. The basis was there for carrying on the same, largely self-sufficient life of the old world. All that was needed was to transfer the old beliefs, customs, and religion. It was accepted that the family was important and that the foundation of the family was land. Because of Pictou Island's small size, there was no agricultural frontier to tame and only those inheriting land had the means for remaining on the Island. This led to a very stable and conservative population.

The new pioneers were usually well educated and often idealistic but unlike the old settlers, they did not arrive with the skills necessary for self-sufficiency on the Island. They came as individuals and formed bonds looser than those of marriage and family. Although land was registered in one name, there was in the beginning an attempt to hold property and farm equipment in common and to share expenses — "the whole pie in the sky idea of a commune" as one of its members put it. Soon it was discovered that there was "always some greedy bastard who was taking more than his share and was not contributing enough." So they said "the hell with it" and from then onward, life became more and more private, and more and more like that of the old Islanders. Individual members now own and maintain the equipment and each person is responsible for his rows in the garden. Like the old Islanders, with their traditional head of the house, the newcomers have discovered that "what you need is a boss," someone to plan and organize the work — although no one seemed to want to take on the task. They have also discovered a need for privacy and have paired off into separate houses. At least one couple has now married and has children.

Unlike the first settlers, the newcomers were able to keep their ties with the world from which they had come and could go back from time to time to earn money. Indeed, the original idea of the commune was that it would be more of a base to come back to than a permanent home. It turned out, however, that there was always so much work to be done that there was little time to get away, and the neopioneers rediscovered what an old resident had always known when he said "I've been working for fifty years and I'm still not even near caught up."

For the newcomers, as had been true of the old residents, the Island increasingly became their world. Now, they, in turn, resent the intrusion of outsiders, especially when they are buying land. By the mid-1970s Island land was owned by residents in several

Canadian provinces and in at least six of the United States. Many owners were speculators who had never seen the Island but who had helped bid up the price of land far beyond its agricultural value. The only future now open to the Island would seem to be as a recreational area. A number of summer cottages have already been built and the Island is becoming increasingly popular with tourists. Thus where the Island was once self-sufficient, it is becoming totally dependent upon the outside world.

PART THREE

Contemporary Small Town Life

GEORGE J. DE BENEDETTI
and RICHARD J. PRICE

Population Growth and the Industrial Structure of Maritime Small Towns, 1971-1981[1]

THE PROMINENCE OF CANADIAN CITIES IN THE national settlement system has meant that little attention is given to the plight of villages and small towns. As Hodge and Qadeer argue, "the promise as well as the problems of the cities attract and hold much of our attention, consume much of our resources, and generate the culture and ideas that promote Canada as an urban society."[2] Yet, small towns continue to play an important role in the social and economic fabric of Canada. Such communities are especially relevant to the Maritimes where a majority of people lives in small towns.[3] In recognition of their importance, this paper both describes and explains some of the trends in Maritime small town population growth between 1971 and 1981. It focuses on the role of industrial structure for interpreting either the growth or decline of the Maritime small town. Two particular questions are addressed. First, do towns that depend on a single industry division (or on a small number of industry divisions) experience distinct population growth or decline patterns? Second, which industry divisions, if any, are conducive to population growth, and which are conducive to decline?

[1] The authors wish to acknowledge the help of our Mount Allison colleagues, Dr. S. Islam, Department of Economics, for reading earlier drafts of the paper and making several helpful suggestions; and Dr. L. D. McCann, Department of Geography, for familiarizing us with census materials and his encouragement. Any deficiencies are those of the authors.

[2] G. Hodge and M. A. Qadeer, *Towns and Villages in Canada: The Importance of Being Unimportant* (Toronto, 1983), p. 1. See also Roy Bowles, *Little Communities and Big Industries* (Toronto, 1982).

[3] *Ibid.*, p. 22.

For the purposes of this paper, a sample of 156 towns in Nova Scotia, New Brunswick, and Prince Edward Island was used. The size of towns varies in population from 156 to 9,684. Ideally, the sample should be based on Poetschke's definition of a community: "...the theory of community does tell us that a community must have an historical existence, a territorial boundary, an economic base, and a population with a sense of belonging. ...In other words, a community is what people say it is."[4] Unfortunately, the reality of census data precludes the adoption of such a definition. The selection criteria were as follows: the town must be reported as a census subdivision in the 1981 Census; and the town must not be part of the urbanized core of a census agglomeration area or of a census metropolitan area. To qualify for census selection, a town must exist as an incorporated political entity. This second criterion excludes towns on the fringe of larger centres where more than 40 percent of the residents work in the larger centre. For these "bedroom communities," it was assumed that population growth would depend largely on interaction with the larger centre, rather than on the local economy itself.

When delineating industries, use was made of the eight census industry divisions reporting the labour force categories for towns of less than 5,000 people (see Table 4). Statistics Canada's definitions of industries are problematic. Fishing, forestry, agriculture, and mining are aggregated into the "primary" division. Such a method obscures, for example, the number employed specifically in harvesting fish. Similarly, the number employed as fish packers is included in the broad manufacturing division. Thus, identifying the extent to which a town is dependent on the fisheries cannot be achieved with any degree of accuracy.

In reaction to the myth of small town extinction, regional scientists have successfully documented a process of small town persistence. Some scholars have even identified a recent period of counterurbanization within the North American settlement system. In the United States, for example, for the first time in this century, the nonmetropolitan population growth rate (10.5 percent) exceeded the growth of metropolitan areas (6.1 percent) between 1970 and 1978.[5] The total small town population in Canada grew

[4] Tom Poetschke, "Community Dependence on Fishing in the Atlantic Provinces," *Canadian Journal of Regional Science*, 7 (1984), p. 214.

[5] David L. Brown and Calvin L. Beale, "Diversity in Post-1970 Population Trends," in Amos H. Hawley and Sara Mills Mazie, eds., *Non-Metropolitan America in Transition* (Chapel Hill, 1981), p. 52.

by more than 25 percent between 1961 and 1981, which is smaller than the rate for urban places in the same period. Although the population growth rate for urban places was more than twice that of small towns between 1961 and 1971, the growth rate was about the same for small towns as for urban places between 1971 and 1981.[6] It would seem that the American pattern of counterurbanization has not characterized the Canadian settlement system. However, the evidence for Canada supports the notion of small town persistence, as it does for the Maritime provinces. Table 1 indicates that small town population has been growing at a lower rate (5.8 percent) than the regional population (8.4 percent). Previously, between 1971 and 1976, the number of small town inhabitants in the Maritimes grew at an identical rate to the entire population, but this trend did not continue. Between 1976 and 1981, while the small town population stagnated, the region's population continued to grow, albeit at a rate half that for the previous five-year period. Moreover, the Maritime's regional and small town population grew more slowly than Canada as a whole.

Table 1

Population Growth Patterns, 1971-1981

Year	Small Towns and Villages in the Maritime Provinces		Maritime Provinces		Canada	
	Population	Percentage Change	Population	Percentage Change	Population	Percentage Change
1971	245,078	—	1,555,158	—	21,568,310	—
1976	259,297	5.8	1,624,050	5.8	22,992,650	6.6
1981	259,198	0.0	1,663,651	2.4	24,343,180	5.9
Overall Growth Rate		5.8		8.4		12.9

Source: Calculated from data in Statistics Canada, *Census of Canada 1971, 1976, and 1981* (Ottawa).

Although the total small town population grew between 1971 and 1981, growth is not equally distributed across the towns — a trend common to other regions as well.[7] The diversity portrayed in Table 2 confirms that generalization about small town decline or

[6] Hodge and Qadeer, *Towns and Villages*, pp. 23 and 25.

[7] See, for example, Brown and Beale, "Diversity in Population Trends."

persistence would be entirely misleading. Some towns have enjoyed a doubling in size, while others have witnessed a greater than 25 percent decline. Nevertheless, when comparing positive and negative growth rates, the distribution of towns by population growth rates is skewed in favour of positive growth. For example, only 10 percent of the towns and villages declined by more than 15 percent, while 26.1 percent grew by more than 15 percent.

Table 2

Population Growth Rates for Maritime Small Towns, 1971-1981

Rate of Population Change	Number of Towns	Percentage of Towns	Cumulative Percentage
Over -25%	3	2.0	2.0
-16 to -25	9	6.0	8.0
-6 to -15	39	26.2	34.2
0 to -5	14	9.4	43.6
0 to 5	19	12.8	56.4
6 to 15	26	17.5	73.9
16 to 25	20	13.4	87.3
Over 25%	19	12.7	100.0

Source: See Table 1.

The initial size of the town appears to affect its growth prospects, as indicated in Table 3. Most towns of less than 1000 and greater than 3000 inhabitants declined, but towns between 1000 and 3000 people made up a disproportionate share of small town growth. However, towns of greater than 3000 people experienced the greatest population stability, with few towns either growing or declining at an accelerated pace.

Diversity in small town population growth trends has been identified but not explained. There are many economic and non-economic variables which could be included in the population growth equation. Proximity to other places, transportation advantages, residential development, industrial inertia, regional amenities, and government subsidization policies are just a few of the factors potentially influencing small town growth.

But what is the role of a town's industrial structure in this matrix of factors? A study by the Department of Regional Economic

Expansion (DREE) identifies towns that are dependent on one company, industry, or industry sector.[8] Although this study does not hypothesize about the effects of single-enterprise dependency on population growth, it did find that in Atlantic Canada, 36 percent of the nonmetropolitan population lives in single industry communities, compared with about 25 percent for Canada as a

Table 3

Average Growth Rates by Population Category and Percentage of Towns Experiencing Growth, 1971-1981

Population in 1971	Average Rate of Growth	Percentage of Towns Growing
0 to 500	-1.4%	50.0
500 to 1000	3.0	53.2
1000 to 1500	19.3	72.9
1500 to 3000	23.3	70.3
Over 3000	.5	39.1

Source: See Table 1.

whole. Maritime small towns tend to be more reliant on one sector or a few sectors, even though the employment structure of small towns in the Maritimes is similar to both regional and national employment patterns (Table 4).

Where the DREE Study found that a large proportion of the non-metropolitan population in Atlantic Canada lives in single industry communities, we attempted in Table 5 to establish the frequency of towns which had varying proportions of their overall employment concentrated in one, two, or three industry divisions. In this table, reference is made to an "ECR" variable, or employment concentration ratio, defined as the proportion of a town or village's total employment engaged in one or more industry divisions employing the largest number of persons in that town. A one industry ECR would be a ratio of the number of persons employed in a town's largest employing industry division to the total number of persons employed in that town. Similarly, a two industry ECR would be a ratio of the number of persons employed in a town's two largest employing industry divisions to the total number of persons

[8] Canada, Department of Regional Economic Expansion, *Single Industry Communities* (Ottawa, 1977).

employed in that town. The higher the value of the ECR, the more dependent economically a town is on a single industry division or a combination of industry divisions. Table 5 indicates, for example, that 14 small towns had 41-45 percent of their employment concentrated in one sector and that 143 or 92.3 percent had less than 45 percent of their employment concentrated in one sector.

Table 4

*Employment in Major Industry Divisions
by Percentage of Labour Force, 1981*

Industry Division	Small Towns and Villages in the Maritime Provinces	Maritime Provinces	Canada
Primary	8.9%	8.4%	7.1%
Manufacturing	19.6	15.4	19.1
Construction	6.2	7.0	6.2
Transportation, Communications and Other Utilities	6.9	8.5	8.2
Total Goods Sector	(41.6)	(39.2)	(40.6)
Trade	17.4	17.0	16.9
Finance, Insurance and Real Estate	3.4	4.0	5.5
Community, Business and Personal Services	29.0	28.7	29.2
Public Administration and Defence	8.6	11.1	7.8
Total Service Sector	(58.4)	(60.8)	(59.4)
Total	100.0	100.0	100.0

Source: Calculated from data in Statistics Canada, *Census of Canada, 1981* (Ottawa).

On average, 34 percent of their employment was concentrated in one sector. For the two sector case, 28 towns had 61-65 percent of their employment so distributed, whereas 87.2 percent had less than 65 percent. On average, 56 percent of their employment was concentrated in two industry divisions. In the three sector situation, 13 towns had 81-85 percent of their employment so concentrated, while 149 or 96.2 percent had less than 85 percent. On average, 71 percent of their employment was concentrated in three industry divisions.

The economic well-being of a town that is dependent on a single industry or on a single industry division is precarious, in that many factors affecting the industry lie outside the control of the local community. It is well beyond the scope of local business leaders to shield the town from external shocks such as declining demand, technological innovations, or changing foreign exchange rates,

Table 5

Small Town Dependency on Largest Industry Divisions, 1981,
by Percentage Employed in Industry Divisions

Percentage of Employed Labour Force	Number of Small Towns		
	One-industry ECR[1]	Two-industry ECR	Three-industry ECR
20-25	16		
26-30	39		
31-35	40		
36-40	35	3	
41-45	14	8	
46-50	3	32	
51-55	5	31	1
56-60	2	33	8
61-65	1	28	23
66-70	0	9	43
71-75	1	6	32
76-80		2	30
81-85		3	13
86-90		1	4
91-95			2
Total Towns	156	156	156
Average ECR	34.0	56.0	71.0

[1] ECR = Employment concentration ratio

Source: See Table 4.

interest rates, and commercial policies. Towns dependent on industries that are sensitive to market fluctuations are especially affected by exogenous shocks. For example, the economic fortunes of a mining town would largely rest on the world price and world demand for the mineral commodity.

To test the hypothesis that dependency on one industry division, or on a few industry divisions, is adverse to town population growth, we employed simple regression analysis. We used the ordinary least squares (OLS) model, regressing the rate of change in population between 1971 and 1981 with respect to various employment concentration ratios (ECRs).

The regression equations can be written as follows:

[1] Percentage change in population =
    .301   -.6228 ECR1
    (2.71)*   (-1.96)*

    R-square = .025

[2] Percentage change in population =
    .556   -.8334 ECR2
    (3.26)*   (-2.76)*

    R-square = .049

[3] Percentage change in population =
    .693   -.8493 ECR3
    (2.78)*   (-2.44)*

    R-square = .039

t values are placed in brackets.
* significant at the 95 percent confidence level, using a two-tailed student t distribution.

The first equation can be interpreted as follows: for every increase of one percentage point in the one industry ECR variable, there would be a decline of 0.6228 percent in the growth rate of population. Furthermore, if 10 percent of a town's employment were concentrated in the largest employing industry division, we would estimate the growth rate in population between 1971 and 1981 to be +23.8 percent. If 60 percent of a town's employment were concentrated in the largest employing industry division, we would estimate the growth rate in population between 1971 and 1981 to be -7.3 percent. The second equation can be interpreted as follows: for every increase of one percentage point in the two industry ECR variable, there would be a decline of 0.8334 percent in the growth rate of population. Similarly, the third equation can be interpreted as follows: for every increase of one percentage point in the three industry ECR variable, there would be a decline of 0.8493 percent in the growth rate of population.

The regressions confirm an inverse relationship between the respective employment concentration ratios and the rate of change in population growth. Although the coefficients of both the intercepts and the ECR variables are statistically significant, the low R-square values indicate that for the variation in the rate of growth in the population of small towns in the Maritimes, the ECR variables explain less than three percent variance in the case of a one industry ECR factor, less than five percent for a two industry ECR factor, and less than four percent for a three industry ECR factor. Nevertheless, to the extent that the ECR variable has influence, dependency on a dominant industry division does adversely affect the population growth prospects of Maritime small towns.

Table 6

Rate of Population Change by Degree of Dependence on Largest Employing Industry, 1971-1981[1]

Percentage Population Change	Least Dependent	Moderately Dependent	Heavily Dependent	Total
Over -10%	17.7%	47.1%	35.3%	100.0%
-5 to -10	16.7	54.3	29.2	100.0
-5 to +5	31.3	28.1	40.6	100.0
+5 to +10	35.7	21.4	42.9	100.0
Over 10	38.5	42.3	19.2	100.0

Raw chi-square = 12.93, df = 8, significant at the 80 percent confidence level

Source: Calculated from data in Statistics Canada, *Census of Canada, 1971, 1976, and 1981* (Ottawa).

[1] The towns were distributed in three equal divisions on the basis of a ranking from least to most dependent.

Another, less rigorous, approach to identifying the relationship between the rate of change in population growth and dependence on a dominant industry division was pursued. This method consisted of crosstabulating these two variables, as shown in Table 6. These results suggest an inverse relationship between the rate of change in population growth and dependence on a dominant industry division. For example, 35.3 percent of the towns that declined by more than 10 percent were heavily dependent on the largest employing industry division, while the same is true for only 19.2 percent of the towns that grew by more than 10 percent. Looked at another way, 38.5 percent of the towns that grew by more than 10 percent were least dependent on a single industry division, while only 17.7 percent of the towns that declined by more than 10 percent were least dependent on a single industry division. This analysis confirms the regression results, that is, there is an inverse relationship between the rate of population growth and the degree of dependency on a dominant industry division. The degree to which a small town is dependent on a single industry division would adversely affect its population growth.

Our regression and crosstabulation analyses support the expectation that the less diversified the economic base of a town is, the smaller will be the rate of growth in population. We next explore whether the growth rate of population is particularly sensitive to employment concentration in particular industry divisions. To do so we employed multiple regression analysis, using the OLS model, to establish the relationship between the rate of change in population — the dependent variable — and the proportion of employment in each of four industry divisions — the independent variables. The four industry divisions were: primary; manufacturing; trade; and finance, insurance, and real estate. We could not include all industry divisions as independent variables without running into the problem of multicollinearity. From the correlation matrix (not reproduced here), we were able to determine the likely existence of multicollinearity from among the four selected independent variables. The finance, insurance, and real estate division variable had a correlation coefficient of 0.42 with the primary activities division variable, and a correlation coefficient of 0.38 with the manufacturing industries division variable. The squares of these correlation coefficients exceed the R-square value of 0.069, which indicates that the finance, insurance, and real estate division variable does not function entirely independently from the primary and manufacturing industries division variables in explaining the growth rate of population.

The regression equation can be written as follows:

[4] Percentage change in population =
$$0.234 - 0.519P - 0.461M - 0.238T + 1.495F$$
$$(1.83)\quad (-1.71)\quad (-2.07)*\quad (-0.49)\quad (1.37)$$
R-square = .069
F-Value = 2.67 (significant at the 95 percent confidence level)

t values in brackets.
* significant at the 95 percent confidence level, using a two-tailed student t distribution.

Equation [4] can be interpreted as follows: for every increase of one percentage point in the proportion of employment in the primary industries division (variable P), there would be a decline of 0.519

percent in the growth rate of population. Similarly, for the manufacturing industries division (variable M), there would be a decline of 0.461 percent in the growth rate of population; and for the trade industries division (variable T), there would be a decline of 0.238 percent in the growth rate of population. For the finance, insurance, and real estate industries division (variable F), there would be an increase of 1.495 percent in the growth rate of population. Only the coefficient of the manufacturing industries division is significant at the 95 percent confidence level. The coefficients of the intercept and the primary industries division are significant at the 90 percent confidence level. The growth rate in population is sensitive to manufacturing, and to a lesser extent, primary activities. The relationship is a negative one, that is, that the growth rate in population decreases as the proportion of employment increases in these industry divisions. The R-square value of 0.069 indicates that only 6.9 percent of the variation in the growth rate in population can be explained by employment concentration in the four industry divisions indicated. However, the overall predictive power of the model is statistically significant, as indicated by an F-value significant at the 95 percent confidence level.

We also employed multiple regression analysis, using the OLS model, to establish the relationship between the rate of growth in population — the dependent variable — and two independent variables: ECR1, the employment concentration ratio in the largest employing industry division; and S, the proportion of employment in the service sector. The service sector comprises the following industry classifications: trade; finance, insurance and real estate; community, business, and personal services; and public administration and defence. Transportation, communications and other utilities as an industry division was included with the goods sector because this industry has very close linkages with the production and distribution of goods.

The regression equation can be written as follows:

[5] Percentage change in population =
 0.076 - 0.554 ECR1 = 0.375 S
 (0.51) (-1.76)   (2.22)*

 R-square = .057
 F-Value = 4.43 (significant at the 95 percent confidence level)

t values in brackets.
* significant at the 95 percent confidence level, using a two-tailed student t distribution.

Equation [5] can be interpreted as follows: for every increase of one percentage point in the proportion of employment in the largest employing industry division, there would be a decline of 0.554 percent in the growth rate of population. For the service sector, there would be an increase of 0.375 percent in the growth rate of population. The coefficient of the service sector variable is significant at the 95 percent confidence level. In this multiple regression model, the coefficient of the employment concentration ratio of the largest employing industry division is significant at the 90 percent confidence level. The growth rate in population is sensitive to the proportion of employment in the service sector. The relationship is a positive one, that is, that the growth rate in population increases as the proportion of employment increases in the service industry divisions. However, the R-square value of 0.057 indicates that only 5.7 percent of the variation in the growth rate in population can be explained by the employment concentration ratio in the largest employing industry division and employment concentration in the service sector. Still, the overall predictive power of the model is statistically significant, as indicated by an F-value significant at the 95 percent confidence level. The correlation coefficient between the two independent variables, employment concentration ratio in the largest employing industry division and the proportion of employment in the service sector, is 0.098. The square of the correlation coefficient is substantially less than the R-square value obtained, indicating a probable lack of multicollinearity.

Table 7

*Rate of Population Change by Degree of Employment
Intensity in the Goods Sector, 1971-1981*

Percentage Population Change	Low Intensity	Moderate Intensity	High Intensity	Total
Over -10%	23.5%	32.4%	44.1%	100.0%
-5 to -10	54.2	16.7	29.2	100.0
-5 to +5	37.5	28.1	34.4	100.0
+5 to +10	28.6	42.9	28.6	100.0
Over +10	25.0	53.9	21.2	100.0

Raw chi-square = 16.91, df = 8 significant at the 95 percent confidence level.

Source: See Table 6.

To complement the regression analysis, crosstabulations were run (Table 7). These show that 44.1 percent of the towns that declined by more than 10 percent had a relatively high intensity of employment in the goods sector. By contrast, only 21.2 percent of the fastest growing towns had a high intensity of employment in the goods sector. Of the faster growing towns, 53.9 percent had only a moderate intensity of employment in the goods sector.

Table 8

Rate of Population Change by Degree of Employment Intensity in the Service Sector, 1971-1981

Percentage Population Change	Low Intensity	Moderate Intensity	High Intensity	Row Total
Over -10%	41.2%	35.3%	23.5%	100.0%
-10 to -5	29.2	20.8	50.0	100.0
-5 to +5	28.1	37.5	34.4	100.0
+5 to +10	28.6	42.9	28.6	100.0
Over +10	21.2	55.8	23.1	100.0

Raw chi-square = 12.63, df = 8, significant at the 95 percent confidence level.

Source: See Table 6.

If the concentration of employment in the goods sector is conducive to population decline, then the opposite should hold for employment concentration in the service sector, when there is an overall positive rate of growth in small town population. The regression equation [5], and the crosstabulations in Table 8 support this conclusion. For example, 41.2 percent of the fastest declining towns are categorized as having had a low intensity of employment in the service sector. By contrast, only 21.2 percent of the fastest growing towns shared the same characteristic of a low intensity of employment in the service sector. However, 55.8 percent of the faster growing towns had a moderate intensity of service sector employment. This complements the earlier finding that 53.9 percent of the faster growing towns had a moderate intensity of employment in the goods sector. Perhaps, in terms of a town's growth prospects, there exists an optimal mix of employment between the goods and service sectors.

The results further indicate that the distribution of employment by various industry divisions does not explain much about small town population growth. Also, as depicted in Table 7, reliance on the goods sector, which includes the primary, manufacturing, construction, transportation, communications and other utilities, has been a partial source of small town decline. More specifically, the higher the intensity of employment in manufacturing, the more likely a town's population declined. Moreover, in contradistinction to the goods sector, a reliance on the service sector appears to have influenced positive small town population growth, although statistically, only one service industry division — finance, insurance and real estate — significantly and positively influenced small town growth.

Maritime small towns in the 1970s were not sheltered from the various structural transformations of the Canadian and global economies. The goods sector, for example, experienced significant change. The decline of the traditional 'smokestack' industries throughout North America has especially affected those towns dependent on manufacturing. Technological change and its concomitant labour market repercussions have included not only the advent of more labour saving modes of production, but a shift in demand towards a more highly skilled and specialized labour force that cannot be provided by most small towns. Tax breaks and incentives which favour more capital-intensive techniques have aggravated the problem in Canada. Such changes have affected traditionally labour-intensive industries, not only in the manufacturing sector, but in the primary sector as well. The fisheries industry, for example, underwent a major restructuring of the productive process in favour of increased capitalization,[9] slowing employment growth because more output could be produced with proportionately less labour input. In other ways, Maritime towns have been unable to attract high technology industries because of a relatively underskilled labour force and a desire on behalf of most firms to take advantage of economies of agglomeration offered elsewhere. Another consideration is that much of the period under study was marked by the global recession of 1973-1982. As the Western world adjusted to the shocks of two rapid oil price increases, there was an overall decline in world demand for the output of the primary and secondary sectors. Towns dependent on

[9] See, for example, L. Gene Barrett, "Capital and the State in Atlantic Canada: The Structural Content of Fishery Policy Between 1939 and 1977," in Cynthia Lamson and Arthur J. Hanson, eds., *Atlantic Fisheries and Coastal Communities* (Halifax, 1984), pp. 78-104.

such industries were generally confronted with shutdowns and layoffs.

Fortunately for the Maritimes, the service sector was conducive to town growth. Part of the explanation lies again with the shift in economic resources, including labour, from goods-producing industries to service-related industries. Canada, like most Western economies, underwent considerable structural change, whereby there was a marked shift of employment from the goods sector to the service sector. Table 9 illustrates this shift for both Canada and the Maritimes, but the trend is wider in scope. A study on the United States economy by David Menchik found that between 1970 and 1977, employment in the service sector grew by 24 percent. This rate is equivalent to four times the growth in the goods-related sector. As well, he found that the rate of growth in the service sector was not only greater for nonmetropolitan areas, but that the service sector accounted for 74 percent of the period's

Table 9

Proportion of Employment in Various Industry Divisions for Canada and the Maritime Provinces, 1971 and 1981

Industry Division	Canada		Maritime Provinces	
	1971	1981	1971	1981
Primary	9.0%	7.0%	9.5%	8.4%
Manufacturing	21.5	19.1	16.0	15.4
Construction	6.8	6.2	7.8	7.0
Transportation, Communications and Utilities	8.5	8.2	9.7	8.5
Total Goods Sector	(45.9)	(40.6)	(43.1)	(39.2)
Trade	16.0	16.9	16.4	17.0
Finance, Insurance and Real Estate	4.5	5.5	3.1	4.0
Community Business and Personal Services	25.6	29.3	24.6	28.7
Public Admin.	8.0	7.7	12.8	11.1
Total Service Sector	(54.1)	(59.4)	(56.9)	(60.8)
Total	100.0	100.0	100.0	100.0

Source: Compiled from data in Statistics Canada, *Census of Canada, 1971 and 1981* (Ottawa).

net gain in nonmetropolitan employment.[10] The significance of
this transformation for the small town economy is addressed by
Thomas Till: "that the service economy is becoming more dominant in non-metropolitan areas is consistent with a passage from an
industrial to a tertiary stage of development."[11]

Clearly, regardless of geographical setting, towns that evolved
with a strong service sector, and towns that were able to adapt in
response to post-industrial social changes, are in a better position to
provide employment opportunities, not only for the indigenous
labour force but for an influx of immigrants.

This paper has examined certain trends in Maritime small town
population growth between 1971 and 1981. The population of
small towns in the Maritimes did grow, despite the occurrence of a
major recession, but not all towns grew at a uniform rate. There is a
relationship between the size of a town and its prospects for growth.
The majority of the towns of less than 1000 and greater than 3000
inhabitants declined, while towns between 1000 and 3000 people
made up a disproportionate share of Maritime small town growth.
Towns with more than 3000 people experienced the greatest
population stability. No attempt was made, however, to explain
how population size itself affected the rate of population growth.

Small towns in the Maritimes tend to be more reliant on either a
single or few industry divisions than for Canada as a whole: 92.3
percent of the small towns studied had almost 45 percent of their
employment concentrated in a single industry division; 87.2 percent had almost 65 percent of employment concentrated in two
industry divisions; and 96.2 percent had almost 85 percent of
employment concentrated in three industry divisions. Because of
this dependency, we tested the hypothesis that dependency on a
single industry division or a few industry divisions was adverse to
small town population growth. Both the regressions and crosstabulations confirmed an inverse relationship between the concentration of employment in one, two, or three industry divisions and the
rate of change in population growth. Although the regression
models accounted for less than five percent of the variation in the
rate of small town population growth, the coefficients were statis-

---

[10] Mark David Menchik, "The Service Sector," in Hawley and Mazie, eds., *Non-
Metropolitan America in Transition*, p. 232.

[11] Thomas E. Till, "Manufacturing Industry: Trends and Impacts," in Hawley and
Mazie, eds., *Non-Metropolitan America in Transition*, p. 197.

tically significant, indicating that highly concentrated employment adversely affected population growth.

Where employment was highly concentrated, it was important to establish which particular industry divisions had the greatest impact on population growth. We found that population growth decreased as the proportion of employment in manufacturing and primary activities increased. The opposite was true for the finance, insurance, and real estate division, where population growth increased as that sector's proportion of employment increased. The coefficients for all three industry divisions were statistically significant: manufacturing and the finance, insurance and real estate divisions at the 95 percent confidence level; primary activities at the 90 percent confidence level. From economic theory and economic base analysis, we would not normally expect to find finance, insurance, and real estate as a leading sector in the economies of small towns. Because of the probable presence of some multicollinearity in regression model [4], the influence of this service division may not be an entirely independent cause of population growth. It could have been possible, for example, that the manufacturing and primary activities divisions adversely influenced the growth of population because technological change was making it possible to produce the same amount of output, but with less labour input. Lower labour input requirements, in the face of expanding output in these industry divisions, would have been conducive to producing a declining growth rate of population. At the same time, because output could have been growing in the goods-producing sectors, the derived demand for services like finance, insurance, and real estate would have been growing. Unlike the manufacturing, agriculture, mining, and forestry industries, it was not likely that technological change in terms of labour saving techniques was occurring as rapidly in finance, insurance, and real estate. The increased output in this service division required more labour input which was conducive to a positive influence on population growth. Thus, we concluded that this particular service division was not acting as a leading sector.

We pursued this issue further in regression model [5], testing to determine whether the service sector was leading growth or simply accompanying it. We found that the growth rate in population decreased as the proportion of employment increased in the largest employing industry division; and also that the growth rate of population increased as the proportion of employment increased in the service sector. More telling was the relatively low correlation coefficient of 0.098 between the independent variables: employment concentration in the largest employing industry division and the proportion of employment in the service sector. From this, we conclude that where a large proportion of small towns in the Maritimes was dependent on a single industry division, it was unlikely that such concentration of employment was in a service industry division. This reinforces our conclusion that the service sector was not an engine of growth in the communities under study.

The crosstabulation results of Tables 7 and 8, like the regression models [4], and [5], revealed that a high concentration of employment in the goods sector was a partial source of small town decline. These results also showed that a majority of the faster growing towns possessed only a moderate intensity of employment in the service sector. In terms of a town's growth prospects, there seems to exist an optimal mix of employment comprising both the goods and service sectors. A moderate concentration of employment in the service sector is a necessary condition — but not a sufficient condition — for growth. Results also indicate that the distribution of employment by various industry divisions explains only a small portion — less than seven percent — of the variation in the rate of population growth of small towns between 1971 and 1981.

Further research should be undertaken, perhaps on an individual town basis, to isolate the many relevant factors, both exogenous and endogenous, which account for population growth or decline. We do know, however, that towns moderately dependent on the service sector grew, and that towns highly dependent on the 'smokestack' and primary industries suffered decline.

PATRICK L. BAKER

Negotiated Objectivity: Weekly Newspaper Reporting and Social Relations in the New Brunswick Communities

For the journalist his sense of what makes news today is the result of long conditioning and subtle training in the knowledge of his audience and medium.... The 'values' of the journalist are established under constant pressures within the society he serves; there is a tension between his existence as a free or creative craftsman and the nexus within which he works.[1]

The people involved in making the news have to fit their activities into a complex social network.[2]

THE GROWTH OF THE MEDIA IN THIS CENTURY has generated both public and academic concern over its influence, as well as questions regarding its impartiality and objectivity. This study takes up these questions in relation to local community newspapers in New Brunswick by investigating the tensions between the journalist's professional ethic of objective reporting and the demands of social relationships in a small community. Weekly newspapers are a long-standing feature of New Brunswick journalism, and several have been in existence for over a hundred years. They therefore merit attention as a traditional aspect of social life in New Brunswick. But they are also part of a more recent phenomenon — the resurgence of the weekly press in Canada in the 1960s. As Paul Rutherford observes, "even the old country weeklies,

[1] Anthony Smith, *The Politics of Information* (London, 1978), pp. 143 and 145.
[2] John Hartley, *Understanding News* (London, 1982), p. 8.

aided by offset printing, had become more professional and more popular."[3] Thus, they merit our consideration for their function in contemporary society.

In the early part of this century there was a broad consensus concerning the media's influence on the public. The rotary press, film, and radio had created new mass audiences, a majority of which were urbanized and industrialized and thus thought to be rootless, alienated, and susceptible to manipulation.[4] In addition, there was a belief that the mass media successfully brainwashed people during the First World War and engineered the rise of Hitler and Mussolini. In this uncomplicated view, analysts revealed the media as powerful propaganda agencies brainwashing a susceptible and defenseless public. After the Second World War and into the 1960s, a second view emerged that was based upon empirical research. This perspective argued that the media had a very limited influence on its audience. People, it was argued, had prior dispositions, and were selective in what they exposed themselves to, and what they actually retained. People manipulated the media; they were not manipulated by the media.[5]

This view of the media was, in turn, challenged from two opposite directions in the late 1960s and the 1970s. On the one hand, empirical researchers argued that disciplined, rigorous research had shown the media to be persuasive in certain circumstances: where the media source is prestigious, trusted, or liked; when information rather than opinion is involved; and when monopoly conditions are more complete.[6] On the other hand, the Marxist and neo-Marxist critical tradition argued that ideological agencies played a central role in maintaining class domination and it was "false consciousness" to deny the media's impact.[7] The

---

[3] Paul Rutherford, *The Making of the Canadian Media* (Toronto, 1978), p. 80.

[4] James Curran et al., "The Study of the Media: Theoretical Approaches," in M. Gurevitch et al., eds., *Culture, Society, and the Media* (London, 1982), p. 11.

[5] See, for example, P. Lazarfeld et al., *The People's Choice* (New York, 1948); E. Katz and P. Lazarfeld, *Personal Influence* (Glencoe, Illinois, 1960); and J. Klapper, *The Effects of Mass Communication* (Glencoe, Illinois, 1960).

[6] See, for example, J. G. Blumer and C. McLeod, "Communication and Voter Turnout in Britain," in T. Leggett, ed., *Sociological Theory and Survey Research* (Beverly Hills, 1974); and P. Clarke and F. G. Kline, "Media Effects Reconsidered: Some New Strategies for Communication Research," *Communication Research*, 1(1974).

[7] See, for example, Tony Bennett, "Media, 'Reality,' and Signification," in M. Gurevitch et al., eds., *Culture, Society, and the Media*; and P. Q. Hirst, "Althusser and the Theory of Ideology," *Economy and Society*, 5 (1976).

conventional characterization of these perspectives as two distinct schools obscures their changing internal differences and the reciprocal influence which each exerts on the other. Among Marxists, there has been a shift away from the perception of the media as a stupefying and subduing force,[8] to a more interpretive view of audience selection from the dominant ideology.[9] This has been accompanied by their increased interest and involvement in empirical research. Reciprocally, those involved in empirical research agree that more attention should be paid to media influence on the ideologies which people use to make sense of their world.

Recently, media research has become interested in how, and for whom, media power is wielded. One line of investigation has examined the structures and practices of media organizations, borrowing from work done on formal organizations. Media organizations are seen to possess most of the characteristics of other large-scale industrial organizations: a hierarchical structure, an internal division of labour, and clearly specified goals.[10] The emphases of these studies are on intra-organizational structures and behaviours, the flow of new materials through the stages of selection and editing, and formal and peer control of media organizations. Their general conclusions have been that power is exercised informally and that the mechanisms of social control are embedded in a series of professional rewards. A second and recent line of investigation, following a fundamentalist-Marxist approach, has focused on the structure of ownership and control of the media. In these studies, the media is seen as a culture producing-industry which should be understood primarily in terms of its economic determination.[11] Here, the content and meaning of the media is found in its economic base. But demonstrating this relationship has been problematical, and there has been a reliance on the "fit" between the implicit ideology of the message and the interests of those in control.

[8] Herbert Marcuse, *One-Dimensional Man* (London, 1972).

[9] R. McCron, "Changing Perspectives in the Study of Mass Media and Socialization," in J. Halloran, ed., *Mass Media and Socialization* (New York, 1976).

[10] See, for example, W. Breed, "Social Control in the News-room: a Functional Analysis," *Social Forces*, 33 (1955); Walter Gieber, "Across the Desk: A Study of Sixteen Telegraph Editors," *Journalism Quarterly*, 34 (1956); and D. M. White, "The Gatekeeper: A Case Study in the Selection of News," *Journalism Quarterly*, 27 (1950).

[11] G. Murdock and P. Golding, "Capitalism, Communication, and Class Relations," in J. Curran et al., eds., *Mass Communication and Society* (London, 1977).

A third type of media study focuses on professional ideologies and work practices of the media. These have developed from early studies of professionalization.[12] One of the attributes of professionalism was the development of a professional ethos or ideology which defined the values and beliefs of the professions, laid down guidelines for behaviour, and so forth. Journalists, in fact, base their claim for professional autonomy on the dictum, "the people have a right to know."[13] Finally, researchers have investigated the interaction of the media with the socio-political environment.[14] Some studies have looked at this relationship from a Marxist perspective, while others have used a pluralist approach. Pluralist analyses emphasize the mutual dependence between media professionals and those in other institutions. Marxists, on the other hand, regard media institutions as minimally autonomous and locked into the power structure.

In summary, two major foci have dominated media studies. One concerns the production of message (content) and the other focuses on the message's effect (impact). In connection with production, a key concern has been the degree to which the media are passive transmitters or active interveners in the shaping of the message, and whether the media are a "mirror to reality." Such a view is held by media personnel who see their role as one of impartial and objective reporting — "getting at the facts." This view is supported by professional ideology as well as by the pluralist view of society in which the media are seen as providing a forum for the contending social and political interest groups that make up society. In this view, based on the notion that facts can be separated from values and that while comment is free, fact is sacred, the media are expected to reflect a multi-faceted reality as objectively and impartially as possible. On the other hand, there are those who use the notion of reflection, but in an inverted sense. Here the images and definitions provided by the media are "false." They are biased

[12] Gaye Tuchman, *Making News* (New York, 1978).

[13] These findings have been interpreted from two diametrically opposed perspectives. The pluralist viewpoint accepts media professionals claims to autonomy and objectivity and sees these as accounting for regulation within the media. Marxist interpretations, on the other hand, discount the claims of media professionalism and emphasize their subservience to a dominant ideology. But both camps share the view that powerful institutions and groups in society have priveleged access to the media.

[14] M. Gurevitch and J. Bulmer, "Linkage Between the Mass Media and Politics," in Curran, *Mass Communication and Society*.

because they are moulded by the interests of the ruling class, and are essentially opposed to the interests of the working class. They are significant because they produce and maintain false consciousness.

Both the masses and the media were products of the industrial revolution. Industry created a largely urban proletariate — the audience for the developing media. It was the effects of this same revolution that provided the central concern of nineteenth century sociologists; and it is clear from the above account that the insights of these sociologists, particularly Marx, have been used to interpret the meaning and role of the media in this century. For a theoretical framework, I propose to use the ideas of another commentator on nineteenth century society who, incidentally, was sympathetic to many of Marx's observations — Ferdinand Tonnies.

Tonnies, like Marx, was interested in persons and in social relations, and not in reified structures and institutions. He saw people as essentially social, relating to others in two ways: in a natural, total way in relationships with family, kin, and neighbours; and in a contractual, partial way in formal relationships with strangers. The importance of the former lies in the shared aspect of relationships which generate traditions, values, common understandings, or feelings of belonging. The significant aspect of the latter is that relations are abstract, formal, and contractually specific in which the medium of exchange is largely money. In this case, there is a veil of politeness — of civilized manners — in these relations, while underneath individuals ruthlessly pursue their own goals. Man lives by making choices and decisions and by organizing his feelings, instincts, and thoughts. In short, he exercises his will. In the former context, according to Tonnies, man uses 'natural will,' weighing the many-sided aspects of community involvement in his decisions. In the latter case, man uses 'rational will,' emphasizing only rational thought directed towards 'artificial' individual action. Feelings are subordinated to reason and custom is not respected.[15]

These two types of 'willing' predominate in two types of context which Tonnies untranslatably called *Gemeinschaft* and *Gesellschaft*. He describes the community *(gemeinschaft)* as made up of members bound together in natural relationships of the kind already noted, who share intimately their work and life within a familiar, valued

[15] On this point, see: Ronald Fletcher, *The Making of Sociology*, vol. 2 (London, 1972).

territory. "It is a broad(er) relationship of solidarity over a rather undefined general area of life and interests."[16] In contrast, *gesell-schaft* is a social world built on a complex network of formally and rationally devised associations. People are members of this world in a contractual sense, but only in so far as they think such associations are useful to themselves as a means to attain certain ends. Thus, "relationships rest[ed] entirely on means-ends assessments, calculations, manipulations, and utilizations."[17] As Parsons argues, "the keynote of *Gesellschaft* is the 'rational pursuit of individual self-interest.' Relationship is to be regarded subjectively as a means by which the individual attains his own ends."[18] Clearly, Tonnies saw *gemeinschaft* as typifying traditional rural communities, *gesell-schaft* the growing industrial society.

Furthermore, for our purposes, as noted above, *gesellschaft* gave birth to the mass media. It was in this *gesellschaftlicht* context that the impartial, objective, aloof, and dispassionate ideal of news reporting was born. Here, the metaphor of the mirror is appropriate. It also leads us to consider the concept of objectivity.

"The concept of the mirror with its attendant series of questions — do the media offer a faithful reflection of reality, or do they mirror the real in a one-sided, distorting way? — has haunted the study of the media since its inception."[19] Such an image of the press is itself an historical product. In the early nineteenth century newspapers existed to persuade their readers and thereby persuade government. Tuchman writes that, "early nineteenth-century newspapers did not carry ads either. Published more regularly, generally as weekly newsletters, these were firmly attached to political parties, purchased by subscription, and circulated among a party's members. Their columns were filled with what we would now call news analyses, including scurrilous attacks on opposition leaders."[20] Readers bought the paper for its opinions and editorial writers were the key to news organization. This was changed by the end of the century. Telegraph and wire services could transmit pictures of what had actually happened, presenting events with apparent impartiality. The task of the newspaper now became to

---

[16] Talcott Parsons, "A Note on *Gemeinschaft* and *Gesellschaft*," in W. J. Calnman, ed., *Ferdinand Tonnies: A New Evaluation* (Leiden, 1973).

[17] Fletcher, *The Making of Sociology*, p. 29.

[18] Parsons, "A Note," p. 141.

[19] Bennett, "Media, 'Reality,' Signification," p. 287.

[20] Tuchman, *Making News*, p. 17.

take this 'factual' picture, to embroider it, rearrange it, and perhaps even propagandize it: "the news agency created the idea of there being an irreducible core of pure fact."[21] As a consequence, an editor no longer used ideology as the source for his writing; he now sought out information.

This is not to argue that newspapers dismissed propaganda as something you did to the news, for there was a terrible carnage of truth in press reporting during the First World War, for example. However, public opinion recoiled in horror at the misuse of the press in 1914-1918, and began to emphasize the responsibility of the newsman. At the same time, there was a drive by newsmen for more professional newsroom control over content in opposition to the interests of the owners. A battle of wills emerged between editors and owners, sometimes of an almost daily nature. Today, the public views the press as being separate from government, standing over government as the Fourth Estate; the readers, as the expression of market forces, are deemed inviolable. Underlying this view is the notion that authority militates against credibility. So, "the twentieth-century journalist . . . came to inherit two contrary sets of duties: on the one hand he was now the agent of opinion, the conscript soldier in the social battle of ideas, the employee of a free press living by controversy; on the other hand he had become tied to an ethic of pure fact, he was expected to put truth before everything else."[22] To handle this dilemma, the basis for journalistic training became the complete bifurcation of fact and opinion and, indeed, the ascendance of fact over opinion. So the journalist, cornered, will mutter that he or she deals in facts, and that "facts speak for themselves!"

The argument, in this paper, is that the media's image of itself, as well as the public's view of their role, has arisen out of *gesellschaft-licht* contexts. The image of the ruthless, objective, story-hungry journalist is the epitome of rational, individual *gesellschaft*. But how do these notions fit into the partial *gemeinschaftlicht* context of New Brunswick communities? It will be argued that the media is not divorced from the community and is, therefore, moulded by the community. The whole notion of control of the media is raised again, but in a different way; not as an investigation of some top-down conspiracy, though this may exist, but rather from the

[21] Anthony Smith, *The Politics of Information* (London, 1978), p. 149.
[22] *Ibid.*, pp. 149-150.

bottom-up, as the notion of an embedded and therefore not free press in a community. Three specific arguments were formulated from these general considerations of the *gemeinschaftlicht* nature of community newspaper contexts and the *gesellschaft* image of their profession. It will be argued that: (1) the media, through its embeddedness in the community's business sector, is thereby 'controlled' by the former, particularly through the need for advertising revenue; (2) the role of the reporter is affected by the context of a small community which has subtle effects on the quest for objectivity; and (3) at an ideological level, newspaper personnel have adopted *gemeinschaftlicht* values and a community world view.

In order to seek answers to these questions, a survey of local papers in New Brunswick was undertaken. The research involved three phases. First, a list of New Brunswick newspapers was compiled from the *1983 Ayer Directory of Publications* and the editors of these papers were identified and interviewed. This phase of the research was designed to yield data on such matters as the history of the paper, its ownership, staffing, philosophy, resources, circulation, difficulties, and relationship to the community. It also provided descriptions of the community in which the paper was produced. In a second phase, six weeks were randomly selected from 1980 and then each paper for these weeks was analyzed for its size, editorials, letters to the editor, features, number of international, national, provincial and local stories, and pieces on sport, women's issues, and hobbies, as well as advertisements and photographs, amongst other material. In all, one hundred and forty-five variables were identified and examined. The data from the content analysis of these newspapers were computerized and analyzed for significant and typical patterns. Finally, Statistics Canada data were used to create additional information about each community. While these data are quite inadequate in comparison with what a detailed community study would reveal, they did yield general characteristics of the community context.

There are thirteen communities in New Brunswick with twenty-two local weekly newspapers, and three cities with five daily newspapers. The former communities vary in size from 1,208 (Grand Falls) to 12,044 (Edmundston). The major industry is primary for six communities; processing for three; service for three; and clerical for one. The communities are relatively stable. They experienced an out-migration rate of just over three percent between 1976 and 1981, but this is biased by the military presence in Oromocto and Chatham where the regular transfer of personnel is commonplace. Excluding these two communities, the out-migration rate is less than two percent. Seventy-two percent of the townspeople were born in New Brunswick and it is likely that a high percentage are natives to their communities. If Oromocto and Chatham are omitted, the New Brunswick-born figure rises to 85 percent.

Although there is a certain stability to these communities, they are certainly not "communities" as defined by Tonnies. Although they may be small in size, this does not mean that they share *gemeinschaftlichte* features.[23] Nevertheless, as Berreman tentatively observes, "scale can be used to refer roughly to the size of a society, as size influences the nature of social organization."[24] So, for the purposes of the argument, the qualitative difference between New Brunswick communities and the larger centres is sufficiently akin to the distinction that Tonnies makes between gemeinschaft and gesellschaft.

In 1980, 27 newspapers published actively in New Brunswick, of which 22 were community weeklies. The combined circulation of these papers was over 262,000, of which nearly 130,000 were community weeklies in non-metropolitan areas. It has been estimated that 75 percent of New Brunswick households in non-metropolitan areas receive a community newspaper. This is considerably higher than the Canadian average of 56 percent.[25] The papers vary in circulation from the *Telegraph Journal's* 98,862 to the *News'* 3,115. They are located in seventeen communities which vary in size from 115,000 (Saint John) to 1,034 (Hartland). Several are the only papers in the community, as in Sackville, Edmundston or Grand Falls for example, or they may be one of three newspapers in a relatively small community, as was the case in Campbellton (Table 1).

The number as well as the circulation of papers has changed with time. Since the beginning of the research, *L'Evangeline*, the French daily, has folded, and the *Moncton Times* and *Transcript* have merged, as have *Le Point* and *Le Voilier*. The *Tribune* has been

---

23 For a discussion of this problem, see: Frederik Barth, ed., *Scale and Organization* (Oslo, 1978).

24 Gerald D. Berreman, "Scale and Social Relations: Thoughts and Three Examples," in Barth, *Scale and Organization*, p. 50.

25 Canadian Community Newspaper Association, *Community Markets: Canada 1985* (Toronto, 1985), p. 205.

bought out by the *Graphic* in Campbellton, and three new papers, the *Citizen* in Saint John and the *Miramichi Headwater* and *Le Voilier — Le Point* in Caraquet have started. The community newspaper business is therefore dynamic. For the 1980 study year, *L'Evangeline* and the *Graphic* were treated as operational, but the *Citizen*, the *Miramichi Headwater*, and *Le Voilier — Le point* were excluded from analysis.

The papers have varied histories. *The Moncton Times*, for example, was started in 1868 by Thaddeus Stevens, becoming a daily in 1877 and serving as an influential Conservative mouthpiece. To coun-

Table 1

Selected Characteristics of Study Communities
and Local Newspapers

| | | | Newspaper Characteristics | | | |
Community	1981 Population	Name	Type	Date Founded	Owner	Circulation
Bathurst	4870	*LePoint*	W	1978	Y. Cormier	4000
		Northern Light	W	1913	Thompson	7934
Campbellton	9818	*L'Aviron*	W	1962	M. Desrosier	6342
		Graphic	W	1908	A. C. Anslow	4000
		Tribune	W	1905	R. Raymond	5965
Chatham	3743	*Miramichi Weekend*	W	1964	D. Cadogan	7780
Dalhousie	2430	*News*	W	1929	D. Cadogan	3115
Edmundston	12044	*Le Madawaska*	W	1913	J. L. Boucher	8639
Grand Falls	1208	*Cataract Weekly*	W	1952	S. J. Merritt	4180
Newcastle	2929	*Miramichi Leader*	W	1906	D. Cadogan	8525
Oromocto	9604	*Post*	W	1906	N.A.	4500
Perth-Andover	1872	*Victoria County Record*	W	1972	D. Henley	3808
Sackville	5654	*Tribune-Post*	W	1872	Tribune Press	3205
St. Stephen	1752	*St. Croix Courier*	W	1865	R. Granville	8568
		Couriere Weekend	W	1978	R. Granville	3619
Sussex	2047	*Kings County Record*	W	1887	D. Henley	8415
Woodstock	1455	*The Bugle*	W	1963	D. Henley	6845
Moncton	54743	*Times*	D	1877	Irving	
		Transcript	D	1882	Irving	
		L'Evangeline	D	1887	Irving	
Saint John	115000	*Telegraph Journal*	D	1868	Irving	
		Times-Globe	D	1904	Irving	
Fredericton	43723	*Gleaner*	D	1880	Irving	

Sources: Canadian Community Newspaper Association, *Community Markets: Canada 1985* (Toronto, 1985); and Statistics Canada, *Census of Canada 1981* (Ottawa).

teract Conservative influence, William Robertson founded the *Transcript* in 1882. For years there was a bitter rivalry between the two papers, but this ended in 1945 when the papers merged, through their purchase by the New Brunswick Publishing Company. Jack Irving then acquired the papers, along with the Fredericton *Gleaner*, in the mid-1970s, and the papers were physically merged in 1984 to form one paper, the *Times Transcript*. The *St. Croix Courier* also has a long history. It was started by David Main in 1865 and is the oldest weekly newspaper in the Atlantic Provinces. Since 1920 it has been run by the Granville family. The *Graphic* of Campbellton, started in 1907, remained a family newspaper. *Le Madawaska* was established in Edmundston in 1913 and bought out by M. Boucher in 1923, the father of the present owner. Other newspapers have shorter histories: the *Bugle* in Woodstock (1963), the *Miramichi Weekend* (1964), the *Victoria County Record* of Perth-Andover (1976), and most recently the *Miramichi Headwater* (1984) and the *Citizen* (1985).

Monopolization characterizes the ownership of both dailies and weeklies. The Irving family own the New Brunswick dailies. Recently, David Henlley has acquired the *Kings County Record* to add to his ownership of the *Bugle* in Woodstock and the *Victoria County Record* in Perth-Andover. David Cadogan now owns four community newspapers: the *Miramichi Leader*, the *Miramichi Weekend*, the *News* and the *Miramichi Headwater*. M. Alphe Michaud, described by one publisher as "the biggest French media man in the province," owns two newspapers and at one time was involved in four. Although these monopoly patterns have been subject to investigation, currently there is more public concern in New Brunswick over government press control, because the provincial government has helped finance the new French daily which replaced *L'Evangeline*. But one Acadian journalist commented that it was all very well for the anglophone press to worry about government control, for they already had three dailies to chose from. Newspapers, he argued, were an important dimension of Acadian life and culture, and government assistance was essential to meet this basic need.

This discussion of media control brings us to the heart of the research problem. It was argued that the community paper may not only be controlled from above, but also controlled through its embeddedness in the community and through the particular outlook it and its reporting staff adopt as a result. These issues are

addressed by examining: (1) the relationship of the paper to
advertising; (2) the role of the reporter; and (3) the ideology of the
community newspaper.

A problem that community newspapers face is that they are
writing for two audiences, the public and the advertisers. Advertising is the major source of revenue. This may be inferred from the
amount of space allocated to advertising. Seventy percent of the
weekly newspapers allotted a 70-30 split: 70 percent advertising
and 30 percent story. Several editors commented that weekly
newspapers initially ran into financial problems with the advent of
television, because the advertisers directed their money towards
the electronic media. With the recent growth of cable television,
however, there has been a marked improvement in newspaper
advertising, because with the accompanying proliferation of stations,
it has become more expensive to reach the public. Now businessmen are again using the weekly newspapers to reach the buying
public. This swing back to advertising in the community newspaper has enabled many papers to bear increased costs of production. Editors interviewed said they will think very carefully before
running a story that is critical of a major advertiser.

Supermarkets are clearly the dominant business to use newspaper space, and in many cases their advertising is crucial to the
paper. Their importance to the newspapers, as well as their
potential influence, is reflected in the fact that the day for publishing the paper is often selected for their benefit. All but four of the
weeklies are published on Wednesdays, specifically giving readers
time to notice the advertisements before shopping on the weekend.
Two papers are published on Thursday, while two others are
weekend adjuncts to Wednesday papers.

In a sense the dailies seem to be somewhat less affected by
advertising. There is not the same fluctuation in their size as a
result of advertising. Although the average size of dailies (32 pages)
and weeklies (28 pages) does not differ markedly, there is a
significantly greater range in size within weeklies in comparison
with dailies. Weeklies may range from 12 pages to 48, whereas
dailies range only from 23 pages to 38. Even more significant is the
greater range in size that exists within a specific weekly paper in
comparison with a specific daily. The greatest range in size for a
daily was 20 pages, for both the *Gleaner* and *L'Evangeline*, whereas
the greatest range in size for weeklies was 66 pages for the *Courier
Weekend* and 38 for *Le Madawaska*. The important point to be made

here is that these page differences are made up largely of advertising. Advertisers judge that a particular event or celebration will be good for business and their demands swell the paper. The data suggest that community newspapers are more susceptible than the dailies to advertising demands, and this accounts for their greater fluctuation in size. This, in turn, supports the argument that the newspaper writes for the advertiser as well as for the public, and thus is controlled to some extent by the former. Are there similar controls exerted on the journalist in his reporting role?

The stereotypical journalist is an individual who gets the facts irrespective of the cost. He stands apart from the story or event, dispassionately observing and portraying what is happening. As noted earlier, this characterization grew out of an industrializing, urbanizing world and is the image associated with large-scale media operations. Media personnel, who work on the studied community newspapers, did not identify themselves with this image; instead, they claimed a role that was different from those who worked for daily newspapers and in urban situations. The emphasis appeared to rest more on maintaining relationships within the community rather than getting the story. They observed that as reporters, they would meet the same people they wrote about on a daily or at least regular basis, and that to ignore this would lead to ostracism in the community. As an ex-reporter observed, "It is easy for dailies to attack important figures, they are usually hundreds of miles away, if not geographically, then at least socially." But, as local reporters observed, this is not the case in a small community where face-to-face *gemeinschaftlicht* relationships have to be maintained. "You are going to meet the same person on the street next day!" These observations clearly derive from the journalist's experience of living in the community in which he or she also works, and indicate that the community, therefore, does exert some control on reporting.

This dimension of the journalist's role in the small community was also alluded to by some editors when they discussed the staffing of their papers. Several editors said that they would prefer to hire someone from within the community who knew the community, rather than someone from a journalism school with all credentials, but who was also a "foreigner" to the community. Indeed, one said that he would prefer to train someone from within the community than have them attend journalism school. In answer to the question why this was preferable, he said that such a person "would

know how to get on in the community." All those interviewed who
had been to journalism school said that when they started work on
the community paper, they had to dissociate themselves from
much of what they had learnt, although they did feel that their
education was still an advantage.

It was noticeable that while the community and most of the staff
on weeklies are relatively stable, there is a high turnover among
reporters. This is usually expressed in terms of "seeking greener
pastures" and "here just getting experience on the job." This may
well be the case, although several editors had worked their way up
to their positions within the same newspaper. But whatever their
motives and however much they have internalized a self-image of a
reporter as a "go-getter of facts," what they report in the weeklies is
not so much a reflection of concern for objectivity, but rather the
editors espousal of community values.

Finally, it can be argued that the community controls the local
newspaper by persuading the personnel to unconsciously adopt the
values of the community. Several editors commented on the
"humane values" that permeate the weekly press. "The community
newspaper is interested in and committed to the community. It has
a character quite different from the dailies." "We are here for the
people. We perform a service to the community." The newspaper
is interested in the "human" angle not so much because this will
sell, but because this is the "proper" angle.

This concern for local values is visible in the focus of the weekly
newspapers. On average the dailies carried 15.7 foreign news
stories, 24.8 national stories, 12.12 provincial stories, and 14.3 local
stories. All carried at least one foreign, national, provincial, and
local story. In contrast, the weeklies carried 2.18 foreign stories, 5.3
national stories, 7.8 provincial stories, and 40.8 local stories. Fifty-
nine editions carried no foreign news at all, 15 carried no national
news, and 20 carried no provincial news.

A comparison of daily and weekly newspapers by topic indicates
that both favour sport in their coverage (18.5 sport stories per
edition for the dailies and 8.4 per edition for the weeklies). But here
the similarities end. Apart from their coverage of sport, the most
frequent stories of the dailies focus on national politics (4.9 stories
per edition) followed by provincial stories (2.6). Comparable
figures for the weeklies are 1 and 1.2. These interests are clearly
different from the most popular topics of the weekly press: community business and local economy (3 stories per issue); the work of

local voluntary associations (2.9 stories); and local entertainment and local education matters (2.6 and 2.7 stories, respectively). Thus, the weekly newspapers carry far fewer political stories than do the dailies, and far more community-oriented stories. In total, the dailies carry 11 political stories per issue, of which less than one on average deals with local politics. The weeklies, on the other hand, carry 5 political stories per issue and usually more than two of these deal with local politics.

At a professional level the press presents an image of impartial objective investigation, but the weekly newspapers in fact reflect community values — they tend not to disturb the peace. They do this by distancing themselves from coverage of power-related, political stories. They also minimize controversial opinions by limiting or omitting local editorial comment in the paper and by running historical pieces or "freelance-opinion" columns by the likes of John Porteous, Roger Worth, or John Fisher. These are written by 'strangers' to the community who usually discuss matters that are only of tangential interests to the community.

The title of this essay indicates an apparent contradiction in terms: objectivity is not open to negotiation. But we see, in fact, that it is, in a sense, negotiated. An implicit, perhaps even unconscious, agreement is reached in the community as to what the role of the community newspaper should be and how journalists should proceed. The title was used to focus on a particular aspect of a particular phenomenon: the problem of impartiality and objectivity in the small town newspaper. It highlights a special strain that the media encounter in this *gemeinschaftlicht* context.

RICHARD PAUL KNOWLES

Guysborough, Mulgrave, and the Mulgrave Road Co-op Theatre Company[1]

G UYSBOROUGH COUNTY, NOVA SCOTIA SEEMS
at first glance an unlikely place to find professional theatre. Occupying the rugged northeast corner of mainland Nova Scotia, the
county is made up of spruce forests, rocky coastlines, and small
fishing villages, with little industry apart from the fish plant in
Canso, and no community exceeding that town's population of
1255. Yet just down the road from Canso is Guysborough town, less
than half the size of Canso and the home of the Mulgrave Road Co-
op Theatre Company.

Mulgrave Road is a small, co-operatively run company founded
in 1977 "to provide theatrical awareness," according to its articles
of incorporation, "which will assist in the socio-economic development of Eastern Nova Scotia, primarily Guysborough County." As
General Manager Ed McKenna wrote in an addendum to the Co-
op's Canada Council application in 1980, "we are first theatre
artists who wish to produce work of a standard equal to theatre
anywhere. But we also exist as a company to practise the art in
Guysborough County where we can help to stimulate the community toward self-awareness and provide it with a means to
articulate its own point of view. In this way we can make a
contribution to the social and economic development of the area,
which, like many rural Maritime communities, struggles to achieve
material progress without sacrificing its heritage, traditions and

[1] The author would like to thank members of the Mulgrave Road Co-op, especially
Ed McKenna, for their generous assistance and hospitality during the preparation
of this article; and the Small Town Life in the Maritimes Research Committee,
especially Larry McCann, for financial and moral support. A shorter version of this
paper appeared in *New Maritimes* 3 (August, 1985), pp. 4-6. A version of this paper
appeared in *Canadian Drama / L'Art dramatique canadien*, 12 (1986), pp. 18-32. The
research uses newspaper clippings and archival material in the possession of the Co-
op. This is usually not footnoted but is referenced in the text when full bibliographic
evidence is available.

values." McKenna writes elsewhere (in a brief to the 1983 Cultural
Policy Conference) that "without culture there can be no community, because without the spirit that culture embodies, [nor] the
character, tradition, and set of values that are shared by members
of a community, a community cannot exist as a distinct entity, no
matter how great its material wealth."

In the short ten years since Robbie O'Neill, with co-founders
Gay Hauser, Michael Fahey, and Wendell Smith mounted *The
Mulgrave Road Show*, the Company has achieved a remarkable
degree of success. Always popular and critically acclaimed in the
Maritimes, their productions of shows such as *The Coady Co-op Show*
and *Bring Back Don Messer* (both with playwright Chris Heide), and
particularly Alistair MacLeod's *The Lost Salt Gift of Blood* and
Robbie O'Neill's *Tighten the Traces/Haul in the Reins*, have received
national attention. Their national success has received financial
recognition, too, in the form of awards from the du Maurier
Foundation as well as the Canada Council, but Mulgrave Road's
audience is not in the first instance a national one. As for many
small regional collectives across the country, the key to their
success is their relationship with their own community. Their
commitment to creating and touring indigenous theatre within the
region was recognized in the fall of 1983 by a special award from
the province.

The Co-op began operations in the town of Mulgrave (population c. 900). Their first production, *The Mulgrave Road Show*, was
based on material gathered from area residents and then shaped
and developed by the actors into a series of scenes and songs that
celebrated the residents' spirit and sense of community, while
making searching comments on the area's history and its political
and economic plight. The show began historically, with a Nova
Scotia that was the most prosperous partner in Confederation and
that traded away its self-reliance for dependence on others. It
moved through a trenchant but hilarious sequence by Wendell
Smith on "The Guysborough County Railroad," a political carrot
in the area for 25 years. Work on the famous "railroad without any
trains" began in 1908, and was finally abandoned in 1931 with
only 22 miles of track laid. It became a symbol of political
manipulation and neglect for the region in the early decades of the
century. The famous Canso Causeway also came under scrutiny in
the show, serving as it did to transform the town of Mulgrave from
a busy port and terminal for the Canadian National ferry to Cape

Breton, to a virtual ghost town, whose main street became known as "plywood avenue" because so many of its stores were boarded up. After the construction of the Causeway the town was left with no movie houses, no community centre, no restaurants, and very few jobs. The message was carried on the feet of some lively verse, this time by Michael Fahey:

> They say that the Causeway was for
> progress comin' through
> But when it came it took away
> everything I knew
> 900 men worked on the railroad
> and on the ferry docks
> But the Causeway came and sealed their fate
> with a mighty pile of rocks
> We called it Black Friday
> and we still recall that name
> For nothing in Mulgrave
> has ever been the same.

Finally, *The Mulgrave Road Show* looked at a present-day Guysborough County, whose only remaining source of income — the fishery — is threatened both by environmental damage caused by the Causeway and by industry brought in to rescue the ailing economy of Cape Breton — those primarily ill-conceived and unprofitable "mega-projects" that are eventually shut down by succeeding governments.

The Guysborough County resident is left with a choice between "goin' down the road," or "goin' on the dole," a choice summarized by a song that framed the show and gave it and the Co-op their name. The lyrics are from "The Mulgrave Road," a poem published in 1951 by Charles Bruce of Port Shoreham, Guysborough County, and named after the shore road that runs between Guysborough and Mulgrave:

> If they stay they stay, if they go they go;
> On the Mulgrave Road it's a choice you make.
> There's an axe in the stump and a fork in the row
> Or a bag to pack and a train to take...

When *The Mulgrave Road Show* opened in Mulgrave on 13 July 1977, with half the population of the town in attendance, the St. Lawrence Parish Hall shook with laughter, applause, and the shock of recognition. Tributes poured in throughout the summer from politicians, journalists, educators, the theatre community, and most importantly, from local residents. The show was described in *The Scotia Sun* (Port Hawkesbury, Nova Scotia) as "a celebration of the sense of community that is today the only remaining asset of this struggling area."

Following this initial success, the group was urged to stay together. With the help of local community development worker Roy Ryan, who provided indirect financial support and helped with the company's application for a Canada Works Grant, Mulgrave Road was kept afloat for a second year. Ryan finally talked Robbie O'Neill into driving to Truro in December of 1977 to register the company as a legal Co-op; it is, I believe, the only theatre group so registered in English Canada. The Company had made the transition from one-show sensation to respectability and recognition, and had at the same time formalized its co-operative structure. Although the details of the artistic direction of the Co-op have changed over the years, the company is still a legal co-operative, and as such is perhaps unique among professional theatre companies in being required to report annually to the provincial Department of Agriculture.

Since 1977 the Co-op's productions have continued to combine humour and song while probing the region's social and economic conditions, viewed usually in a historical context. In 1978, *Let's Play Fish* (a show based directly on a winter spent in Canso town among the fishermen) examined the plight of the inshore fishery through the eyes of a Canso family over two generations. The play follows the evolution of a traditional way of life caught between the pressures of urbanization and the increasingly corporate nature of the fishery. The central character, Gerald, moves in the course of the play from baby to neophyte fisherman, to disillusioned trawlerman, to young alcoholic, to going down the road, and finally to returning to the community as a government official trying to explain new fisheries department programmes to his confused father. His role ends with his attempt to run for political office. In spite of problems finding appropriate personnel for the production — theatre people in Nova Scotia, like fishermen, tend to go down the road — the show opened in Canso on 1 July 1978 with Mary Vingoe, Gay Hauser, Robbie O'Neill, and Barry Dunn in the cast. It received very favourable reviews, many of which commented on the importance of a company "who create their material," as the Halifax *Chronicle-Herald* reviewer remarked, "from the experience of the people they work and live with. The images utilized by the actors are not pre-packaged in Toronto or New York, but originate in local Nova Scotian experiences."

The exploration of Nova Scotian experiences continued in 1979 with a revival of *The Mulgrave Road Show* and a production of *The Coady Co-op Show*, developed with playwright Chris Heide. The show dealt with the Antigonish movement, Fathers Moses Coady and Jimmy Tompkins, and the founding of the co-operative movement in eastern Nova Scotia. It was mounted collectively and performed in the familiar presentational style of the Co-op. Its narrative line — the stories of the founders and of the people themselves — was interspersed with speeches by Mackenzie King, Coady, and Tompkins, as well as by songs and skits that carried the bulk of the political and historical import. There were impressive comic sequences, including a satiric co-operative family supper and a hilarious and highly theatrical physicalization of the co-operative message. For this scene, three actors banded together to play a guitar, a banjo, and a fiddle in an octopus of arms and legs as each chorded one instrument while strumming, picking, or bowing another. The show was sponsored in part by Co-op Atlantic and it celebrated the founders of the movement to which Mulgrave Road belongs. But as the reviewer for the *Scotia Sun* (4 July 1979) said: "the show didn't lose sight of the fact that the grand ideas of the founders have since been supplanted." It lodged "the sensible plea that they be re-examined."

In 1979, the Co-op moved from Mulgrave to Guysborough, the county seat and home of the county museum. Though an even smaller town (population 512), it was a place that the Co-op felt was more appropriate for their purposes and closer to the heart of the community.

One year later, in 1980, the Co-op presented productions of *One on the Way* and the popular *Bring Back Don Messer*, written by Chris Heide. *One on the Way* was the Co-op's first production outside of what had been its Summer/Fall touring season. Created collectively by the cast — Gay Hauser, Nicola Lipman and Mary Vingoe, with director Svetlana Zylin — it dealt with the often neglected subject of the roles, pleasures, and problems of rural women, taking its title from the refrain of one of its songs: "She may not have known it / And not always shown it / But there was always one on the way." The show grew out of a powerful quilt-making sequence by Gay Hauser in *The Mulgrave Road Show*, and its mosaic of monologues, skits, songs, and interviews involving women of different ages and situations resembled the structure of the quilt itself.[2] The composite, sometimes moving and often amusing was, like a quilt, more than the sum of its parts, and it portrayed a strong and linked community of women as the backbone of Guysborough County. And as reviewer Greg Dennis wrote in the *The Chronicle-Herald* (6 June 1980), "*One on the Way* was not elaborate or fancy — but then again, neither is life in Guysborough, N.S."

Bring Back Don Messer was in some ways a departure for the company. Because of the popular and controversial nature of the material, including the infamous cancelling of *Don Messer's Jubilee* in 1969 by the C.B.C., the show was booked to tour not only the usual smaller centres throughout Nova Scotia, but also larger centres throughout the Maritimes, including Halifax's Rebecca Cohn Auditorium, the Confederation Centre in Prince Edward Island, and the cavernous Convocation Hall at Mount Allison University in Sackville, New Brunswick. The company, at this stage in its development, was clearly not ready for this type of exposure, and this was reflected by mixed reviews in Halifax and elsewhere. Nevertheless, as an attempt to produce a completely scripted two-act play that also involved a playwright fully in the collective process, the show was a step forward for the Co-op. It was clearly their most ambitious offering up to that time.

Bring Back Don Messer was conceived and first researched by Chris Heide with director and company manager Ed McKenna between the fall of 1979 and the spring of 1980, and was then written by Heide in an early version at the Banff Playwrights Colony under the direction of Larry Lillo. The script was then workshopped in Guysborough for ten days, six weeks prior to the regular rehearsal period. The result was a serious play with a more coherent and controlled dramatic structure than the Co-op's usual song-and-sketch format, and one that posed with considerable technical skill a central question, summarized in *The Chronicle-Herald* (1 August 1980) by Michael Fahey as, "are we no longer participants in cultural life, [but] merely consumers of pre-packaged entertainment?"

Playwright Heide focused on a single family in Goldboro, Nova Scotia, whose members stay the same age as the years pass from

---

[2] See Cindy Cowan, "A Message in the Wilderness," *Canadian Theatre Review*, 43 (1985), p. 106.

1914, in the opening scene, to 1969, the year the Messer show was cancelled, at the end of the first act. In the second half, which brings the action up to the present, the characters age a year with each scene. Unlike John Gray's recent and heavily nostalgic play, *Don Messer's Jubilee, Bring Back Don Messer* wisely and cleverly avoided putting Messer and his Islanders on stage, focussing instead on Messer's typical audience in Guysborough County. The play moves from an early scene in which a family and a community entertain one another with songs, stories, and dances; and progresses through the advent of radio and television to the days of imported, pre-packaged entertainment that isolates and fragments — rather than welds together — its audiences. If the show itself was perhaps under-rehearsed, the script was ambitious, serious, and effective. In performance it provided its own alternative to the kind of mass entertainment that it so tellingly probed. Michael Fahey remarked that "we hope to be able to bring to each community some of the excitement and spirit which accompanied the Islanders wherever they toured," and it was not accidental that, as *The Evening News* of Stellarton reported (26 September 1980), the tour followed a schedule "reminiscent of the tours once conducted by Don Messer himself."

In 1981, *Guysborough Ghosts* drew on the local oral tradition in a lighthearted, collective creation directed by a co-founder of the Co-op, Wendell Smith, that nicely balanced the same year's production of *Victory! The Saga of William Hall, V.C.*, directed by Graham Whitehead. *Guysborough Ghosts* was highly entertaining comedy, and its subject was as much story telling itself as it was of ghosts. Reviewers within the region all expressed pleasure at seeing familiar people and events and in hearing familiar accents and folklore; but as a script, the pastiche of songs and skits was more notable for planting the seeds of later shows than for its own qualities. Its most notable character, Leo Kennedy, would later inspire the Co-op's most widely popular show, Robbie O'Neill's *Tighten the Traces / Haul in the Reins*; and its best story was later developed by Cindy Cowan, like O'Neill an actor in *Guysborough Ghosts*, into the intricate and haunting poetry of *Spooks: The Mystery of Caledonia Mills*. But perhaps the most significant feature of *Guysborough Ghosts* was its set, conceived and executed by the Co-op's resident designer Stephen Osler, and described by the reviewer of Thunder Bay, Ontario's *Chronicle Journal* (2 June 1981): "eerie red and orange lighting displays misshapen walls of weathered drift-

The main street of Guysborough town and, in the foreground, the converted theatre, once Henry Marshall's general store.

THADDEUS HOLOWNIA

wood draped with torn streamers of old cloth, and at the back is a
cloth-shrouded window where shadows form and just as mysteri-
ously disappear. Howls and screams echo in the growing dusk."

Stephen Osler's design was also a prominent and effective
feature of *Victory!* This design made excellent use of a ship's mast
and yard arm to capture the spirit of the days of sail as background
for the story of William Hall, the first Nova Scotian, the first
Canadian sailor, and the first black man to win the Victoria Cross.
The actors sang ringing sea songs while hauling anchor or raising
sail; and they made effective use of a versatile cannon, as well as a
fog machine and strobe lights during the central battle at Lucknow,
where Hall won his medal. The script, developed by the cast and
director.from a draft by journalist Mike Paterson, was conceived as
"a celebration," according to director Whitehead, "rather than
... an introverted debate with racial overtones" (*The Chronicle-
Herald*, 22 August 1981). Nevertheless, it was unstinting in its
presentation of the times in all of their hardship, including a
brilliantly performed sequence by Buddy Doucette on the cat
o'nine tails. And the celebration was never simplistic or naive. The
scene in which Hall was awarded his Victoria Cross, in fact, was
ironically interspersed with a description of the brutality by which
the British avenged atrocities committed during the Indian mutiny,
atrocities which were themselves graphically described. As the
reviewer for the Nova Scotia Dramatists' Co-op *Newsletter* (October,
1981) wrote: "these scenes... reinforce the irony of history, its
tragedy and its farce, the personal heroism and the racism. For
racism is at the root of imperialism." The show was celebratory in
tone, and its portrayal of William Hall was sympathetic, dignified,
and full of good humour. In terms of design and of subject matter, it
represented a further broadening of Mulgrave Road's scope. As
the coherent narrative of an individual life contained within the
familiar framework of songs and skits, it represented a further and
successful experiment using dramatic structure within the collective method.

At the end of 1981 the Co-op could look back on five successful
years of creating and touring new Nova Scotian plays within the
region, years in which it had never ceased to experiment and
expand. They were poised to enter their most successful year, and
to face the changes that inevitably accompany success.

In early spring, 1982, Mulgrave Road presented the first version
of Robbie O'Neill's *Tighten the Traces/Haul in the Reins*, an affec-

tionate portrait of Canso native Leo Kennedy that followed his
growth from a boyhood struggle with cerebral palsy, polio, and
prejudice, to a manhood characterized by strength, dignity, and
good humour. *Tighten the Traces* was a one-man collective, shaped
by O'Neill but derived almost entirely from stories told to the actor
by Leo Kennedy himself, with music provided by Nathan Curry.
The show was originally intended for school audiences, but it met
with so much success that it was remounted for a week of lunchtime
performances at Neptune Theatre in Halifax, where it received
rave reviews. The Co-op remounted the show again the following
spring, at which time Nathan Curry was replaced by Cape Breton
fiddler Ronald MacEachern, who wrote and performed new music
and songs. At the same time, David Gibbons was hired to design
lighting and sets, and one of Canada's best directors, Peter Froeh-
lich, was brought into work with O'Neill on the performance and
script. It was this version that was taken on tour across the country
and into Maine, England, and Scotland, and that served as the
basis for the C.B.C. television production that won O'Neill a
Thespis award for best performance from the Atlantic region of
ACTRA. Producer Kent Stetson won the same award for best
production. Performed together with a stage adaptation of Alastair
MacLeod's short story, "The Boat," the show received very favourable reviews and standing ovations across Canada and abroad.
When performed at the National Arts Centre in 1983, it won for
O'Neill a best male actor award from the Ottawa Drama Critics
Association. The show was later nominated for the Chalmers
award for best Canadian play performed in the Toronto area in
1984, and for a national ACTRA award for best television production of the year.

Also in the spring of 1982, the Co-op offered *Another Story*, a
collective creation that looked at the incongruence between the
lives of the beautiful people on the T.V. soaps and those of the
Guysborough County residents who watch them. Scenes and songs
by unemployed and uninspired members of the community were
juxtaposed with scenes based on the soaps themselves, complete
with commercial breaks. A song by area residents with the refrain
"the anger and despair I feel is real," followed tellingly in the wake
of the earlier lyric, "with a sunny smile and fresh-washed hair/You
too can be a millionaire." Elsewhere, a group of rural women sang
of the dislocation and dissatisfaction bred by the continuing presentation of "another world" as reality:

.The passion, the sex, the infidelity,
Wish that some of this could be happening to me,
But I live in another world.

The strength of the show, in fact, derived in large part from its
music and lyrics, composed by Marsha Coffey and director Jan
Kudelka. The closing song provides a good contrast between the
entertainment offered by the Co-op and the escapism of the soaps:

Tell me a story
    that's different from mine
That I can get lost in
    passing the time.[3]

After a production of *Road Reviews*, a compilation by Chris Heide
of highlights from their earlier shows directed by Don Allison and
sponsored by the Province of Nova Scotia for Nova Scotia's Old
Home Summer in 1982, the Co-op mounted what became its most
ambitious and effective show. This success was a stage version of
Cape Breton author Alistair MacLeod's *The Lost Salt Gift of Blood*,
the collection of stories, and the production, from which "The
Boat" was drawn. The script received its first workshop with
Alistair MacLeod and director Svetlana Zylin in June 1981, after
which MacLeod and Robbie O'Neill took it to the Playwrights
Colony in Banff before rehearsals began in Guysborough in September 1982, under the direction of Hans Boggild.[4] The resulting
production was a haunting, poetic piece of narrative theatre that
received enthusiastic reviews wherever it was performed. The first
act was a montage of sequences from a variety of stories, focussing
on images of loss and loneliness. It climaxed with a deeply moving
dramatization of "The Road to Rankin's Point," featuring a
riveting, gut-wrenching performance by Nicola Lipman as an
elderly woman approaching death. The production was note-
worthy for the author's resonant, poetic prose, for excellent performances from Nicola Lipman, Robbie O'Neill, John Dart and
Carol Sinclair, for the music of Ronald MacEachern, and for
designer J. P. Camus' evocative, earthy set. It moved powerfully
beyond the particulars of time and place in the second-act drama-

---

[3] I am indebted in my account of *Another Story* to Sine MacKinnon's review in *The Casket* (Antigonish, Nova Scotia), 21 April 1982.

[4] For a detailed discussion of *The Lost Salt Gift of Blood*, see Richard Paul Knowles, "Co-operative Theatre on Mulgrave Road," *Canadian Theatre Review*, 37 (1983), pp. 51-54.

tization of "The Boat," when one man's attempt to come to terms
with his Cape Breton past became the ritual enactment of the
death throes of a culture.

The production set a new standard for the Co-op, and presented
them with new problems as well. The size of the show raised
questions about the appropriateness of their usual venues — it had
to be performed at their rented Guysborough location, the local
Masonic Hall, on the floor space usually reserved for the audience,
while the audience was relegated to the small stage at one end of
the hall. This raised, too, the whole question of audience: did they
wish to perform in the region's small town and village movie
theatres and in local high school auditoria, or was their proper
audience the more sophisticated habitués of arts centres in larger
towns and cities? Equally vexing were the problems raised by sheer
success. There was talk of moving to Halifax; of seasons that
included more scripted work, perhaps work from outside the
region, or outside Canada; and of relaxing their mandate to do
only new work. The company's increasing artistic success also
raised new audience expectations and new ambitions and goals
among Co-op members. The Co-op's gradually increasing government funding, moreover, created tensions with the home community, some of whom resented the spending of government
money on theatre in an economically depressed region where so
many were unemployed. Some of these concerns were softened in
the spring of 1985 in a characteristic way, as the Co-op mounted a
rollicking old-fashioned collective on unemployment called *Occupational Hazards*, directed by Carol Chrisjohn. The show was
inspired by a short story by Lesley Choyce, but based once again on
interviews, this time with Cape Bretoners, and molded into shape
by the cast and director, with the assistance of *Fighting Days*
playwright Wendy Lill. The production, like the collectives of
old — though with a tighter structure and consistent characters —
was a witty, sympathetic, and timely representation of the concerns
of its own audiences. A sardonic programme note expressed concern about cutbacks in arts funding, remarking that "the members
of this company are frequently unemployed."

In the wake of *The Lost Salt Gift of Blood*, several organizational
changes were made. The evolving shift to a regular winter season
was consolidated. There was an acceleration of what had been a
gradual increase in the broadening of Co-op membership, as new
personnel such as Carol Sinclair, Mary-Colin Chisolm, Wanda

Graham, and future artistic directors John Dartt and Gary Vermier, were brought in to work on *Another Story*, *The Lost Salt Gift of Blood* and productions of the 1983-4 season. Two scripted works were produced in that season, and the only collective was the annual Christmas show. Unfortunately, neither Mary Vingoe's *Holy Ghosters* in the Fall nor Cindy Cowan's Spring offering, *Spooks: The Mystery of Caledonia Mills*, received very favourable reviews, even though audience response was good. Both were relatively large-scale, non-musical shows produced after the fashion of *The Lost Salt Gift of Blood*.

Holy Ghosters was the first non-collective by the Co-op. It used a period setting and costumes to explore the plight of Nova Scotians in 1776 who were caught between the unpopular British and the invading rebels from America. Inspired by Thomas Raddall's novel, *His Majesty's Yankees*, the script was a sensitive treatment of complex issues, and it encompassed the very different points of view of the recently-expelled Acadians, the rebel sympathizers, those loyal to the British throne, and those attempting to survive the conflict through compromise or delay. Reviewers praised the powerful presentation of the play's strong central women, played by Wanda Graham and Mary-Colin Chisolm, but many, perhaps unaccustomed to seeing famous men in supporting roles,[5] were critical of the presentation of Richard John Uniacke, who was to become one of Nova Scotia's most prominent and respected political figures, as a vacillating though pivotal minor character. Reviewers also expressed some confusion over the play's organization, confusion caused by what the playwright herself describes as excessive doubling, which forced director Jan Kudelka to link the play's fourteen scenes by means of slow-motion changes and musical bridges, the latter provided by composer Marsha Coffey. The doubling, of course, was done out of economic necessity. While displaying the impressive skills of the company, it undermined some of the qualities of a script that is among the best that the Co-op has produced. It has since been revised at the Banff Playwrights Colony, and will hopefully receive a second production in the near future.

Cindy Cowan's play *Spooks: The Mystery of Caledonia Mills* dealt with Mary Ellen MacDonald, a Guysborough County girl whose "spook farm" was the subject of international press attention in

[5] See Cowan, "A Message," p. 108.

1922, and who excites controversy in the region even today. The script was workshopped in September 1983, and again in a "text personalization" workshop with voice and movement coach Rita Howell, before it opened in Guysborough on 8 March 1984. It deals with unusual events, including mysterious fires that took place at Alex MacDonald's house in Caledonia Mills, Nova Scotia — events that remain debated but unexplained. Based on extensive archival research by Cowan, the play is nevertheless far from documentary in style, pitting as it does the "facts," as represented by prominent American parapsychologist Dr. Walter Franklyn Prince, who investigated the case, against other, perhaps deeper truths. As Cowan writes in her notes to the unpublished script, "*Spooks* is a folktale about a culture's colorful and imaginative response to what they don't understand." Unfortunately, many reviewers came expecting the suspense and excitement of a traditional ghost story rather than the play's probing of the roles of myth and faith in a scientific age, and they consequently found the play as directed by Linda Moore "neither particularly scary nor the compelling puzzle it purports to be" (Barbara Senchuk, *The Chronical-Herald*, 17 March 1984).[6] There was, nevertheless, praise for excellent performances by Carol Sinclair, Mary-Colin Chisolm, Gary Vermier and John Dartt, as well as for the always effective sets of Stephen Osler.

In the wake of the 1983-4 season, and now faced with tension over the direction the Co-op should take and with the resignation as co-artistic director of founder Robbie O'Neill, the Co-op met in September of 1984. The task was to review its position, to find a workable administrative structure, and to discuss mechanisms for the artistic direction of the Co-op. Several options were discussed in a weekend-long meeting, but it was finally decided that the Co-op would meet each fall to select an artistic director from among the membership — defined at the meeting as all those who had worked with the Co-op. This director would run the company on behalf of the group and according to principles and guidelines

---

[6] See also *ibid.*, pp. 108-09, where the playwright says that "I tried to reveal the true story of a young girl unfairly accused of setting fires in her parents' home. I attempted that the girl's story had been manipulated by the media to promote newspaper sales and, in the same way that journalists sought out the 'thrills and chills' of the story in 1921, they again sought them in the play. Expecting spine-chilling 'ghosts and spooks' they criticized the play for not living up to their expectations."

outlined by the membership at the meeting, for a thirteen-month period beginning the following May. The meeting also unanimously reaffirmed the Co-op's dedication to new work by Nova Scotians and about Nova Scotia — they workshop several new scripts per year — and to the co-operative principles on which the company was founded. There was also commitment to a physical and visible presence in the town of Guysborough. They decided to purchase the building — the town's old fire hall — in which the meeting was held.

These decisions, in spite of the pressures of success, seem to have been wise ones, and the purchase of the old fire hall — their first purchase of real estate — has also helped to solidify the Co-op's relationship with its home community. With the help of a federal job creation grant, the Co-op hired six people (a significant number in a town with a total population of 512) to work throughout the spring and summer of 1985 on the renovation of the building, including restoring the Main Street facade to its nineteenth-century appearance when the building served as Henry Marshall Jost's store. As explained in the Co-op's April newsletter in 1985, their hope is that "the preservation of this structure will contribute in a very positive way to the attractiveness and continued redevelopment of Guysborough's Main Street. . . . And, of course, the greater profile our theatre will gain in the community will be a real benefit to us."

Mulgrave Road, like Saskatoon's 25th Street Theatre in *Paper Wheat*, or Theatre Passe Muraille in *The Farm Show*, not only produces theatre that is about the people that are its audience, but because it draws on local stories, characters, and history, it produces theatre that reflects that audience as co-creators. In a supplementary letter to their Canada Council application for 1980, Michael Fahey and Ed McKenna explain: "Because we use the "collective creation" process to produce "indigenous theatre", we require the participation of a great many members of the community as resource persons, who will be open with us about their experiences and attitudes, and permit us to use this information in our shows. The people of Guysborough County have been very generous with us in allowing us to use material of a highly personal nature, and have shown a confidence in our abilities to handle such material with sensitivity, for which we are very grateful. Without this generosity, we could not function in the way we do, and we could not produce our theatre."

In speaking so immediately to, and on behalf of, its community as audience, the Co-op returns theatre with unusual naturalness and directness to its spiritual roots.

Unlike many other regional collectives, Mulgrave Road is very much a part of the community it celebrates and reflects. In the fall of 1984, their production of *In My Father's Footsteps* was a disturbingly personal look at the generation gap in the county, explored by the re-enactment of Robbie O'Neill's visit with his father the previous summer to the site of O'Neill Sr.'s wartime service as a member of the "Devil's Brigade," an elite Canadian-American commando unit that fought in southern Italy. In spite of the workshopping of the script with Michael Fahey and Paul Thompson, Robbie O'Neill's closeness to the material was the source of the production's significant weaknesses as well as its emotional impact. The production, housed in designer Stephen Osler's stylized hotel room and framed by jagged barbed wire and sand bags, veered between psychological naturalism and a symbolic, expressionistic style new to the Co-op. The transition between the two styles was occasionally uncomfortable. However, the use of expressionism extended the limits of the form itself — essentially a one-man collective after the fashion of *Tighten the Traces / Haul in the Reins* — even as it allowed O'Neill and the audience some distance from the personal applications of the material. O'Neill's willingness to take significant risks, both as an actor and as a playwright, is characteristic of his work and that of the Co-op, as is the closeness of the artists and audiences to one another and to the material that serves as subject matter for the shows.

Many members of the Co-op have roots in the region, and the Co-op members share the same working and living conditions as the people for whom, and about whom, they produce their shows. Ties with the community are cemented by shared struggles and mutual support. Ed McKenna, a mainstay of the company since joining as General Manager in 1978, has said that, while his commitment to the Co-op is strong, "I doubt very much that I would work in the theatre outside of Guysborough." Together with his role in the Co-op, McKenna is president of the local historical society, and is at work on a history of the county. The Co-op's contributions to the community are many. *One on the Way* began as a workshop with students in the high school in Guysborough, where Gay Hauser mounted a show based on the student's own families and lives, in which two student actors wrote their own material and presented it to their peers. It was then developed further and taken on tour by the Co-op. In 1977 the Co-op went so far as to use area residents as actors in a radio production of Al Pittman's play, *A Rope Against the Sun*. The cast was drawn from a wide cross-section of the population, from the very young to the very old; none had any professional experience.

The company has also done a community Christmas show every year since 1980, which they take into many of the county's two- and four-room schoolhouses, bringing theatre to children who might otherwise never see it. The first two of these were called *Everyman's Christmas*, and both combined traditional Christmas Mummerings, adaptations from medieval morality plays, Christmas traditions from the region, and a nativity scene, all presented within the framework of a troupe of travelling minstrels and with the aid of songs, tumbling, juggling, and puppetry. *The Night Before*, in 1982, was a complete rewriting of the same material, together with stories from Dickens, O'Henry, and Dostoevsky, and for it the Co-op enlisted the aid of Peter Cumming, a writer from Cape Breton with a special interest in children's theatre. In 1983 and 1984 Gary Vermier and Carol Sinclair wrote and directed new scripts, *Presents* and *Holly and the Blizzard Barn*, both of which were favourably received by reviewers and welcomed enthusiastically by adult audiences as well as by the region's schoolchildren. The Co-op sees the annual Christmas show as an important part of its responsibility to the county and the province, and in spite of the difficulties and dangers of winter travelling in remote areas, the show tours for a full month. It is among the Co-op's most popular offerings.

The community reciprocates, helping the company by providing office, storage, and rehearsal space, typing and bookkeeping services, and moral support. McKenna's grant application to the Canada Council in 1979 bears witness to this, and provides refreshing reading in what are usually dry documents. He tells of lighting scaffolds welded for the company by Little Dover Boat Builders for "the price of a few pieces of pipe," and of "Clayton Digdon, garage proprietor, who, with the aid of tools such as a ball peen hammer and a bar of soap, kept our rusty Ford on the Road the last two years, for not much more than the price of a few beers and free tickets to the shows."

The Co-op, then, shares the plight of a proud, self-reliant community that has fallen on hard times. Their shows resemble their subjects, in that they are produced on a shoe string budget, and they reflect the intimacy and informality of the people. As Robbie O'Neill said in an article for *Atlantic Insight* (July, 1979), "you can just get by doing theatre in Guysborough County ... but just getting by is what everyone's trying to do here."

The difficulties following in the wake of their national success are in part simply growing pains, but they also spring from the Co-op's refusal to do "tourist theatre," as 1984-5 artistic director John Dartt puts it, that would support the local economy by bringing in summer audiences while selling out the local culture. Their return to first principles as articulated in September of 1984, is a recognition that their national success is a product of their strong roots in their own culture. At their best, they find universal truths in regional metaphors, and the finely observed detail with which they reflect their home community has a resonance that reaches beyond Guysborough County, and beyond the Maritimes. As Westerner Randy Burton said of *The Coady Co-op Show* in *Western People* (2 August 1979), "fishnets don't have the same feel as a steam driven thresher, but 50 cents for a pound of fish isn't far distant from 50 cents for a bushel of wheat, when the rent comes due."

The greatest accomplishment of The Mulgrave Road Co-op, however, and one that they have recognized and reaffirmed, may well be their very operation as a co-operative venture. Jim Lotz, in an article for *Arts Atlantic* (Winter/Spring, 1980) entitled "Theatre and Regional Development," commented that "in proving the power of collective creativity in a region marked by divisions ... the players are not simply representing another reality — they are living it." He goes on to say that "the Mulgrave Road Co-op shows how new ways of acting can lead to new ways of being. Their message ... makes much more sense in providing direction for Atlantic Canada than all the current utterances of politicians, economists, and planners. ... The Mulgrave Road Co-op has not simply recaptured the past; it has shown everyone in Atlantic Canada how to get a firmer grip on the future." And it has done so by speaking in the voice of the people.

CHRISTINE STORM,
THOMAS STORM and
JANET STRIKE-SCHURMAN

Obligations for Care:
Beliefs in a Small Canadian Town[1]

IN SPITE OF IMPROVEMENTS IN THE HEALTH OF THE elderly, many old people will suffer disabling illness which leaves them chronically unable to attend easily to the routine needs of their daily lives.[2] In spite of the improved private and public pension plans and an affluence which permits more old people to accumulate savings for their retirement years, financial resources will be inadequate for many.[3] In spite of the incidence of centres for senior citizens and similar facilities, many old people will be socially isolated. These conditions can be anticipated by most people for themselves, or for their relatives, and friends.

The recent and future growth of the older population has been widely publicized, together with its implications for society at large.[4] However, it is not clear whether people in general have addressed the personal implications of the information. Changes in the structure of the kinship system and its social context create major difficulties for the family as the primary support system for the aged.[5] Alternative support systems have progressed very little beyond the level of pilot and demonstration programmes.[6] Institu-

---

[1] We wish to acknowledge the research assistance of Patricia Finley, Nancy Mac-Kenzie, and Ker Wells.

[2] R. Wilkins and J. Adams, *Healthfulness of Life* (Montreal, 1983).

[3] National Council of Welfare, Government of Canada, *Sixty-five and Older: A Report by the National Council of Welfare on Incomes of the Aged* (Ottawa, 1984).

[4] Government of Canada, *Fact Book on Aging in Canada* (Ottawa, 1983).

[5] See the discussions in: E. M. Brody, "'Women in the Middle' and Family Help to Older People," *The Gerontologist*, 21 (1981), pp. 471-82; and J. Treas, "Family Support Systems for the Aged: Some Social and Demographic Considerations," *The Gerontologist*, 17 (1977), pp. 486-91.

[6] S. R. Blum and E. Mindler, "Toward a Continuum of Caring Alternatives," *Journal of Social Issues*, 36 (1980), pp. 133-52.

tional alternatives, in particular, continue to be regarded as the
least desirable on both economic and psychological grounds,
although the rate of institutionalization in Canada remains among
the highest in the world.[7]

This study is concerned with general perceptions of responsibility
towards the old, rather than personal intentions or actual behaviour. These perceptions are one of several determinants of behaviour. A summary of findings is difficult because of wide variations
in the specific questions asked of respondents and the populations
sampled. Nevertheless, two perceptions are commonly found. Old
people and younger adults seem to agree that independence for the
old person is desirable whenever possible.[8] In addition, there is a
clear consensus that children should maintain close contact with
parents, and a less clear consensus concerning material assistance
and physical care.[9] The "government," "children or relatives," or
old people themselves, in that order, were volunteered by both a
general sample of the adult population and a sample of old people
as responsible for the care of older people.[10]

Research on actual sources of assistance to old people shows that
adult children provided support and services. For example, Cantor
found that frail elderly received significant care from children (30
percent), other relatives (19 percent), and also from friends and
neighbours (12 percent). She documented a regular order of
sources of support: with spouse and children preferred, next, other
relatives, then, friends and neighbours, and last, formal organizations.[11] Care-giving by children, according to Shanas, is most likely
to involve visiting and psychological support and an exchange of
services.[12] Children and other relatives are most likely to help the

---

[7] C. W. Schwenger and N. J. Gross, "Institutional Care and Institutionalization of
the Elderly in Canada," in V. W. Marshall, ed., *Aging in Canada* (Don Mills, 1980).

[8] See, for example, S. L. Hanson, W. J. Sauer, and W. D. Seelback, "Racial and
Cohort Variations in Filial Responsibility Norms," *The Gerontologist*, 23 (1983),
pp. 626-631.

[9] See, for example, Hanson et al., "Racial and Cohort Variations;" and G. F. Strieb,
"Family Patterns in Retirement," *Journal of Social Issues*, 24 (1958), pp. 48-60.

[10] F. Shanas, *The Health of Older People* (Cambridge, Mass., 1962).

[11] M. H. Cantor, "Strain Among Caregivers: A Study of Experience in the United
States," *The Gerontologist*, 23 (1983), pp. 597-604.

[12] F. Shanas, "Older People and Their Families: The New Pioneers," *Journal of
Marriage and the Family*, 42 (1980), pp. 9-15.

old person with health and physical problems by contacting and mediating with community agencies.[13]

The present study included perceptions of obligation on the parts of the major sources of potential assistance suggested in the literature, and also investigated the influence of potential modifying factors, such as geographical proximity and financial ability. Previous studies have not directly compared the major sources of potential support, taking into account the type of assistance and other relevant circumstances. In addition, since most of the available data are based on urban or national samples, this study contributes data from a small town in Atlantic Canada.

Twenty women from each of four age groups were interviewed. Young adults (18-25 year olds, mean age 22 years) were selected from under-graduate students. Mature and middle-aged adults (30-45 year olds, mean age 38 years and 50-65 year olds, mean age 56 years, respectively) were sampled from a list of volunteers obtained by approaching church and social club groups. Old adults (65-85 year olds, mean age 77 years) were selected from private apartment complexes whose tenants consisted largely of old people.

The sample was restricted to women partly because studies indicate that women typically play a larger role in maintaining contact between the generations and partly because women were more readily available.[14] All subjects resided in Atlantic Canada in a small town. The area is one in which there has been a long history of out-migration by the young due to limited employment opportunities. As a result of this out-migration, the children and other younger relatives of the elderly are especially likely to live in other communities, often at considerable distance.

Social characteristics of the four age groups differed. Most of the young adult group were single students with only part-time, usually white-collar, occupations. The two middle groups were largely married, the majority homemakers, and the others worked at traditional female occupations. None of the elderly group was currently employed and most of them were widowed. Socio-

---

[13] S. O. Daatland, "Use of Public Services for the Aged and the Role of the Family," *The Gerontologist*, 23 (1983), pp. 650-656.

[14] See, for example, S. M. Abu-Laban, "The Family Life of Older Canadians," in V. W. Marshall, ed., *Aging in Canada* (Don Mills, 1980); and J. Hendricks and C. D. Hendricks, *Aging in Mass Society* (Cambridge, Mass., 1977).

economic status based on the husband's current or former occupation was middle-class, largely small business and professional. The students came from similarly middle-class families.

Each subject was interviewed in her home or in a university room by one of three trained undergraduate research assistants. The procedure took approximately one hour and had two parts. The first was a partly structured interview in which subjects were asked to imagine a hypothetical old person, whose circumstances and resources were described, followed by a series of questions about care for the old person's needs. The second part was a paper-and-pencil questionnaire consisting of a set of items representing systematic variations in potential sources of assistance and conditions affecting their ability to provide help. Subjects rated the degree of obligation for each combination of source and circumstances. Demographic information for each subject was obtained and additional questions concerning the subject's own experience with the elderly were asked.

The rationale for this order was that the interview would make salient the issues and alternatives involved and ensure that ratings of obligation were thoughtful. Conversely, the spontaneous reactions of subjects during the interview would not be affected by any implicit structure suggested by the questionnaire.

The interview began with the presentation of a hypothetical case of an old person who was represented as physically disabled, with no income other than the old age pension, and with two children and two siblings, church membership and several close friends. [15] For half of the subjects in each age group, the old person was presented as a woman, for the other half, a man.

After this basic description, the interviewer asked a set of questions concerning responsibility for physical care and help with everyday needs, financial assistance, and social-emotional support. A set of suggested follow-up questions was prepared; it was designed to encourage subjects to expand on their answers and to explore the limits on their perceptions of responsibility. For example, if a subject did not spontaneously mention financial resources of children to whom she assigned responsibility for financial assistance, she would be asked: "Suppose they have financial problems of their own?" In every case subjects were allowed to expand spontaneously and additional probes were employed only when required.

[15] Verbatim instructions and standard questions can be obtained from the authors.

Following completion of the interview, subjects in the three younger groups completed the questionnaire. The oldest group did not because many found the task too onerous. The questionnaire consisted of three forms. Each form began with the sentence: "The old person is alone, not well, and without financial resources." One form asked: "What is the obligation to help with physical needs;" the second replaced physical by "financial needs;" and the third "psychological needs (company, emotional support, and interest — companionship)."

For each type of need, subjects were asked to rate the amount of perceived obligation of various relatives and an old friend on a five point scale: 0 = no obligation whatsoever; 1 = some obligation, but only if it is easy and doesn't conflict with other obligations; 2 = definitely obligated to try to help; 3 = strong obligation to help, even if it means some personal sacrifice; and 4 = morally obligated to help at almost any cost. The relatives were classified as son, daughter, brother, or sister, and each was presented as "living close by" or "living far away"; "in good financial shape" or "in poor financial shape" (e.g., "son, living close by in good financial shape"). This yielded twenty items per form. In two additional items per form, subjects were asked to rate the degree of obligation of the church and the government. The order of form presentation was counter-balanced across subjects. Finally, subjects were asked a series of questions concerning their amount of personal contact with old people, including relatives. The oldest group, themselves old, were asked to relate their experiences with parents and grandparents when they themselves were younger. All subjects were asked to compare current conditions for the elderly with those of previous decades.

Statistical tests were then applied to the questionnaire data. A separate 3 x 5 x 2 x 2 between-within factorial analysis of variance was performed for each type of need (physical, financial, and psychological). The between-subject variable was age (young, early middle-aged, and late middle-aged). The within-subject variables were: relationship (son, daughter, brother, sister, friend); financial circumstances (good or poor); and distance (near or distant). These analyses permitted a comparison, according to need, of the perceived obligations of various possible personal sources of assistance depending on their proximity and financial circumstances. The variables of proximity and financial condition are not applicable in the same way to social institutions like the government and church. Therefore, ratings of their perceived obligations were compared separately to the personal sources. In the results presented below, all significance levels reported are less than .001, except where otherwise stated.[16]

The main effect of age and interactions involving age were not significant for any of the three types of needs. So far as these ratings indicate, therefore, the age groups did not differ in their perception of relative obligation. Therefore, means and standard deviations presented in Tables 1-3 are collapsed across age groups.

We first consider personal sources of obligation. Degree of perceived obligation varied with type of relationship. Planned comparisons showed that children were more obligated than others including siblings who were, in turn, more obligated than old friends. Sex of the children or of the sibling made no significant difference. These effects were obtained for physical, financial, and psychological needs. All were significant.

Whatever the type of relationship, obligation decreased significantly with increasing geographic distance for all three types of needs. The effect of distance was larger than any other effect in the case of psychological needs, in contrast to financial and physical needs. For physical and psychological needs, there was a greater difference between personal sources of assistance in degree of obligation if they lived close by than if they lived at a distance. For psychological needs, the effect of distance on degree of obligation was less when the financial condition of the source of assistance was good rather than poor. No interactions involving distance were significant for financial needs.

Financial status had a major effect on the degree of obligation assigned. The greater the financial resources, regardless of relationship, the greater the obligation to assist. The interaction of financial status with type of relationship was significant for physical and financial needs, but not for psychological needs. Differences among sources with good financial resources were greater than among sources with poor financial resources. Other interactions were nonsignificant.

What is the perception of institutional obligation? In the case of physical needs, the perceived obligation of church and government was not significantly different. These institutions were seen as more obligated to assist than old friends, siblings with poor financial

---

[16] Analysis of variance tables are available from the authors.

resources, or children with poor financial resources who live far away. They were seen as less obligated than children with good financial resources.

In the case of financial needs, the perceived obligation of government to provide was significantly greater than the church ($t(59)*23$, $p < .01$). Only children, if they had the financial resources, were assigned greater obligation than government. Siblings, if they were in good financial shape, were intermediate between church and government in obligation, but differences were small. In the case of psychological needs, the church was perceived as more obligated to meet the psychological needs than was the government ($t(59)*71$, $p < .01$). Children were somewhat more obligated than the church if they lived nearby, and siblings who lived nearby somewhat less than the church. The church was more responsible than relatives living far away or friends. The responsibility of government for meeting psychological needs was intermediate — similar to that of friends who lived nearby, children or siblings who lived far away, but clearly less than that of children or siblings who lived nearby.

Table 1

Perceived Obligation to Assist with Physical Needs:
Means and Standard Deviations

Condition/Proximity	Personal Sources									
	Son		Daughter		Brother		Sister		Friend	
	M	SD	M	SD	M	SD	M	SD	M	SD
Good financial condition/ living close	3.33	0.75	3.35	0.73	2.60	0.87	2.63	0.86	1.60	0.85
Good financial condition/ living far away	2.93	0.95	2.92	0.94	2.30	0.85	2.35	0.90	1.27	0.92
Poor financial condition/ living close	2.48	0.85	2.47	0.93	1.75	1.04	1.75	0.94	1.05	0.89
Poor financial condition/ living far away	1.92	0.93	1.90	0.99	1.43	1.00	1.38	0.98	0.77	0.83

Institutional Sources

Church - *M* 2.55 *SD* 1.17   Government - *M* 2.63 *SD* 1.07

Note: The higher the score the greater the degree of perceived obligation.

We now consider the findings of our interviews. These results were consistent with the questionnaire results in the sources of assistance suggested and the degree of obligation assigned. As in the questionnaire, responses varied according to the type of need. Sex of the old person made no systematic difference. There were, however, differences in nuance and attitude underlying the assignment of obligation within the same age groups and, to some degree, between age groups, which were not revealed in the questionnaire. These will be elaborated below.

Table 2

Perceived Obligation to assist with Financial Needs:
Means and Standard Deviations

Condition/Proximity	Personal Sources									
	Son		Daughter		Brother		Sister		Friend	
	M	SD	M	SD	M	SD	M	SD	M	SD
Good financial condition/ living close	3.30	0.93	3.32	0.89	2.53	0.93	2.58	0.91	1.57	0.98
Good financial condition/ living far away	3.27	0.92	3.27	0.92	2.43	0.91	2.55	0.91	1.33	0.99
Poor financial condition/ living close	1.97	1.02	1.97	1.09	1.42	1.01	1.40	0.98	0.80	0.86
Poor financial condition/ living far away	1.78	1.04	1.78	1.04	1.28	0.99	1.28	0.96	0.70	0.87
	Institutional Sources									
	Church - M 2.25 SD 1.24 Government - M 2.92 SD 1.12									

Note: The higher the score the greater the degree of perceived obligation.

With a few exceptions, subjects spontaneously hedged their assignments of obligation with qualifications and contingencies, often illustrated from the subject's own experience. The effect of these qualifications was that the obligations, apparently clear, were, in fact, ambiguous; the solutions to the needs of the elderly were problematic and dependent on specific circumstances. The older and the more experienced the subject, the more true this was although, again, there were exceptions. Most subjects felt that the family, with the aid of community agencies supported by government — particularly the Victorian Order of Nurses and Meals-on-Wheels — could and should care for the everyday needs of the elderly person. Most of these subjects said that children were the family members primarily obligated. The predominant feeling seemed to be that the family was collectively responsible, but that the actual care should be given by whichever family member was most able to provide it. Children were considered responsible for making contacts and arrangements with the community agencies available. A minority of subjects expressed the opinion that the elderly person him/herself really should be responsible for arranging care when it was required. Neighbours, friends, church groups, and social clubs were often mentioned as resources that might well help an old person unable to care for his/her daily needs, and older subjects, in particular, gave many examples of such assistance. These sources, however, were always discussed in terms which made it clear that no obligation was implied. Only a few subjects made any distinction on the basis of sex in assigning responsibility to family members. For those who did, however, the daughter rather than the son, the sister rather than the brother, were described as the natural caretakers.

The consensus with respect to meeting financial needs was that children specifically, rather than other family members, bore the obligation; and that if children were unable or unwilling to aid financially, the government should cover the basic financial needs. There was a widespread feeling that with free medical care in Canada and pension provisions, government was, in fact, providing, and that there really should be little need for additional assistance. Similarly, many respondents felt that reasonable attempts to save and judicious use of money should preserve the elderly person's financial independence. Thus, a definite responsibility was placed on the elderly person. No distinction was made between the financial obligation of son or daughter.

Although all groups assigned major responsibility to the family for meeting the physical and financial needs of the old person, and, within the family, primarily to the children, there were some differences within and between age groups in this respect. A few subjects in the two oldest age groups specifically absolved the family of any obligation, citing family members' other commitments to jobs, younger dependents, and their own lives. Many subjects, however, elaborated on the family members' obligations in a way that recognized conflicting demands, essentially weaken-

ing the obligation. At the other extreme, a very few insisted on the
absolute obligation of children towards their parents regardless of
sacrifice. Recognition of the difficulties experienced by family
members in meeting their obligations was most commonly expressed by women in the oldest group and somewhat less commonly in the two middle-aged groups. The young adults, however,
showed much less awareness of these complexities. They were more
absolute in assigning responsibility to children, regardless of special
difficulties or special circumstances. They were less diffuse, assigning responsibility specifically to the children without mentioning
the possibility of other sources of aid. In the case of physical care,
though not financial aid, older subjects were more likely to regard
the family as a unit responsible for determining which members
were best able to assist.

Table 3

*Perceived Obligation to Assist with Psychological Needs:
Means and Standard Deviations*

Condition/Proximity	Personal Sources									
	Son		Daughter		Brother		Sister		Friend	
	M	SD	M	SD	M	SD	M	SD	M	SD
Good financial condition/ living close	3.43	0.81	3.55	0.72	2.98	0.91	3.03	0.90	2.43	1.01
Good financial condition/ living far away	2.70	1.01	2.82	0.98	2.38	1.09	2.42	1.05	1.88	1.06
Poor financial condition/ living close	3.23	0.96	3.30	0.87	2.73	1.04	2.73	1.01	2.23	1.11
Poor financial condition/ living far away	2.20	1.12	2.30	1.11	1.92	1.09	1.97	1.09	1.53	1.14
	Institutional Sources									
	Church - M 3.20 SD 0.88 Government - M 2.20 SD 1.34									

Note: The higher the score the greater the degree of perceived obligation.

   In contrast to financial and physical needs, the assignment of
responsibility for meeting the psychological needs of the elderly
person was much more diffuse. Children and grandchildren were
felt to have an obligation for such matters as visiting, calling, or
writing on a regular basis. Siblings were much more often men-

tioned in connection with psychological needs. Friends, neighbours, and non-governmental institutions, especially the church, were mentioned just about as often as family members. Formal governmental agencies were much less likely to be mentioned, with a single exception — Senior Citizen Centres were often mentioned as a partial solution to problems of loneliness.

It was clear that the type of need labeled "psychological" was considered by respondents to be the most common problem of the elderly, but that the responsibility to remedy this problem lay primarily with the elderly person him/herself and his/her use of the social resources available. Others should be concerned and try to provide the stimulation and companionship needed, but this responsibility was spread very widely and was less obligatory than the responsibility to meet physical or financial needs.

The most common reason for regarding children as responsible was *reciprocity*, that is, children, having been cared for by the parent, should return that care. Some older subjects suggested explicitly that if parental care had been poor, children's obligations would be reduced. Many subjects regarded care for an elderly parent or other relative as the natural outcome of affection. Once again, older subjects occasionally suggested that such affection might not, in fact, exist. The young group did not raise this possibility. Older subjects often mentioned their own experience in caring for elderly parents or grandparents, drawing one of two conclusions. Some felt that, since they had sacrificed for their own relatives, someone should be prepared to sacrifice for them. Those few who absolved children of responsibility, however, felt that the disruption they had experienced in their own lives should not be inflicted on their own children or other young people.

Many subjects in the oldest age group expressed the view that conditions for the elderly and resources for their care were considerably improved over earlier decades. Many felt that government pensions, even without substantial personal savings, were reasonably adequate; that free medical care eliminated a major concern; and that government and community agencies would always be available if extra-ordinary needs arose. At the same time, these same subjects clearly felt that modern conditions made it more difficult for children and other relatives to provide assistance. They spontaneously mentioned such factors as smaller homes, larger distances, dual careers, and increased costs of raising a family. In contrast, the youngest subjects felt that times had

changed for the worse in that family ties were weaker and that
children were less responsible towards their parents. They felt that
impersonal agencies could not substitute for family attentions.
(These student subjects seemed convinced that the elderly enjoyed
and needed the company of young people like themselves. The
oldest group was more likely to stress the importance of friends of a
similar age.)

Subjects in all age groups mentioned nursing homes for the
physically disabled old person, but always as a last resort if all
forms of personal assistance were ruled out. Perceptions of nursing
homes were clearly negative. Attitudes towards living with children were ambivalent. Most of the oldest group preferred independence both for themselves and others, but at the same time
most saw living with a child, particularly if they lived nearby, as a
reasonable possibility, preferable to the nursing home, and felt the
children should be prepared to provide that opportunity.

Although the predominant view was that families (especially
children) and the government (through financial support and
community agencies) should share responsibility for meeting the
needs of old people, this view was hedged with so many qualifications and contingencies as to make the solution of any individual
case very problematic. Subjects were explicitly aware of this
situation. They would ask about the circumstances of the (hypothetical) old person, clearly implying that solutions and responsi-
bilities were contingent on a wide variety of material, social, and
psychological factors.

What can we make of these findings? The expectation that
children would be perceived as the primary source of assistance
regardless of type of need was clearly confirmed. Son or daughter
received significantly higher ratings of obligation than any other
source of assistance and were invariably named as the first resource
by subjects in the interview. However, this obligation was strongly
affected by circumstances. Children in poor financial shape, for
example, were regarded as less obligated to provide financial aid
than siblings with adequate financial resources. Both financial
status and distance affected the degree of obligation of children
whatever the nature of the old person's need. The effect of financial
circumstances and physical proximity on the obligation of children
was anticipated, but the magnitude of this effect was somewhat
surprising. The influence of these circumstantial factors was not

limited to the structured questionnaire, but was apparent through-out the unstructured interviews in subjects' spontaneous responses. In this more open task, subjects, in fact, were likely to elaborate on related circumstantial factors conflicting with the children's obli-gations towards the parent. The size of the children's own family, the need to provide for their education, the need for privacy, and the possibility that caring for an elderly parent might place undue strain on a marriage — these and many other factors were men-tioned. Clearly, the obligation of children is unambiguous only in the abstract. As soon as subjects start to consider concrete cases, ambiguities arise.

In every case, the obligation of government was regarded as substantial, equal to or greater than that of any more personal source of assistance except for children in favorable circumstances. The interviews strongly suggest that, failing personal sources of assistance, the obligation of government is perceived to be absolute. As indicated above, even when family is able to provide assistance, the degree of sacrifice expected is limited and the feeling strong that government should assist.

In general, age differences were not marked. Older subjects were no more likely than younger subjects to emphasize the role of children, other personal relationships, or church in providing assistance; and they placed no less emphasis on government. There were, in fact, no significant age differences in the results from the structured questionnaire. The impression from the interviews was that, if anything, older subjects were more likely than younger to raise factors which might make assistance difficult for family and to stress conflicting obligations which, to some degree, reduced re-sponsibility. Even the church was exempted by many older subjects on the basis that the burden of caring for all the elderly who might require aid would be unreasonably great.

While there was no evidence in the structured questionnaire for any stereotypic division of responsibility on the basis of gender, a minority of the older subjects made it clear in the less formal interview that the stereotype survives. If gender was mentioned at all, women were assumed to be the primary caregiver.

Any generalizations that emerge from this study are limited, of course, by the fact that the subjects were all women, all resident in a small town. We expected, however, that these characteristics of the sample would be related to more conservative attitudes, that is, to greater emphasis on family and neighbourly responsibility and less on government, than in an urban population. The findings reflect a less conservative attitude than expected.

The consensus appears to be that children should be aware of the needs of their elderly parents and organize assistance. (However, the interviews indicated that most of the respondents were not at all clear about the nature of services available, the eligibility requirements or costs, or the steps required to mobilize the available resources.) Everyone agrees that the children themselves should be prepared to make some sacrifice. The extent of that sacrifice is very unclear and subject to differing interpretations. The responsibility of anyone other than children or government agencies is very limited — a matter of personal temperament and convenience, rather than obligation.

The literature on altruism, while largely limited to factors affecting assistance given to strangers, may be of some relevance here. It suggests that the greater the ambiguity, the less likely that assistance will be received — and the less adequate it will be.[17] With respect to the elderly, there seems to be little ambiguity about who should assist, but considerable ambiguity about when, how much, and by what means they should assist.

---

[17] See, for example, B. Latane and J. Rodin, "A Lady in Distress: Interesting Effects of Friends and Strangers on Bystander Intervention," *Journal of Experimental Social Psychology*, 5 (1969), pp. 189-203.

Notes on Contributors

Patrick L. Baker is Head of the Department of Sociology and Anthropology at Mount Allison University. He has done research on Africa, the Caribbean and Canada, and is presently writing an ethnohistory of Dominica, West Indies.

Jill Burnett graduated from Mount Allison in 1984 with a B.A. honours degree in Geography and History. A Rotary International Fellow who studied in Africa after graduation, she is currently working as a grants officer with UNESCO in Ottawa.

Gwendolyn Davies, whose research focuses on the literary culture and history of the Maritimes in the 18th and 19th centuries, is Head of Mount Allison University's English Department. She has published important articles in journals such as *Acadiensis, Canadian Literature*, and *Essays on Canadian Writing*.

C. Mark Davis teaches history and Canadian Studies courses at Mount Allison University. He is presently completing his Ph.D. dissertation on "Temperance and Prohibition Movements in Maritime Canada, 1830-1930."

George J. De Benedetti has taught economics at Mount Allison University since 1968, where he is now department Head. His chief research interests are community and regional economic development. He is Vice-President of the Atlantic Canada Economics Association and is a frequent commentator on C.B.C. Radio.

Berkeley Fleming teaches in Mount Allison University's Sociology Department. He has written about the sociology of rental housing markets and is presently interested in the history of social theory. He is actively involved in a number of professional organizations.

William G. Godfrey is Dean of Arts and a member of the History Department at Mount Allison University. Amongst his many publications is the book, *Pursuit of Profit and Preferment in Colonial North America: John Bradstreet's Quest*.

Thaddeus Holownia is a well-known Canadian photographer whose photographs can be found in many private and public collections in North America. He has just completed a term as Head of Mount Allison University's Fine Arts Department.

Dean Jobb is a former history student at Mount Allison University who, since graduation in 1982, has worked as a free-lance journalist and as a reporter for several Halifax newspapers.

Richard Paul Knowles has contributed articles on Canadian theatre and on Shakespeare to a variety of publications, including *Canadian Theatre Review* and *Canadian Drama/L'Art dramatique canadien*. He teaches both English and Drama at Mount Allison University.

Larry McCann is Davidson Professor of Canadian Studies at Mount Allison University. He has written extensively on the regional and historical geography of the Maritimes, and is editor of *Heartland and Hinterland: A Geography of Canada.*

Carrie MacMillan teaches English at Mount Allison University where she specializes in Canadian literature. She has published articles in *Studies in Canadian Literature* and *Essays on Canadian Writing*, and continues research on the 19th century Canadian and Maritimes novel.

Richard Price earned a B.A. honours degree in Economics from Mount Allison in 1985. He is presently completing a law degree at the University of Toronto.

John G. Reid now teaches history at Saint Mary's University, but before that he was Winthrop Pickard Bell Research Fellow at Mount Allison University. He is the author of a number of books, including *Mount Allison University: A History*, and has just published a book of critical decades in the history of the Maritimes.

Eric Ross has taught in the Geography Department at Mount Allison University since 1972. A world traveller, he has lectured in Japan, Scotland and Australia, and is presently researching the expansion of Scottish settlement in several new world contexts.

Christine Storm teaches in Mount Allison University's Psychology Department. She has published several articles on aging and continues active research on friendship and support networks across the lifespan. She is active in organizations concerned with women's issues.

Thomas Storm has taught psychology at the University of British Columbia, Mount Allison University and Saint Francis Xavier University. He is presently a consultant to the Health Promotion Directorate, Health and Welfare Canada, but continues to do research on aging and social and interpersonal relations.

Janet Strike-Schurman earned her B.A. honours degree in Psychology from Mount Allison in 1983 and her M.A. from the Université de Moncton in 1985. She is presently working as a clinician in Quebec.